Liberal Peace Transitions

LIBERAL PEACE TRANSITIONS

BETWEEN STATEBUILDING AND PEACEBUILDING

Oliver P. Richmond and Jason Franks

EDINBURGH UNIVERSITY PRESS

First published in 2009 by

Edinburgh University Press Ltd
22 George Square, Edinburgh
www.euppublishing.com

This paperback edition 2011

Reprinted 2012

Typeset in Sabon
by Servis Filmsetting Ltd, Stockport, Cheshire, and
printed and bound in Great Britain by
CPI Antony Rowe, Chippenham and Eastbourne

A CIP record for this book is available from the British Library

ISBN 978 0 7486 4297 7(paperback)

Contents

Acknowledgements

This study is the result of a research project conducted by the Centre for Peace and Conflict Studies (CPCS) at the University of St Andrews. This project, which ran from 2005 to 2007, critically examined 'liberal peace transitions' in a number of different peacebuilding contexts. It was funded by the Carnegie Trust and the University of St Andrews, to whom we are grateful. See www.st-andrews.ac.uk/intrel/ for more details. We would like to thank the many individuals who contributed or helped during the research and fieldwork necessary for this book including our interviewees and assistants in all of our case studies, as well as the individuals who commented on our subsequent work, especially John Groom, Roger Mac Ginty, Michael Pugh, Chandra Sriram, Ian Taylor, Alison Watson, Keith Webb, Andrew Williams, and the members of the various panels and workshops around the world where this work was presented. We would like to thank especially the members of CPCS, our students and interns, and the members of the steering group that was convened for this project. We would also like to thank Stefanie Kappler who helped with some onerous administrative tasks, and of course, the staff at Edinburgh University Press. Finally, thanks to Kulturstudier and its staff and students in Pondicherry, India, and to the School of Politics and IR, University of Queensland, Australia, where the final revisions to this manuscript were carried out.

Acronyms

AAK	Alliance for the Future of Kosovo
ABRI	Angkatan Bersenjata Republik Indonesia (Indonesian military)
ACT	Alliance for Conflict Transformation
AD	Alliance of Democrats
ADB	Asian Development Bank
APODETI	Timorese Popular Democratic Association
BHAS	Bosnia and Herzegovina Agency for Statistics
BiH	Bosnia and Herzegovina
CIVPOL	Civilian Police
CNRT	National Council of Timorese Resistance
CPP	Cambodian People's Party
CSD	Centre for Social Development
DFID	Department for International Development
DK	Democratic Kampuchea
DoP	Declaration of Principles
EIC	Economic Institute of Cambodia
EU	European Union
EULEX	European Union Rule of Law Mission to Kosovo
FDI	foreign direct investment
F-FDTL	National Defence Force of Timor-Leste
FRY	Federal Republic of Yugoslavia
FUNCINPEC	National United Front for an Independent, Neutral, Peaceful, and Cooperative Cambodia
GPA	Governance and Public Administration

HAER	Humanitarian Assistance and Emergency Rehabilitation
HAK	The Foundation for Law, Human Rights and Justice
HDI	Human Development Index
HDZ	Croatian Democratic Union of Bosnia and Herzegovina
HPI	Human Poverty Index
HRW	Human Rights Watch
ICG	International Crisis Group
ICRC	International Committee for the Red Cross
IDP	internally displaced person
IFIs	International Financial Institutions
IFOR	Implementation Force
IMF	International Monetary Fund
INGO	international non-governmental organisation
InterFET	International Force East Timor
IOs	international organisations
IPTF	International Police Task Force
IR	international relations
KFOR	NATO-led peacekeeping force in Kosovo
KLA	Kosovo Liberation Army
KP	Return Coalition – 'Povratak'
KPNLF	Khmer People's National Liberation Front
KPS	Kosovo Police Service
LDC	least developed country
LDK	Democratic League of Kosovo
LDP	Liberal Democratic Party
LNGO	local non-governmental organisation
NATO	North Atlantic Treaty Organisation
NDI	National Democratic Institute
NGO	non-governmental organisation
OCHA	UN Office for the Coordination of Humanitarian Affairs
OHR	Office of the High Representative
ONUSAL	United Nations Observer Mission in El Salvador

OSCE	Organisation for Security and Cooperation in Europe
PA	Palestinian Authority
PASSIA	Palestinian Academic Society for the Study of International Affairs
PDK	Democratic Party of Kosovo
PDP	Party of Democratic Progress
PIC	Peace Implementation Council
PISG	Provisional Institutions of Self-Government
PLC	Palestinian Legislative Council
PLO	Palestine Liberation Organisation
PNA	Palestinian National Authority
PNC	Palestine National Council
PNTL	East Timor National Police
RS	Republika Srpska
SIDA	Swedish International Development Cooperation Agency
SME	small and medium-size enterprises
SNC	Supreme National Council
SOC	State of Cambodia
SRP	Sam Rainsy Party
SRSG	Special Representative of the Secretary-General
TFGWB	Trust Fund for Gaza and the West Bank
TMK	Kosovo Protection Corps
UCK	Kosovo Liberation Army
UDI	unilateral declaration of independence
UDT	Timorese Democratic Union
UN	United Nations
UNAMET	United Nations Mission in East Timor
UNDAF	United Nations Development Assistance Framework
UNDP	United Nations Development Programme
UNHCR	United Nations High Commissioner for Refugees
UNICEF	United Nations Children's Fund
UNMIBH	United Nations Mission in Bosnia and Herzegovina

UNMIK	United Nations Interim Administration in Kosovo
UNMISET	United Nations Mission of Support in East Timor
UNMIT	United Nations Integrated Mission in Timor-Leste
UNOTIL	United Nations Office in East Timor
UNPROFOR	United Nations Protection Force
UNRISD	United Nations Research Institute for Social Development
UNSC	United Nations Security Council
UNTAC	United Nations Transitional Authority in Cambodia
UNTAET	United Nations Transitional Administration in East Timor
UNTAG	United Nations Transition Assistance Group
USAID	United States Agency for International Development
WFP	World Food Programme

Introduction: A Framework to Assess Liberal Peace Transitions

Introduction

Since the early 1990s, the projects of peacebuilding and statebuilding have increasingly been integrated. Since the early 2000s, this has been mainly an outcome of the United States and the United Kingdom's support for an active, muscular and humanitarian liberal internationalism. This has thrown up similar internal anomalies and inconsistencies that can also be observed in liberal forms of imperialism, as Hobson so accurately characterised at the start of the twentieth century.[1] As such issues have emerged, criticism has become more pronounced from a range of commentators, both local and international, policy and academic. This study examines the discourses of peace implicit in the theoretical and policy literatures relating to these debates, and investigates their impact in the context of a number of specific case studies chosen to represent the range and diversity of liberal peacebuilding. To date, there has been little research that has specifically focused on peace, as opposed to war or order. As a result, systematic inquiries into peace are rare and unsurprisingly there is an inadequate understanding of the contemporary conceptualisation of peace, nor its empirical dynamics. Both academics and policymakers, however, often see the advantage of a clearer understanding of the concept of peace as an alternative, a liberal assumption or an ideal type, both in theory and in empirical terms.

This study explicitly examines the nature of the peace created through different aspects of, and the praxis of, contemporary peacebuilding. It examines the development of the discourse of the liberal peace and compares this evolution with the development of practical approaches for peace, in the context of peacebuilding, the work of international organisations, donors, agencies, non-governmental organisations (NGOs) and the contributions of key liberal states. It reflects on a set of concepts developed in the context of the liberal

1

peace project. In particular, it examines these concepts via a reflection on their deployment in a selection of post-conflict peacebuilding case studies. The aim of this approach is to develop a firm understanding of the nature of the peace that contemporary peacebuilding actors are in the process of creating.

The research and fieldwork for this study focused on a selection of case studies in the post-Cold War period until late 2007 when fieldwork for the project also came to end (so providing the cut off date for our empirical analysis). The case studies include Cambodia, Bosnia, Kosovo, East Timor and the Middle East, and were selected to represent a wide chronological range of liberal peacebuilding examples that also reflect a range of issues and conflict characteristics, though not necessarily a large range of different actors or approaches (with the exception of the case of the Middle East). This data is used to develop and evaluate a more nuanced understanding of the liberal peace project than has been common until recently, and potentially to contribute to the production of a set of intellectual and policy guidelines relating to the actions of peacebuilding actors in the context of construction of the liberal peace. The research presented in this study also endeavours to underline the ontological, epistemological and normative aspects of these debates in an attempt to open up the conceptualisations and imaginings of peace as a serious research agenda, which represents a more balanced engagement with questions of peace in post-violence polities. It also raises the question of what is the alternative to the liberal peace if its problems are more far reaching than is often generally thought?

We are particularly concerned with the nature of liberal peace that is commonly used as the model for post-conflict statebuilding, and is employed by the international community to reconstitute states after conflict. This study adopts a particularly critical approach to the one-size-fits-all paradigm which is generally used (even though the existence of such a model is often defended or even denied), and which has been employed since the end of the Cold War to bring peace and democracy to conflict zones. It draws heavily on the theoretical framework developed in its sister volume by Oliver Richmond, *The Transformation of Peace*.[2] This study places these theoretical and conceptual frameworks into an empirical context and explores the actual forms of 'liberal peace' that exist following a brokered peace process and a peacebuilding operation in our five different cases. It does so by breaking down liberal peace theory into the main constituent parts identified in Richmond's previous study.

Assuming an ever-present engagement with a range of state security and human security issues, these constituent parts of the liberal peace include democratisation, human rights, civil society, the rule of law and economic liberalisation in the form of free-market reform and development. Through this process, we develop a critical and theoretically informed empirical exploration of the 'technology' of the liberal peacebuilding process, particularly with regard to our case studies.

Such an approach enables an examination, from a grounded perspective, of the discourses of peace implicit in the theoretical and policy literatures relating to war and conflict in the peacebuilding and statebuilding endeavours represented by our cases. This is not based mainly on survey or quantative forms of data collection and methodologies, as is generally the case in other related comparative research,[3] but mainly on first hand interviews and observations on the ground and amongst the international peacebuilding community as well as a range of primary documentation.

Through this mode of analysis we endeavour to examine explicitly what the nature of the peace created through different aspects of peacebuilding is in each context in order to draw more general comparative conclusions. This is juxtaposed and contrasted with our presentation of the development of the discourses and practices of the liberal peace, or liberal peacebuilding, and increasingly of neo-liberal statebuilding. We aim to establish a basis for a far better and more nuanced understanding of the nature of peace that a wide range of actors in the field, both local and international, are contributing to, both for intellectual and policy clarification.

As a point of departure for this critical study of the liberal peace, this introductory chapter next outlines in more detail the foundations and intellectual origins of liberal peace theory. It then moves beyond this literature by introducing a conceptual framework for 'liberal peace transitions' that explains both the individual components of liberal peace and the different forms of liberal peace that can be derived from these components. It is this conceptual framework that is applied, critiqued and assessed throughout this study using the data collected from fieldwork in our case study areas.

The Liberal Peace Framework

The liberal peace framework has emerged through a complex evolution within a very specific political, economic, social, conceptual and methodological environment, which has universal ambitions, nevertheless.[4] As the Cold War ended, UN peacebuilding, humanitarian and donor assistance, the role of the World Bank and other international financial institutions, the UN Development Programme, and the role of national institutions and experts began to expand toward a broader project of engaging with conflict through the construction of the liberal state. Wildly ambitious and normatively more sensitive than what had preceded it, problems soon emerged in locations as diverse as Somalia and Cambodia in the early 1990s. Yet, this optimism in the face of emerging difficulties and even rejection led to the liberal peace being conceptualised as being predicated upon the cornerstones of democratisation, the rule of law, human rights, free and globalised markets, and neoliberal development. The response to any subsequent problems that have emerged has tended to focus on better integration of, and efficacy in, these areas, rather than a broader questioning of the liberal peace model itself, or of its assumptions.

The liberal peace is a discourse, framework and structure with a specific ontology and methodology. It provides a liberal epistemology of peace and its projected reform of governance entails a communicative strategy on which depends its viability and legitimacy with its recipients. This operates both at a social and a state level and cannot be achieved without significant resources. The allocation of those resources, the power to do so, and their control, has become the new site of power and domination in post-conflict societies. Thus, it must be asked how this can be so while at the same time remaining true to the emancipatory claims of the liberal peace for its subjects or citizens within liberal states. Paradoxically, it is the case that the NGO and agency personnel, those in the UN and World Bank, diplomats and officials, generally show great commitment to the countries they are working in (often in difficult, uncomfortable and dangerous conditions) and are to a large degree implicitly, if not explicitly, aware of the problems of the liberal peace model.[5] Many of the peacebuilding 'international civil service' are thoroughly committed to the idea of 'peace' as both desirable and theoretically and practically possible. They are also careful to avoid the creation of external dependency, they endeavour to be sensitive to the needs of local ownership and to local conditions, and are very careful not to upset sensitive local political and social customs or arrangements where these are deemed to be viable within the liberal peace. Sometimes they may also feel that interests and politics are blocking their progress but are reluctant to intervene directly. They are sensitive to such problems while also recognising that their professional roles or the projects they are part of are in many ways inadequate and create forms of peace that are far from ideal, or even what they consider to be within the realms of what is possible. What little is done is normally better than nothing in such terms. They may adhere to the injunction 'do no harm',[6] written into the mandates of United Nations Development Programme (UNDP) or the World Bank for example, in order to protect the sanctity of the notion of peace, to protect the fragile balance that might already exist in a given post-conflict location, and also to protect the integrity of legitimacy of the liberal peace framework. Often, though, the priority is the international or regional dynamics of the liberal peace rather than its local quality.

Within this liberal peace framework, four main strands of thinking have evolved. These are the victor's peace, the institutional peace, the constitutional peace and the civil peace.[7] The victor's peace has evolved from the ancient argument, predating the Roman raising of the city of Carthage, that a peace which rests on a military victory and upon the hegemony or domination of that victor is more likely to survive. The institutional peace rests upon post-Treaty of Westphalia attempts to anchor states within a normative and legal context in which states multilaterally agree how to behave, on international norms and international institutions, and how to enforce or determine their behaviour. The constitutional peace rests upon the post-Enlightenment argument, most famously made by Kant, that peace rests upon democracy, trade and a set of cosmopolitan values that stem from the notion that individuals are ends in themselves, rather than means to an end. Finally, the civil peace is derived from the phenomena of direct action, citizen advocacy and mobilisation (often transnationally) in the attainment or defence of basic human rights and values, often for reasons of social justice and human emancipation. These aspects of the liberal peace are both contradictory and complimentary, and each brings with it a certain intellectual and empirical baggage. Together they reflect the liberal aspiration for freedom and for mutual regulation. The fine balance between these broad aspirations in the context of state sovereignty produces the liberal peace. This peace rests upon the resultant framework provided by democracy, the rule of law, human rights, free trade and development.

The different strands of thinking about peace outlined above draw on debates in political theory and philosophy, the constitutional peace plans of the Enlightenment period, the empowerment of civil society, and the institutional peace plans of the imperial and post-colonial periods. They have recently converged on a contemporary notion of 'peace-as-governance'[8] whereby the liberal state provides the framework for the creation of peace at local, state and international levels through governmentalism and its relation to institution building. This has become the most common form of peace, applied by international actors through a methodological peacebuilding consensus in conflict zones. Such international actors draw on the epistemic knowledge systems and communities that liberalism supplies and represents in order to reorder the distribution of power, prestige, rules and rights. Peace-as-governance in state-building terms focuses on the institutions of state as the basis for the construction of the liberal peace. For NGOs and agencies, it focuses on the governance of society. In terms of bottom-up peacebuilding, different actors contribute to the liberal peace model by installing forms of peace-as-governance associated with the regulation, control and protection of individuals and civil society. The balance of power, hegemony, institutionalism and constitutionalism, and civil society converge in this version of peace in an era of governmentality, which is super-territorial and multilayered.[9] It incorporates official and private actors from the local to the global, institutionalised in the alphabet soup of agencies, organisations and institutions.

Boutros-Ghali's early policy conceptualisation of peacebuilding in *An Agenda for Peace* was indicative of an emerging and loose 'peacebuilding consensus' about a liberal peace.[10] It envisaged multiple levels of governance to provide early warning systems, preventative diplomacy, peacemaking, peacekeeping, peacebuilding, as well as peace-enforcement capacities in order to enable the UN to become engaged in addressing the 'deepest causes of social injustice and political oppression'.[11] Implicit in *Agenda* was a coordinated strategy that spanned these approaches as part of a general commitment to a broader notion of peace and security on behalf of the 'international community', involving a long-term commitment to post-settlement environments including disarmament, the repatriation of refugees, the restoration of order, election monitoring, the protection of human rights, reforming and strengthening governmental institutions, and 'promoting formal and informal processes of political participation'.[12] This was to occur through four key mechanisms: the insertion of political and economic liberalism into peace settlements; providing expert advice during implementation; conditionality attached to economic assistance; and proxy governance.[13] These mechanisms contributed to the liberal processes outlined in the triptych of the UN's

Agendas, and also acted as a carrier for the neoliberal, marketisation, free trade dimension of peacebuilding that was also inserted into the liberal peace through various forms of conditionality.[14]

There are many obvious problems with the different intellectual strands of the liberal peace. Because the victor's peace framework has often resulted in territorial and strategic over-extension, greed and an inability to control unruly subjects despite its impositionary qualities, it is not generally now seen to be a viable basis for peace. The civil peace discourse, on the other hand, is often seen to be limited and suppressed by state elites or of secondary importance to security, and institutional and constitutional, dynamics of the liberal peace. The civil peace is often invisible even though it may be propagated by non-state actors motivated by human security and social justice frameworks. The institutional peace discourse has difficulty coping with many discordant interests and voices, and the enormity of its systemic project, which requires the consent of a broad range of actors and the mediation of a range of interests. Its development and implementation has drawn the UN system, international financial institutions (IFIs) and agencies into the quagmire of multilateral governance with its attendant political interests and material inefficiencies. As a result, as an approach to peace, it has struggled to create consensus or to communicate with those involved at the civil level, or to receive and respond to various types of feedback emerging about its overall project. The constitutional peace is often perceived as a threat to those in post-conflict polities who do not want to share power in domestic constitutional situations, and who do not want the certainty of domestic legal structures that might outlaw or undermine their often predatory activities. It has often fallen victim to the simple binaries it depends upon – the territorial inside/outside, and the identity of friend or enemy.

Derived from the four strands of thinking within the liberal peace framework outlined above, there are different graduations into which the liberal peace project can be broken down. The most authoritarian approach is represented by the *conservative* model of the liberal peace, characterised by top-down approaches to peacebuilding and shaped by techniques of coercion, domination and hegemony. This tends to be operationalised via military intervention, political conditionalities and the imposition of a state-led peace, which diplomats are fond of describing as the 'art of the possible'.[15] Often reflected in non-UN peacekeeping, or the conditionalities built into the roles of the World Bank or the UN, as well as in recent US unilateral statebuilding efforts, it has become an expression of external interest. The conservative model has often been thus accompanied by military action, as has been the case in Somalia, the Balkans, Afghanistan and Iraq. This is a clear reflection of the victor's peace, at least in the preliminary stages of intervention.

The *orthodox* model of the liberal peace represents a discourse and praxis focused on statebuilding, on liberal institutions, and one that is also more sensitive of local ownership. This model is indicative of an eagerness of the liberal international community to transfer its ideas, methodologies, objectives and norms into a new post-conflict framework aimed at governance via consensual negotiation. Although striving for balance and for multilateralism, this model imagines peace as being state led and institutional in terms of involving international organisations, institutions and NGOs, as well as the creation of the mechanisms of democracy, the rule of law, human rights and the free market. Representing a top-down and bottom-up approach at the same time, this model juxtaposes needs-based and rights-based approaches to peace, yet with a clear emphasis on the top-down dimension, which is operationalised via conditional models and practices of donors, organisations and institutions, as well as projecting the vested interests of major states and donors. This model has emerged mainly from the UN family's practices after the Cold War, dealing with peacebuilding and governance reform, and culminating in temporary UN sovereignty over East Timor. In this regard, the orthodox model concurs with the conservative model in that it rests on an initial provision of security, and then builds a peace based upon the international assumption of technical superiority over its subjects via the claim of the normative universality of the liberal peace.

As a third discourse, the *emancipatory* model of the liberal peace assumes a more critical stance, especially as far as the role of coerciveness, conditionality and dependency is concerned. As an alternative to the top-down security and institutionally focused approaches of liberal peace orthodoxy, it emphasises a much closer relationship with the subjects of the liberal peace, focusing on local ownership and consent. Therefore, it offers a bottom-up, emancipatory approach, allowing for a stronger concern for social justice and people's needs and an assumption of far greater local agency. Though still assuming a significant degree of universalism, it accentuates discursive and locally negotiated requirements. This in turn allows for a more nuanced consideration of the various actors involved, mainly local and international NGOs in association with major agencies and some state donors, according to the respective phase the conflict and peacebuilding process is situated in. Equating to the civil peace, the emancipatory model is not merely internationally or state led, but rather shaped by private actors and social movements.

These main aspects of the liberal peace model often tend to be combined in the 'peacebuilding consensus',[16] which can be viewed as a loose agreement on peacebuilding amongst a wide range of actors, with their respective courses of action depending upon priorities associated with dominant state interests, donor interests and the capacity of peacebuilding actors. But this consensus does not stand up to very close scrutiny except in very general terms. The peacebuilding consensus loosely represents an agreement amongst peacebuilding agencies, donors, states and most NGOs that democracy, free markets, the rule of law and human rights, and developmental processes are necessary to produce a sustainable solution to conflict. This concurrence has, over the last eighteen years or so, been extended and is assumed to lie in the context of liberal/neoliberal statebuilding, of which Afghanistan and Iraq are notable recent examples, and Cambodia, Bosnia, Kosovo and East Timor are more orthodox examples.

The post-Cold War peacebuilding consensus has generally allowed third parties to initially impose the liberal peace framework via very specific qualifying moves (e.g. the adoption of free markets, elections, human rights). Disputants who fail to accept this form of intervention and its conditionalities are often excluded economically and politically from the peace process. The more difficult it is to get the range of local actors to cooperate, the more governance functions are taken on by external actors, and the more coercive liberal peacebuilding becomes. Peacebuilding has essentially become a process where establishing democracy, human rights and the market are seen as the ultimate goal.[17] However, the installation of a liberal democracy resting on human rights, humanitarianism and an agreement on what constitutes development and a globally integrated economy is the only governance formula the international community will currently invest in. This means that there is often external consent for the principles of this sort of intervention, but internal consent is clouded by the particularistic political, social and economic practices that may not survive such an intervention.

The components of the liberal peace have been critiqued from several different perspectives. These have focused upon the incompatibility of certain stages of democratisation and economic reform; the ownership of development projects and 'thick and thin' versions of the liberal and neoliberal agenda; the possible incompatibility of post-conflict justice with the stabilisation of society and human rights; the problem of crime and corruption in economic and political reform and the establishment of the rule of law. These terrains are relatively well explored.[18] Yet the nominal unity of the peacebuilding consensus often breaks down exactly because of internal competition, interests and the capacity of its different components. The graduations of the liberal peace may contradict and undermine each other, leading to inconsistencies and contradictions in the broader peacebuilding process.

Despite blending into each other, those graduations have often been conceptually employed successively during different stages of peacebuilding. Hence, the conservative version of the liberal peace is likely to be resorted to during an emergency period in order to preserve or reinforce the sanctity of the liberal peace model in the international realm and support the activities of the liberal international community. In post-conflict reconstruction phases, official actors may gradually shift to the orthodox version of the liberal peace, attempting to respond to the interests of the general population, but also redefining the state by focusing on the development of institutional relationships, institutions and constitutions. Being dependent on both local and donor consent, this model is conducive to forms of cooperation between agencies and NGOs, which are more wary of conservative approaches, and their associated actors, who in turn tend to focus on reasonably immediate results rather than on the longer-term sustainability of their approaches. Yet, once sustainability becomes a key issue in the post-emergency phase and internationals begin to think about their exit strategies, even top-down actors begin to move towards the more critical, emancipatory models of the liberal peace. Despite its breadth and relative lack of parsimony, this latter graduation in turn appears to be the most legitimate one in terms of allowing for sustainability and reducing external intervention and conditional forms of governance. Yet, all these graduations of the liberal peace tend to be presented as emancipatory and highly legitimate in policy discourses, given that such rhetoric creates the impression of a higher degree of capacity, knowledge and so legitimacy for those guiding the peacebuilding process.

The Framework for Assessment

It is vital to identify the graduations of the liberal peace that are being constructed in the different liberal peacebuilding contexts around the world, through different types of intellectual and policy analysis, and by different actors. This should enable the evaluation of both their effectiveness in their own terms and their sustainability according to a more critical analysis of peacebuilding approaches. This will enable a more sensitised reflection of the legitimacy of peacebuilding in these contexts. These goals are represented by a configuration of the main four discourses of peace, and the four graduations of the liberal peace outlined above. This process, we argue, will lead to a better understanding of (1) the type of peace being created, (2) impediments to peace, and (3) the sustainability of this peace. Conclusions and comparisons drawn from this analysis consequently may open the way for a greater intellectual and policy understanding of the agendas inherent in the different aspects of the liberal peace project.

What the various examples of contemporary peacebuilding seem to illustrate is that entry into a conflict zone is often predicted on a conservative version of the liberal peace, with the aspiration of moving towards the orthodox graduation. A significant number of examples can be provided for this expectation, but a significant number also remain mired within the conservative graduation of the liberal peace. No examples of liberal peacebuilding have so far achieved an emancipatory graduation of the liberal peace, and indeed, a serious deficiency with respect to social justice, socio-economic well-being and development mars all such international efforts in the post-Cold War era. The tendency has been for international peacebuilding actors to enter a conflict environment somewhere within the conservative graduation of the liberal peace framework. This involves a removal of self-government and self-determination first, in order to achieve their aspiration for orthodox or emancipatory graduations after a period of international tutelage. Theoretically, this allows the internationals to withdraw more easily, safe in the knowledge that peace has been achieved. However, experience has shown that where force is used in a hyper-conservative initial approach, even in the name of liberal peacebuilding, moving along the liberal peace axis towards the orthodox graduation tends not to occur. The best illustrations of this appear to be the cases of Bosnia and Kosovo, where the political entity (state or not) is weak, as well as socially and economically unsustainable, despite the length of time the internationals have been involved.[19] Somalia and Afghanistan are other similar examples. Where international entry is based upon a peace agreement with broad consent and consensus, it often occurs within the conservative graduation but moves rapidly towards the orthodox; however, progress beyond this has generally not occurred.

This raises the question of what the requirements are for the construction of a specific graduation of the liberal peace, which may then shift from the conservative to the orthodox version? It also raises, what is for us, an even more important question of how to develop a more emancipatory version of peace? The liberal peace discourse focus may provide the basis for a more sophisticated form of peacemaking. In practice, however, in the cases examined in this study, liberal peacebuilding processes have created very weak states that have been capable of providing limited security with international assistance, and institutions with similar international support. Civil society has been marred by joblessness, lack of development, nationalism and the often tortuous slowness of the shift from the pre-intervention situation to even the most limited form of the liberal peace. Local conditions have benefited from better security, but progress in other areas has been slight so far. In these conditions, a lack of confidence in the new polity and in the economy are often key problems, as well as suspicion of the intentions of both international and local actors. For instance, throughout the Balkans, there has been suspicion of the intentions of internationals, of local politicians, as well as a lack of confidence in constitutions and institutions, the viability of the states being formed, and acute problems relating to both unemployment and ethnic chauvinism. This is despite the lengthy presence of the many internationals and their now long-running multidimensional peacebuilding operations.

Most of the various approaches deployed by international actors claim to be emancipatory. They all find their *raison d'être* in the identification and response to specific threats identified to the liberal peace project and its reliance on the liberal state itself. Furthermore, they exist side by side and in tension which each other. The conservative notions of liberal peace and the critical notions act, in theoretical, conceptual and policy terms, as brakes upon each other and upon the worst excesses of hegemony, domination and relativism. This has tended to produce a form of quasi-liberal statehood in many of its instances, representing a compromise of the international version of the orthodox liberal peace, and local and deep-rooted patterns of politics, both disrupted by war and peacemaking, reformative or re-asserting themselves in spite of, or through, liberal peacebuilding. The emancipatory wing of liberal peacebuilding, visible in theory, has not emerged in practice. This raises the questions of what practical and local forms of emancipation might look like; who might enable them; how they are understood and if necessary, transferred; who is most receptive to them and why; and what impact they have upon the recipients' identity? Again, these open questions underline the subjective ontology of peace in practice even despite liberal peacebuilding's attempt to produce an objective and universal peace system.

Building upon the above framework and critiques of the liberal peace in post-violence statebuilding, in this study we examine the key areas of the liberal peace in each of our case studies. In particular, we assess the process of democratisation, the development of the rule of law, of human rights, civil society, and free market reform and development in each case. We measure the achievements of these in the context of their claimed objectives, but also of their actual outcomes and consequences. This two-pronged process of assessment allows us to determine the basic type of liberal peace that has been developed according to the typology and graduations outlined above. What becomes clear as this study progresses is that peacebuilding and statebuilding are not necessarily comfortably matched. Indeed, it has become clear that some aspects of the contemporary statebuilding agenda do not support peace, even of a conservative or orthodox liberal graduation – or at least anything more than a very crude and negative peace.

Chapter Outline

In the context of the above framework, the first chapter in this study turns to an examination of the nature of the peace that has developed in Cambodia since the early 1990s. Despite the best efforts of international donors and the NGO community, liberal peacebuilding in Cambodia has so far failed in many of its key aims. It has also been modified by a combination of local political, economic and social dynamics, international failings, and the broader limitations of the liberal peacebuilding praxis. There have been some important advances, but serious doubts remain as to whether this project has been or can be successful, not least because of the ontological problem of whether the liberal peace is transferable into non-western or non-liberal polities. This raises the question of what type of peace has actually been built? We argue that the result of international efforts so far has been to produce little more than a virtual liberal peace.

Chapter 2 examines the effect of the Dayton Peace Accords by unpacking the components of liberal peacebuilding in Bosnia and questioning if the current situation is the result of a failure of liberal peace praxis. In particular it explores the nature of the relationship between international (sovereign) governance, the national/local political leadership, and the Bosnian peoples, which is the site of a clear disconnect, if not a continuing struggle. We show how this lack of cooperation is derailing liberal peacebuilding and the construction of a multi-ethnic and democratic state in Bosnia. The resultant political stalemate between nationalist groups, particularly in parliament, has led to a stagnation of the liberal statebuilding process. The result may see Bosnia left to fester in a virtual form of liberal peace with the causes of the conflict left unresolved amidst a chronic socio-economic crisis and a fragile security situation.

Chapter 3 extends these arguments to provide a critical examination of the effort to build a liberal peace since 1999 in East Timor. This illustrates that to a large degree the liberal peace model has failed the East Timorese people in producing anything remotely representative of a social contract or the 'good life'. There are two aspects to this: the first is the failure to construct a social contract between society and its institutions of governance. This is related to the broader issue of the social legitimacy of, and contract with, international actors derived from society and its complex groupings. The second is the failure, at least in the transitional period, to respond to the experiences of everyday life and welfare requirements of the new state's citizens.

Chapter 4 examines how the liberal project, even on the scale and depth employed by the international governance of Kosovo, is susceptible to local co-option, particularly where one group can adopt the language of the liberal peace and has strong support from, and credibility in the eyes of, the international community. This has led to a focus on achieving statehood for Kosovan Albanians, the marginalisation of other identity groups and their agendas (most vocally Kosovo's Serbs), and consequently the undermining of the pluralist goals of peacebuilding with the implicit cooperation of liberal peacebuilders. Given Serb opposition to statehood for Kosovo, there is a danger that liberal peacebuilding has encouraged the partition of Kosovo rather than created a pluralist polity, as it has already contributed to the emergence of a highly contested declaration of independence.

Chapter 5 examines the Oslo peace process as the first attempt to introduce the liberal peace framework in the Middle East, and the later, more limited engagement with the construction of a viable peace between the Israeli state and the Palestinians. It argues that the 'thin' liberal peace model employed in the Middle East peace process is problematic due to its exclusive nature. It builds states for liberals, and thus excludes and indeed, often simply ignores non-liberal others. Indeed, it may also be the case that some of the obstacles to a viable framework for peace stem, not just from local political and cultural dynamics, but also from the liberal peace paradigm's engagement with the region itself.

Finally, the Conclusion sums up our findings and arguments from the case-study chapters and charts the development and achievements of liberal peace theory as a method for creating a self-sustaining peace in post-conflict states. It re-examines the liberal peace framework, identifies its strengths and weaknesses, and offers some thoughts on some possible responses to the problems we have identified. Far from supporting the orthodoxies of liberal peacebuilding, as the reader might have by now realised, the conclusion to this study is highly critical. It suggests the need for modifications or alternative approaches for making peace, perhaps through greater cultural sensitivity and local ownership and with a focus on the agency, rights, needs and welfare of the communities and individuals concerned rather than on overly securitised institutions and states. This is not to abandon the liberal peace project, but to see it as part of an interwoven tapestry in which there are many patterns of peace, all of which share – if they are successful – high levels of local, regional and international legitimacy amongst citizens. The liberal peace has shown in its statebuilding forms to have very limited capacity where these three levels of legitimacy become diluted by a wide range of problems. This fragility in its legitimacy is related to different dynamics of local, regional and global politics, but it is also derived from internal inconsistencies and incoherencies in the liberal project that are amplified as it is exported into the non-liberal milieu. Some aspects of the liberal peace may well be universal (the desire for self-government, self-determination, democratic participation, forms of human rights, a rule of law and prosperity) but such claims mask much dissensus about their detail, contextuality and the mechanism of governance, control and power that put them in place for others. As we have seen in this study, this can very easily come to be seen as patronising tutelage, and impositionary. What seems to have emerged in our case studies at least, and via or perhaps despite such top-down, institutional and state-centric obsessions, is a liberal-local hybrid of positive and negative characteristics. International conditionality and hegemonic prescriptions coexist with local elites and everyday struggles for self-government, rights and welfare. The liberal peacebuilding community would do well to heed and perhaps facilitate these developments, rather than to ignore or resist them.

Notes

1. J. A. Hobson, *Imperialism: a Study* (London: Nisbet, 1902).
2. Oliver P. Richmond, *The Transformation of Peace* (Basingstoke: Palgrave Macmillan, 2005).
3. See, in particular, Roland Paris, *At War's End* (Cambridge: Cambridge University Press, 2004); Michael W. Doyle and Nicholas Sambanis, *Making War and Building Peace: United Nations Peace Operations* (Princeton, NJ: Princeton University Press, 2006).
4. See Richmond, *Transformation of Peace*, among many others, for more on this evolution. This section is based upon the conclusion of *Transformation of Peace*.
5. This is clearly the case when one considers the scope of the official reports and documentation released by international organisations (IOs), agencies, IFIs and NGOs on their aims and objectives, though they must also be read in the context of their need to work within their own constitution frameworks, which have normally been constructed with a previous set of priorities and constraints in mind. Boutros-Ghali's *Agenda for Peace* was perhaps the best example of this: Boutros Boutros-Ghali, *An Agenda for Peace: Preventive Diplomacy, Peacemaking and Peacekeeping* (New York: United Nations, 1992).
6. For an influential study on this, see Mary B. Anderson, *Do No Harm: How Aid Can Support Peace – or War* (Boulder, CO: Lynne Rienner Publishers, 1999).
7. For more on these contributory strands, see Richmond, *Transformation of Peace*, chaps 1 & 2.
8. For a development of these components of the liberal peace, and the notion of peace-as-governance, see Richmond, *Transformation of Peace*, esp. conclusion. See also Chandra Lekha Sriram, *Peace as Governance: Power-sharing, Armed Groups and Contemporary Peace Negotiations* (Basingstoke: Palgrave Macmillan, 2008).
9. Michel Foucault, 'Governmentality', in Graham Burchell, Colin Gordon and Peter Miller (eds), *The Foucault Effect: Studies in Governmentality* (Chicago, IL: Chicago University Press, 1997), pp. 87–104.
10. For a development of this line of thought, see François Debrix,

Re-envisioning Peacekeeping: the United Nations and the Mobilization of Ideology (Minneapolis, MN: University of Minnesota Press, 1999), p. 56.

11. Boutros-Ghali, *An Agenda for Peace*, A/47/277-S/24111, para. 55.
12. Ibid. A/47/277-S/24111, para. 55
13. Roland Paris, 'International peacebuilding and the mission civilisatrice', *Review of International Studies*, 28: 4, 2002, pp. 642–5.
14. This is essentially what Mandelbaum calls the combination of peace, democracy and free markets: Michael Mandelbaum, *The Ideas that Conquered the World: Peace, Democracy, and Free markets in the Twenty-first Century* (New York: Public Affairs, 2002), p. 6.
15. This cliché was often quoted to us during interviews with officials during the fieldwork for this project.
16. See Oliver P. Richmond, 'UN peace operations and the dilemmas of the peacebuilding consensus', *International Peacekeeping*, 10: 4, 2004.
17. United Nations, *Report of the Panel on UN Peace Operations* (New York: UN, 2000). Available at http://www.un.org/peace/reports/peace_operations/, 21 August 2000.
18. Kofi Annan, 'Democracy as an international issue', *Global Governance*, 8: 2, April–June 2002, pp. 134–42; A. Bellamy and P. Williams, 'Peace operations and global order', *International Peacekeeping*, 10: 4, 2004; D. Chandler, *From Kosovo to Kabul: Human Rights and International Intervention* (London: Pluto, 2002); J. Chopra and H. Tanja, 'Participatory intervention', *Global Governance*, 10, 2004; M. Duffield, *Global Governance and the New Wars* (London: Zed Books, 2001); R. Paris, *At War's End* (Cambridge: Cambridge University Press, 2004); M. Pugh, 'Peacekeeping and critical theory', Conference Presentation at BISA, LSE, London, 16–18 December, 2002.
19. This was the conclusion reached by many of our interviewees, official and non-official during fieldwork in the Balkans in January 2005.

Cambodia: Liberal Hubris and Virtual Peace[1]

> What is, is, what is not, is not.
> The Tao is made because we walk it,
> things become what they are called.
> Chuang Tzu[2]

Introduction

In 1993 there seemed to be an early post-Cold War triumph for the
United Nations, and for the liberal peace. Following the proclamation of the Cambodian constitution and the creation of the new government of Cambodia, the United Nations Security Council declared
the successful completion of the mandate of the United Nations
Transitional Authority in Cambodia (UNTAC)[3] and pulled out.
This heavily publicised (and much criticised) withdrawal was hailed
as a great achievement for the UN and the 'new world order,' as it
seemingly replaced a particularly brutal intrastate conflict with the
concept of liberal peace. However, as this chapter argues, the liberal
peacebuilding project in Cambodia has been far from successful
and has created little more than a virtual peace.[4] Leaving aside the
ontological problem of whether the liberal peace is at all viable, or
whether its export through a weak peacebuilding consensus is possible, why is it that the liberal peacebuilding project in Cambodia has
failed after so many years to move beyond the virtual? The liberal
peace seems mainly to exist in the minds of the international elites
who are attempting to steer its reform and development and is at
best incompatible with the indigenous Cambodian political, social,
cultural and economic structures. Applying the liberal peace to
Cambodia is analogous to using a square peg for a round hole.

The UNTAC mandate was both revolutionary and unprecedented
for the UN with regard to the mission aims and intrusive methods
it employed to achieve them. Acting broadly to accomplish a comprehensive political settlement of the Cambodian conflict and with a
budget of $1.7 billion, UNTAC sought to establish overall command

of the Cambodian socio-political and economic infrastructure by taking control of seven components.[5] These components, comprising human rights, electoral, military, civil administration, police, repatriation and rehabilitation elements,[6] amounted to a statebuilding exercise underwritten by the principles of the Wilsonian liberal peace, combined with contemporary neoliberal principles. This approach was not necessarily new, building upon the peacebuilding ideas already in practice in Namibia (UNTAG) and El Salvador (ONUSAL).[7] A longer historical view might also point to similarities to the US experiences of state reconstruction in both Germany and Japan after 1945, and of their engagement in reconstruction for allied states.

The departure of the UN from dealing with the symptoms of conflict via peacemaking and peacekeeping to approaching the root causes via 'peacebuilding' was fully articulated by Boutros-Ghali in *An Agenda for Peace* in June 1992.[8] In this report, with respect to peacebuilding Boutros-Ghali argued that the need was to 'identify and support structures which will tend to strengthen and solidify peace in order to avoid a relapse into conflict'.[9] This is perhaps reflective of the post-Cold War liberal peace optimism of the 'end of history',[10] which supposedly heralded a 'new world order' also proclaimed by US President Bush Senior, as the UN became involved in statebuilding enterprises in the early 1990s. Despite notable setbacks for UN liberal peace missions, such as in Somalia, the liberal peace thesis has permeated through UN doctrine, forming the mainstay of *Supplement to an Agenda for Peace* (1995),[11] the Millennium Development Goals (2000)[12] and the High Level Panel Report (2004)[13] and is equally instrumental in the imminent creation of a permanent peacebuilding commission at the UN.

The example of peace in Cambodia, as an early test of the validity of the liberal peace thesis and indeed the resolve of the UN, is an important one. Significant questions have to be asked. Fourteen years after the declared success of the Paris Peace Accords and the withdrawal of UNTAC, and following $200 billion worth of investment and the involvement of national governments, IOs and untold NGOs, it is questionable whether the liberal peace has taken root in Cambodia.

This chapter examines the nature of the peace that exists in Cambodia by deploying the liberal peace framework. This in turn allows for an assessment of the Cambodian peace in regard to its perceived position, relative to international understanding, focusing particularly on UN, governmental and international donor organisation perspectives. We argue that the perceived position of the achievements of peacebuilding in Cambodia as an 'orthodox liberal peace', perhaps even progressively moving to embrace an emancipatory liberal peace model, is an illusionary and mythical construct – a 'virtual peace' which so often is camouflaged by the liberal peace. As the reconstruction of peace in Cambodia was based upon a comprehensive peace agreement, it was assumed that it would achieve an orthodox liberal peace soon after elections were held. In fact, as we show, the peace prevalent in Cambodia is much more limited and at best is a conservative liberal peace. Far from embracing liberal peace, the peace in Cambodia, despite the best efforts of international donors and the NGO community, has probably moved little from its status during the UNTAC period. However, it is clear that the potential for an orthodox liberal peace is present mainly because of the array of international actors who have remained engaged in the liberal peace project in Cambodia since the early 1990s. In light of this claim, this chapter will aim to analyse the current peacebuilding situation and explain why peace in Cambodia may resemble an orthodox and therefore externally sustainable (rather than self-sustaining) peace, while in actual fact there are many important contra indications. It will critique the liberal peace thesis in its application to the case of Cambodia and ask what type of peace actually exists, whether this is a sustainable form of peace, and ascertain why this is so.

Cambodia and the Liberal Peace

When the mission was launched, UNTAC promised a 'comprehensive peace' settlement in Cambodia.[14] Indeed the Paris Peace conference adopted a wide-ranging agreement on a political, social and economic settlement of the conflict. This included political institutions such as sovereignty, independence and territorial integrity and the renovation of both society and the economy via a declaration on rehabilitation and reconstruction.[15] UNTAC's intention following a ceasefire was to bring the four warring factions together and create, via democratic elections, a power-sharing government, whilst rebuilding state infrastructure managed by liberal democratic institutions. The Paris agreement, which formed the basis for the UNTAC mandate, was composed essentially of liberal peace components, including a ceasefire and disarmament, maintenance of law and order, repatriation of refugees, the protection of human rights (via a new constitution), the control of administrative machinery, as well as, crucially, the organisation, conduct and monitoring of elections.[16] The most important element of these was of course elections, which were intended to create a power-sharing political alternative to the violent power struggle of the civil war. Indeed the battle for power between rival factions is widely considered to be the root of the Cambodian conflict, compounded perhaps by the geo-political interests of regional and international actors. As Heininger points out, 'unlike most post-cold war conflicts, neither ethnic nor tribal hatreds drove it. Rather it was a simple struggle for political power by different factions',[17] consisting of the Cambodian People's Party (CPP) led by Hun Sen, Prince Sihanouk's FUNCINPEC party, the Khmer Rouge and the Khmer People's National Liberation Front (KPNLF). These power structures led Chandler to suggest that the political history of Cambodia can be described as a struggle among factions between three visions of order: royalism, parliamentarianism and socialism.[18]

The underlying assumption of the UNTAC mission was that if elections were imposed on the Cambodian political system and a measure of power sharing was established between the groups, coupled with the implementation of liberal reforms in society and a market economy, liberal order would naturally follow and Cambodia would be guided from civil war into a situation of sustainable peace. This approach represents the liberal peace thesis that has its roots in Kantian thinking about perpetual peace and, as Paris points out, is a working example of the Wilsonian hypothesis.[19]

In order to achieve such a form of liberal peace, the international community charged the UN with the political and economic restructuring of a member state[20] into a liberal democracy. UNTAC was to supervise the transition from a one-party state and war-torn society to a peaceful multi-party democracy.[21] Consequently, UNTAC faced a mammoth statebuilding task. For this, it received a budget of $1.5 billion, $595 million of which was assigned to 'restore a sustainable degree of economic and social stability'.[22] UNTAC then intended to re-establish and in some cases actually create state institutions through which political power could be centralised and controlled by the rule of law. This was to be achieved, as Lizee explains, by substituting the political control exercised by factions or sub-factions with that of a newly centralised means of governance. This new system of governance would operate under a replenished state apparatus that would exercise state power according to democratic rule.[23]

The nature of peace that UNTAC intended to introduce in 1992 closely followed a conservative liberal peace according to the typology presented in the introduction to this book. It was to be achieved by force and diplomacy and existed as a constitutional peace, conceived, instituted and imposed on Cambodia entirely from 'outside'. Social and developmental aspects of the new peace were less significant, though NGOs and other actors did give an 'orthodox peace' element to the peacebuilding process. Nevertheless, the expectations for a political transformation in Cambodia were surprisingly high, and perhaps rightly so, as the liberal peace model claims a proven ontology of sustainable peace and good democratic governance. The obvious problem, however, was the lack of historical and cultural models in Cambodian society for such a socio-political system. Many considered it unrealistic to expect a UN operation to rebuild Cambodia as a democracy in a relatively short period of time because it was a country with no history of free elections and power sharing.[24] As a result, many still feel this is unrealistic.[25]

However, the UNTAC mandate, which itself represented an exercise in social engineering, had a proven liberal lineage in the development of western states and the belief that peace follows the development of democracy. The key to liberal peace in Cambodia and the success of the UNTAC mandate was believed to be in the centralisation of power through elections and the regulation of violence. Hence, the structure of peace UNTAC intended to create was to be achieved by remodelling Cambodia on the example of the western state.[26] What is more, UNTAC was expected to provide relatively quick results given that a peace agreement had already been arrived at, and was focused upon the holding of 'free and fair' elections. This was intended to provide the exit point for UNTAC and would dismantle its control of key aspects of governance. A system of political power was to be established which was to be based on 'a centralised and far-reaching managerial apparatus, allowing an administrative supervision and indeed regulation of Cambodian society without any resort to force'.[27] Furthermore, political rights expressed through state power would be developed containing provisions for human rights that would shield individuals from the arbitrary use of violence by state agencies.[28] This would in turn be complemented by the development and promotion of liberal economic market forces and a capitalist economy which would 'serve to instil the notion of freedom of economic choice leading to the freedom of political choice'[29] and the thus social empowerment of the individual.

These political and economic developments were intended to complement the creation, development and growth of civil society, which would cement the liberal peace in Cambodia. The emergence of civil society has been a slow process but it has been aided by the availability of donor funding[30] and the creation of pressure groups and organisations, some purely political, but the majority non-governmental. These included 'advocacy, watchdog, and single-interest groups such as professional associations, community groups; credit societies; and user groups'.[31] In this context, NGOs attempted to encourage

> participation and awareness, help reduce poverty at the grassroots level, promote peace, democracy and human rights; assist in safeguarding democratic processes, observe in elections, strengthen the government's understanding and knowledge of rule of law, and help in dispute-solving.[32]

Indeed the role played by NGOs has been particularly significant since the UNTAC period in developing and sustaining the liberal peace by significant contributions to the rebuilding of Cambodian society. In fact the presence of NGOs, especially indigenous ones, has been interpreted as a positive indicator of the (re)emergence of civil society in Cambodia.[33] According to Pact, an international NGO, over 400 Cambodian NGOs are working throughout the country. This increasingly strong and responsive local NGO sector contributes significantly to Cambodia's development and its civil society.[34] They are also an important source of funding. For example, between 1992 and 2001 the donor community has disbursed more than $4 billion to and through NGOs.[35]

Clearly, the international community and especially the United Nations have a vested interest in maintaining the perceived success of the UNTAC mission and the maintenance of liberal peace in Cambodia. As a result, and perhaps due to the level of interest in the Cambodian liberal experiment, there is a growing volume of work analysing the UNTAC mission. The consensus of opinion seems to suggest that despite the enormity of the project, UNTAC was a success.[36] This is due primarily to the unexpected ability of the mission to achieve organised elections with an impressive 90 per cent electorate participation, establish national self-determination and independence, end civil war, and repatriate 370,000 refugees.[37] It is also noted in the literature that UNTAC was more than just a peace-keeping mission but a peacebuilding process to 'implant democracy, change values and establish a new pattern of governance based on multi-partism and fair elections'.[38] UNTAC was envisioned as a fully fledged peace operation, conditioned by the expectation that it would withdraw after elections, and that the peace process itself was more or less determined by the holding of elections. Yet it is debatable whether the withdrawal of UNTAC following the elections suggests that an orthodox liberal peace had emerged, as the international community expected.[39]

In accordance with the orthodox liberal peace graduation, the vacuum created by the departure of UNTAC enabled peacebuilding actors to focus on the state. This is illustrated by the fact that between 1992 and 2001, eighteen major bilateral donors[40] and several other multilateral ones, including UN agencies, the World Bank, the International Monetary Fund (IMF), the Asian Development Bank (ADB) and the EU have provided funding of more than $4 billion to promote various liberal peace projects in Cambodia.[41] In 1992, the IMF introduced an economic stabilisation programme to cut capital and social spending, followed up by a structural adjustment loan, designed to stimulate market reforms.[42] Consequently, although economic development is very poor, the economy has shown signs of progress. For example, from 1992 to 2002 it grew by 7 per cent per annum in 1995–6 with an average growth rate of 4.6 in 1993–2000.[43] UNTAC had tried to stimulate the Cambodian economy via a massive aid programme, which was intended to develop markets and industries in Cambodia.[44] Any success here was primarily due to UNTAC's financial impact as its presence stimulated the local economy in construction, trade and services for foreign consumption, not all of it salubrious.[45]

Doyle suggests that UNTAC's overall success was due to its multi-dimensional character. He points to a number of 'successes' including the elections and rehabilitation programme, as well as state and civil society development via the control of state finances, currency and budget.[46] He also highlights the development of human rights via the adoption of the main human rights covenants, re-education programmes and the granting of freedoms of press, association and movement.[47] According to these perceived successes an orthodox liberal peace should have taken root in Cambodia. The next section examines why this may not be a fair representation of the local reality.

Virtual Peace?

Thirteen years after the withdrawal of UNTAC and the investment of over US $5.66 billon in aid (by 2003)[48] from donors and lenders,[49] some of which has funded the activities of over four hundred or so

NGOs, has a self-sustaining (liberal) peace taken root in Cambodia? Not so, according to John Sanderson, the former UNTAC commander, who suggested in 2001 that 'the Cambodian people find themselves in a state which remains largely lawless some nine years after the Paris peace agreements, due to less than successful attempts through the ballot box in producing a form of properly consensual government'.[50] As with the literature on the successes of UNTAC there is also a substantial body of work discussing the failures of the mission – although much of the analysis in this literature relates directly to an assessment of the mechanics and logistics of the actual UN operation itself, such as lessons of UNTAC.[51] Nevertheless, because we intend to examine the nature of the peace that currently exists in Cambodia it is important to be aware of the perceived shortcomings of the UNTAC project, as it is from these roots that the current situation in Cambodia has grown.

Consensus on the main failures of the UN mission focuses principally on the inability of UNTAC to obtain a complete ceasefire and fully disarm, demobilise and canton 70 per cent of the military forces of the four main factions.[52] Indeed the loss of the Khmer Rouge from the power-sharing settlement (they withdrew from the Paris agreement, electoral process and disarmament in the summer of 1992)[53] can be seen not only as a fundamental failure of the democratic and liberalising political process, which relied upon the actual representation and participation in government of the various factions, but also of the attempt to revolutionise the existing political culture and break the stranglehold of the traditional political system that exists. This system, as we have suggested, rests upon contention for absolute political control. It is perhaps the essence of elite politics and is typified by the chronic struggle for political power and hegemonic dominance. This understanding of state power by Cambodian political actors as a zero sum commodity is an important factor and part of the reason why democratisation is proving such as Sisyphean task.

The difficulty in reconciling these factions is related to further problems attributed to UNTAC and the development of liberal peace, focusing on the weakness of UNTAC in dealing with the state. Despite the comprehensive scope of the mandate, UNTAC failed to comprehensively achieve its terms and thus fully instigate the required political, social and economic structural changes that could help facilitate the accommodation of liberal peace. The key failure once again relates to the factions and UNTAC's inability to control them by persuasion, coercion or even force (the latter being a method that UNTAC were clearly reluctant to employ). Doyle argues that whilst UNTAC had a broad mandate, it did not exploit or fully enforce it. He suggests a central failure was the inability of UNTAC to control the civilian administration and prevent the break down of law and order and political neutrality.[54] The problem was that the Paris Peace Accords were reliant on the good faith and voluntary cooperation of the factions in the Supreme National Council (SNC). However, the factions cooperated only when it suited their individual interests and party agendas. This obviously caused complications for affective administrative control. For example, UNTAC was unable to control the provinces without the aid of the factions who often circumvented UNTAC bureaucracy to achieve their own agendas. Furthermore, the collapsed condition of the state of Cambodia meant that in some regions it had lost effective control anyway and de facto authority had slipped to provincial governors and generals.[55] Doyle sums up the problems of UNTAC's inadequacy by pointing out that 'the UN agreed to do much more than monitor but less than replace'.[56]

UNTAC's role in the introduction of the mainstay of liberal peace – democratisation – has proved to be far from successful. It would be perhaps unfair to apportion all the blame to UNTAC for this, but nevertheless the inadequacies of the UN mission certainly were a contributory factor. Indeed, since UNTAC's withdrawal it has proved decidedly difficult to introduce liberal democracy in a lasting and sustainable form to Cambodia, especially since the government that was created by the democratic elections in 1992, 1998 and 2003 has not proved to be particularly representative. Although UNTAC's 'free and fair' elections of 1992 were enough to satisfy the mandate,[57] it did not go far enough in breaking the dictatorial nature of the Cambodian political system. Indeed, Hun Sen's State of Cambodia (SOC)[58] used the elections to democratically legitimise the monopoly of power. As the Khmer Rouge claimed at the time (they used it as a reason for their departure from the peace process), real political power had not been transferred to the SNC. Hence, the SOC, dominated by the dictatorial Prime Minister Hun Sen, and the CCP, still had a monopoly of state apparatus to serve its own ends; this was especially relevant in the control of the security forces and the secret police.[59]

Although FUNCINPEC won more votes than the CCP and King Sihanouk became head of state, Hun Sen never relaxed his hold on the reigns of governmental power. In fact, on the contrary, he progressively increased, centralised and strengthened his own personal grip. Heder has charted the growing consolidation of power of Hun Sen and the current reality of the Cambodian state – 'not as a vehicle for good governance, but for serving the interests of Hun Sen and his entourage, a maze of patronage, corruption and repression.'[60] Hun Sen, consolidating on a coup in 1997, established himself in an unrivalled position of power following his gradual erosion of FUNCINPEC strength and the increasing repression of the Sam Rainsy Party (SRP), both of whom formed the opposition movement Alliance of Democrats (AD) after the 2003 election. The apparent endgame occurred after the results of the 2003 election, when, sensing defeat, Hun Sen orchestrated a virtual 'palace coup' in which he formed a government that destroyed FUNCINPEC power and exiled the SRP.[61] This led Sam Rainsy to ironically remark, 'As a fake democracy, Cambodia is a country with only a democratic façade, made up of apparently democratic institutions, which are functioning in fact in the most autocratic way.'[62] Liberal peace in Cambodia is clearly a virtual peace.

The paralysis of democratic government and civil society in Cambodia, incorporating the tenets of liberal peace (democracy, political representation and participation, rule of law and human rights), is widely attributed to the problem of corruption. Although the main accusations of corruption are focused at government level, it is undoubtedly an enormous problem. USAID suggested $300–500 million is 'diverted' from government coffers every year, a figure approximately equal to that of annual donor assistance.[63] Corruption as perceived within the liberal peace framework seems to be accepted at many levels of society. The Centre for Social Development (CSD), an indigenous NGO campaigning against corruption, recognises the institutionalisation of corrupt practices. In a particularly detailed survey of 'everyday forms of corrupt practices', the CSD cites detailed examples of daily corruption ranging from public services such as water and electricity, through to education and health, business licensing and police, customs and the judiciary.[64] Given that free market reform and neoliberal models of development underpin liberal peacebuilding, such practices are clearly meant to impede the taking root of the liberal peace – to the extent that this might even be a purposeful collusion on the part of actors who see the liberal peace as undermining their traditional privileges.

Corruption is a central problem for Cambodian development and democratisation. This concern is illustrated by the main funders and donors who see corruption as a major drain on their resources. Some organisations are resigned to the futility of the problem and have imposed conditionality, in the form of governance indicators, on loans;[65] others have even withdrawn from funding some areas altogether.[66] Nevertheless, the UN, World Bank, USAID, ADB and alike, are still heavily investing in anti-corruption plans, ranging from – ironically – cash funding, to education, awareness and action programmes. Furthermore, according to the UN, who identify corruption as a key area requiring 'urgent attention', the government of Hun Sen has established fighting corruption as its first priority in its 'good governance' programme tied to the Cambodia Millennium Development Goals.[67] Yet the effectiveness of anti-corruption legislation and the willingness of the Hun Sen government to enforce it remains to be seen. Unsurprisingly its record to date does not inspire optimism. Indeed, corruption exists in almost every facet of Cambodian politics and society, being largely understood and accepted as a cultural norm, as a lubricant of the Cambodian machine – without which nothing would function.

Apart from fighting corruption, another vital pillar of the structure of liberal peace – human rights – is not in a much better position. In 1992, UNTAC promised extensive initiatives to respect, observe and protect the human rights and freedoms of Cambodian citizens.[68] However, according to Human Rights Watch (HRW) 'Cambodia in 2005 saw a sharp reversal in progress towards observing human rights and developing political pluralism since the signing of the 1991 Paris Peace Accords.'[69] Despite the best intentions of UNTAC in 1992 and the continuing work of human rights NGOs, local and regional organisations and the United Nations Development Programme (UNDP, which invested $13 million in a democratic governance programme in 2004), Cambodia still has a particularly poor human rights record. This includes political intimidation, especially against political opponents of the government, such as the SRP, but also against independent media and civil society.[70] The judiciary are also widely viewed as corrupt, incompetent and biased. According to HRW, they continue to be used to 'advance political agendas, silence critics and strip people of their land'.[71] In fact, in a report on human rights, the CSD gives the judiciary and courts the most dishonest institution rating (almost off the scale), closely flowed by the customs and the police.[72]

Also extensively contravened are freedoms of association and assembly, as 'threats to human rights defenders have intensified, with grass roots activists and human rights workers being subjected to harassment, intimidation, restrictions of movement, legal action, and physical violence'.[73] Perhaps in response to these continuing problems UNDP launched a development assistance framework (UNDAF) for the period 2006–10. In conjunction with the World Bank, ADB and the Department for International Development (DFID), they intend to promote good governance and the promotion and protection of human rights,[74] but once again, the success of this programme requires close government cooperation.

The failure to successfully plant human rights and freedoms in Cambodian soil can be attributed to the inability of the UNTAC mission to enforce corrective measures on the Cambodian government during its tenure. However, a growing, and in many ways more developed, human rights programme has been underway in the last thirteen years, so aside from UNTAC, why has a central branch of the liberal peace failed to take root? To answer this question it is perhaps important to examine the social, historical and cultural nature of Cambodia and question whether the predominantly western political and social constructs encapsulated in the liberal peace are compatible with the Cambodian structure. As Jenny Heininger points out, in a country with a history of human rights abuses bordering on genocide it would be an uphill task to educate the population and develop indigenous human rights organisations and mechanisms.[75] This is an issue central to the understanding of liberal peace and its compatibility with developing and post-conflict countries with little or no history of human rights and will also be dealt with in the next section.

Has the economic liberal peace – free and globalised markets and neoliberal development – become sustainable in Cambodia? Once again, the facts are not encouraging. According to the Economic Institute of Cambodia (EIC) the annual growth rate of the economy (GDP) for 2005–6 was around 5 per cent – down from 7.7 per cent in 2004 and 5.2 per cent in 2002. Inflation was set to continue to rise. The exchange rate of the Riel against the US dollar has also been weakened by an economic slowdown in rural areas. This is not helped by worsening health statistics and the fact that there seems to be a steady growth of the poverty rate. Based on earning US $1 per day, 36 per cent of the population were on or below this in 1997, 39.4 per cent in 2000 and 42.4 per cent in 2004 – the most recent figure (this amounts to approximately 6 million people out of a population of 13 million).[76] Incidentally, according to UNDP statistics, 78 per cent of the Cambodian population live below US $2 per day. This rates Cambodia eighty-one (out of 103) on the Human Poverty Index (HPI) making it the worst performer in East Asia and the Pacific.[77] According to UNICEF, the child mortality rate is also increasing: for under 5 year olds it is 141 per 1,000 (2004) compared to 115 in 1990. Infant mortality is 97 per 1,000 (2004) compared with 80 in 1990.[78] The average life expectancy currently stands at 57.4 (2001).[79] These disturbing statistics rate Cambodia 130 out of 177 on the UN Human Development Index (HDI), ranking it second lowest in Southeast Asia as a least developed country (LDC).[80]

These figures have not resulted, however, from the international community fiddling whilst Cambodia burns. As we outlined above, Cambodia has been the recipient of foreign aid since 1993 totalling over US $5.66 billion, the results of which have not been all bad. As the EIC suggest, '[T]hese assistances have greatly contributed to the reconstruction of Cambodia, boosting economic growth, financing trade and budget deficits and, to some extent, to alleviating poverty.'[81] Quite what the economic situation in Cambodia would be like now without these extensive aid packages, also incorporating institutional and technical assistance, is perhaps all too easy to imagine. Nevertheless, an economic liberal peace in Cambodia is still far from reality. Criticism for this has been directed at both the donor community and the government. The EIC suggest that the simple reason for the lack of high economic growth performance is the absence of an automatic mechanism to ensure simultaneous growth and poverty reduction. As a result they and other institutions such as the World Bank, ADB and IMF have recommend extensive structural reforms;[82] however, once again these are dependent on the willingness of the Hun Sen government.

Criticism has also been levelled at the international community, especially at the emphasis of investment, which the EIC suggest should be focused more on agricultural development, health care, education and fundamental infrastructure.[83] It has also been pointed out that the financial aid entering the country often goes directly to the salaries of foreign advisors and technical specialists: it therefore leaves the country and does not benefit either the economy or the development of indigenous employment and local capacity. Thus, EIC recommend that technical assistance should be provided by Cambodian professionals or via a local partnership with foreigners.[84]

UNTAC, too, has not escaped criticism for having a retrogressive effect on the fragile economy, which paradoxically it was created to strengthen. As Mayall argues, 'The UNTAC presence was economically and socially destabilising because it fuelled an artificial boom and generated massive inflation.'[85] Kato also identifies the 'distortionary effects' of UNTAC, and suggests that the economic effect of the mission was to make some Cambodians very rich, while many more suffered a fall in standard of living, due to insecurity and inflation.[86] A further social consequence of UNTAC was the artificial boom created by the relative wealth of its staff. This had obvious local effects but also created an influx of Vietnamese immigrants, especially prostitutes. This not only exacerbated ethnic tensions but is also arguably responsible for the introduction of the HIV epidemic to Cambodia,[87] which now stands at a worrying 1.9 per cent.[88]

Almost all observers of the current Cambodian economy identify a concerning growth in the gap between the rich and poor.[89] Peou suggests that this is a 'consequence of liberalisation without adequate state intervention or protection'.[90] Many also point to the functioning of an 'informal' economy that neither is controlled by nor contributes to the development of the state. Furthermore, there is a distinct lack of unemployment figures available for the Cambodian economy suggesting a widely accepted understanding that it is a subsistence economy[91] and therefore western (liberal) forms of measuring it are irrelevant. World Bank officials estimate that 85 per cent of the population are still subsisting on small strips of land ironically distributed by the Khmer Rouge in an attempt to end feudal land ownership, even after over a decade of development initiatives.[92] Certainly the implications of applying a free market system to a state that perhaps lacks the capacity to coordinate it may in fact be responsible for the stagnating economy and be the reason for the growing disparity between socio-economic groups.

The next section of this chapter examines three questions. First, why and for what reasons has liberal peace not become self-sustaining in Cambodia, at least in the manner that the international community hoped for? How far is what is recognisable as a liberal form of peace in Cambodia dependent upon the support of external actors, and how far is the current peace actually a virtual peace? Thirdly, it seeks to discover what 'type' of peace actually exists in Cambodia.

Liberal Peace: Can you Get There from Here?

The question that now arises is, if the orthodox version of the liberal peace has not been created after more than a decade of peacebuilding involvement, what kind of peace actually exists? Is the liberal peace virtual in the case of Cambodia, simply acting as a superficial overlay and mainly identifiable to the internationals present, making little impact upon the indigenous polity, its components and citizens?

In comparison to western philosophy, which operates a predominantly linear ontology in accordance with western cultural traditions of progress from one place to another along an established or preordained line or axis to an end result, eastern philosophy is generally holistic and perhaps more accommodating, advocating acceptance of where one actually is as a result of the effects of the natural order, created by the influence of the environment in which one exists. Is Cambodian politics progressing according to the technology of governance offered by the liberal peace or is it merely existing as is, or developing into a hybrid form – which western peacebuilders sometimes describe in rather frustrated fashion as passivity?

Essentially, as we have demonstrated above, liberal peace is a western linear concept that relies upon the actor progressing along a set or preordained path to the end result of emancipated liberal peace, which Fukuyama calls 'getting to Denmark'.[93] The difficulty with the Cambodian situation, as we have outlined thus far, is that there are cultural obstacles associated with traditional configurations of power, knowledge and institutions, which may be obstructing the liberal peace 'journey'. This is perhaps because the tenets required by liberal peace are actually incompatible with the Cambodian social and political milieu, which effectively nominates and perpetuates structures that, even within the milieu of the liberal peace, resist deep-rooted reform. In the next sub-sections we discuss what has 'gone wrong' with the liberal peace in Cambodia and why the gap exists between real and virtual liberal peace. Essentially we will be asking: can Cambodian politics develop from where it is assumed to be now, to the desired orthodox liberal peace, which was so clearly imagined in the Paris Peace Accords and the mandate of UNTAC and which has clearly not yet been achieved? If not, is the concept of liberal peace actually compatible with the Cambodian cultural political system, and if not, why not? In what follows, we focus on the compatibility of some of the key individual components of the liberal peace framework.

Democratisation and Good Governance

As we argued above in the examination of the imposition of democratisation on Cambodia, first by UNTAC and since then by the various agencies of democracy operating within it, the sustainability or even existence of democratisation is tenuous. This, it seems, is due primarily to the strong political and cultural traditions of power (and violence) that are inherent in Cambodian society. We should not excuse or accept the lack of democracy in Cambodia via an inherency or culturalist argument but should acknowledge the existence of a Cambodian political system, though one that is not organised via the territorial boundaries of the sovereign state necessarily. This is particularly important because despite popular misconceptions of its non-existence, it has proven a powerful influence on Cambodian affairs since at least the Angkorian period twelve hundred years ago.[94] The belief or at least assumption that an indigenous political system and indeed economic system does not exist in post-conflict 'failed states' such as Cambodia (even since the destruction wrought by the Khmer Rouge and the civil war) is an oversimplification.

The assumption that a post-conflict 'collapsed' state has no socio-economic or political system often legitimates the installation of the liberal peace framework. This establishes 'peace through governance', in which liberal modes of governance for a state's key characteristics are inculcated by international actors. The difficulty with Cambodia is that recognised or not (by internationals), the dynamics of the existing (cultural and historical) political system in Cambodia are not presently closely compatible with the liberal peace. Consequently, attempting to impose a totally new system – especially one so culturally different – where one already exists and functions is proving difficult. One of the shortcomings of UNTAC was its failure to legitimately and completely remove the existing political system – that of absolute domination of power by one party (leaving aside the problem of whether the new liberal peace framework is viable at all, for the moment).

Perhaps an even more fundamental issue than the imposition of a new political system lies in the question of whether the roots of the conflict have been addressed, with the Cambodian conflict being rooted in the contention for power and the monopoly of violence. Part of the liberal peace framework involves the creation of a Weberian state in which violence is monopolised by the state on the assumption that it will not exploit this role. However, as Roberts argues, imposed elections and the democratic process 'merely changed the vehicle for communicating hostility and confrontation, from war to elections',[95] hence the monopoly of violence was of benefit to the incumbent in this process. Yet originally, the democratic procedure is based on the assumption of 'good government' and the notion of 'loyal opposition', requiring the elected 'losers' in the democratic government to back the majority and have an interest in supporting the decision for the good of the country. Conversely, the 'winners' need a level of magnanimity and interest in power sharing in government and need to include all sides in the political process. However, aside from the notional acceptance of the royal family as head of state, the incumbent Cambodian regime has never done this. In fact – quite the opposite – they operate as an autocratic dictatorship. But should we be surprised by this, given the nature of Cambodian politics? Roberts illustrates the point:

> The significance of the [Cambodian] conflict has not changed. It remains a vital struggle for political power in an extremely hostile environment where the consequence of absolute defeat and marginalisation could be dire. Power in Cambodia, traditionally and contemporarily, has been of an absolutist nature, with little tolerance of opposition.[96]

This assumption on the nature of the existing Cambodian political system clearly has very serious implications for future of the liberal peacebuilding project in Cambodia. The notion of political power and the contention for its sole domination are deeply embedded in Cambodian culture and form the framework around which the social structure is constructed. Power and violence are not centralised in the mechanics of the state but are institutionalised in governance and therefore monopolised by the ruling party, which acts as a natural block to the process of democratisation. This is because liberal peace is based on the understanding that society moves to embrace non-violence and the institution of the state, with a strengthened structure that is legitimised by democratic elections and which centralises and monopolises the means of violence. This is the basis of the social contract – the surrender of violence by individuals and groups to the state in defence of its citizens and ultimately of democracy.

Lizee argues that it is for this reason that the 'logic' of peace in Cambodia is deeply flawed. Indeed, the imposition of peace in Cambodia is a political rather than merely a technical problem: the requirement for a political framework is that it would render the contest for power in Cambodia non-violent. Yet this type of social structure does not exist in Cambodian society.[97] If we accept that the liberal peace project is viable we need to accept that this process is a comprehensive form of social engineering. Such a peace is about institutionalising liberal forms of governance, particularly associated with democratisation and the economic system. Due to the inherent difficulties in the organic development of democracy, this is becoming central to the development of liberal peace and its crucial component of statebuilding. Thus a lexicon that increasingly accompanies the language of liberal peace is that of statebuilding, which provides the shell in which governance is instituted along liberal lines to create the liberal peace, focusing on the centralisation of power, the monopoly over the means of violence, the establishment of democratic and corruption-free governance to protect the individual, as well as to promote their rights and interests through the creation of state capacity. Fukuyama suggests that the dimensions of liberal 'stateness' revolve around 'state function' and 'state capacity', whereby the functions of states and the ability to carry them out are crucial. In his view, model states have a number of essential functions of government (scope) and have high capacity to achieve them (institutional capacity or strength).[98] The Cambodian state – a weak state in this instance – has a very limited scope of government functions and a low capacity to achieve them. The obvious difficulty in Cambodia is the imposition of liberal democratic post-conflict statebuilding reforms on a state with a distinct lack of capacity (government institutional strength) to achieve them. In terms of good governance, the democratic process is clearly being interfered with, corruption is rife and the general population has little agency, politically, economically or socially, other than in limited and very localised contexts.[99]

This raises a number of issues about how democratic institutions are to be built and 'good governance' made sustainable. Perhaps the most important question revolves around the role of the internationals. IOs, ROs, as well as international and local NGOs are all integral parts of the liberal democratic peace process. Following the extensive UNTAC remit, these organisations were drawn into the reconstruction vacuum created by the departing UN mission. NGOs provided essential support to the country's rehabilitation and reconstruction by supplying financial and technical assistance, plus training and capacity building activities.[100] Yet,

> most international NGOs do not support local NGOs and few have well-developed plans for capacity building and institutional support. They are unclear about the future and have no handover strategies, leaving the sustainability of their programmes in doubt. Also, their assumptions about developments in Cambodian society are unclear and their methods of working with the government are inconsistent.[101]

Despite these withering criticisms, the NGO community has become the de facto or virtual state in Cambodia and represent *the* liberal democratic peace in the statebuilding process. It is a widely held belief that if the internationals left the country, Cambodian liberal peace would quickly disintegrate.[102] For example, international donors, frustrated with the endemic corruption and weakness of state governance, circumvent the bureaucratic inefficiency of government and instead fund NGOs directly. Although this has obvious short-term gains, it not only undermines the capacity building of the government department – which is supposed to be a primary objective of the NGO – but it also exacerbates the problem it is supposed to resolve because no indigenous capacity is developed and no knowledge, experience and sustainability of governance is created. Fukuyama calls this 'capacity destruction' and suggests that it cannot be fixed unless donors make capacity building their primary objective instead of the services that capacity is meant to provide.[103]

Other international organisations such as the IMF, World Bank and ADB are also tiring of the corruption in government and therefore attach conditionality to their loans and grants.[104] Although this is intended to 'fight' corruption the only losers are the fledgling Cambodian organisations that again suffer a loss of capacity. Although there is a strong argument that conditionality is a failed strategy that does more harm than good,[105] it still features in strategies of the ADB and World Bank in Cambodia.[106] So, far from the situation improving, the intent of Cambodia's main donors is for a 'draw down' due to a sense of imposing a 'failed plan [on Cambodia]',[107] which in itself is a condemnation of the transition to liberal peace. Perhaps even more damning is Robert's belief that the failure of democratic transition in Cambodia is actually due to the liberal peace itself. He believes this represents the continuation of western arrogance based 'on the continuity of such thinking and assumptions as underpin the Liberal Project and the flawed conclusions upon which that agenda rests'.[108] Conclusively, Hughes and Conway suggest 'foreign investors and the aid system still have little confidence in the stability of Cambodia's current political arrangements. The prospect for an active and committed development role for the state . . . is still very remote.'[109] Democracy and good governance are very much virtual qualities of Cambodia's liberal peacebuilding project, which have little in the way of linkage with the population.[110]

Rule of Law and Civil Society

Institutionalised corruption is a central feature of Cambodian society and a factor that greatly influences the success of building liberal peace, especially the components of the rule of law and civil society. According to the former Australian Ambassador to Cambodia in 1994, 'corruption at every level of society has again become a way of life in Cambodia. Every business deal must have a cut for the relevant minister and every transaction involves a percentage for the relevant official.'[111] It seems that corruption – or the western understanding of it – is at the core of Cambodia's hierarchical socio-political framework. This is constructed and operated on a feudal basis, at the heart of which is the patron-client relationship. Anthropologist Lindsay French observes: 'political power and control has traditionally involved the accumulation of an entourage of assistants, employees, and loyal followers who provide support in exchange for various forms of protection and assistance.'[112] The attainment of the hegemonic domination of political power underwrites the patronage system and allows networks to be constructed from the top down, based on loyalty and rewards. Political defeat, even through democracy, and the possibility of marginalisation from power has enormous consequences for the nature of Cambodian society. This is particularly significant in a society where resources are scarce, thus competition for political domination is of paramount importance.

At every level individuals replicate the 'system' by creating their own patronage networks. This accounts for the high levels of corruption and explains the flow of rent-seeking arrangements that exist throughout Cambodian society. Hinton argues that the notion of power dispensed by patronage has its roots in Theravada Buddhism. This introduced the concept of *dhamma*, which can be related to 'an animating energy that generates vitality and power'.[113] The Cambodian understanding of *dhamma* is implicit in the notions of power and merit. Power, according to Hinton encapsulates concepts such as authority, skilfulness, strength, influence, rank and prowess and can exist as 'raw power/authority, hard power and potent power, and skilled efficacy'.[114] Merit relates to a moral source of potency that a person is perceived to have accumulated. Thus in Theravada Buddhism the law of karma holds that one's position in the present relates to their actions in the past. Those in positions of power therefore are assumed to have achieved this through merit and consequently are ascribed with potency, which explains the existence of associations and networks to and from power holders. Hinton explains, 'Cambodians frequently search for signs of such potent centres both to avoid offending these potentially dangerous beings and because they may hope to increase their own power and status through association with them.'[115]

Lizee also argues that historically Cambodian political society is not orientated towards institutionalised politics but draws on other forms of praxis. Society has developed a deep mistrust of centralised political organisation, especially since the Khmer Rouge period. The hierarchical Cambodian political system has been shaped by the legacy of the French colonial period and the influence of Brahmanism – a Hindu Brahamic cult that created a pyramid-like system of social order.[116] Lizee also suggests that this type of caste system[117] was equally influenced by the fatalism of Theravada Buddhism, having the combined effect of establishing a hierarchical political system but removing the individual from the process – hence creating an inescapable and inevitable individual human destiny associated with fatalism and passivity in the face of authority.[118]

While these are sweeping claims to make about another society and culture, it appears the Cambodian polity is overlaid with a micromesh network comprising of multi-dimensional clientelism and patronage networks linking individuals to power centres. As Hinton explains, these relationships of personal dependency may involve moral authority, emotional bonds and kinship ties and involve a relationship whereby the patrons protect the clients and provide them with resources, which may enable them to rise in status. In return, the clients make offerings and provide general support, loyalty and service.[119] Roberts identifies the 'system' of patronage and clientelism as a structure of 'loyalty for security', which ensures the preservation of the elite's socio-economic position by the lower ranks, thus perpetuating the lineage of power and position. The linkage in these networks is known as strings or *khsae*. Although *khsae* have been re-established in the post-Khmer Rouge period, their existence helps to explain the nature and process of the Cambodian genocide: when a political-power holder was targeted and removed by the Khmer Rouge his or her entire string was unearthed and subsequently eradicated.[120]

These networks provide the main means through which ordinary Cambodians tap into the state apparatus, which is supposed to guarantee a personal social security net.[121] This would suggest that the attainment of a liberal democratic civil society in Cambodia is very difficult and hence, far from plotting progression down the 'path' to a 'liberal civil society', Cambodia apparently is in a completely different position relative to its own historical and cultural environment. The creation of liberal peace would therefore not only require a replacement for *khsae* but a viable alternative to an absolutist political system – in other words, fundamental political and socio-cultural structural changes.

It is widely argued however, that 'civil society' does exist in Cambodia. It emerged, according to Curtis, in the UNTAC era facilitated by donor funding and consisted of 'many groups, political parties and NGOs . . . the range of which was both impressive and exciting'.[122] Yet, in light of the societal existence of the institutions of clientelism and patronage, doubts plague the actual existence of this new 'civil society'. This is particularly with regard to the access and political influence that groups have and also the limitations of the sustainability they are creating, due to being partly and in some cases wholly beholden to donor funding.[123] It can actually be argued that the liberal civil society is quite possibly an illusionary 'virtual' or 'parallel' society created by the presence of, and funding streams provided by, the internationals and mainly visible to international eyes. This is a situation that far from aiding the development and sustainability of an indigenous civil society is in fact undermining the peace process by failing to build local capacity and local demand, where reliance is on the external, not the local actor. A report by the United Nations Research Institute for Social Development (UNRISD) pointed out:

> As a result of its politicisation and militarisation, humanitarian assistance has taken ever more massive and spectacular forms and tends increasingly to substitute and destroy local resistance and coping mechanisms and institutions rather than to support and enforce them.[124]

These fears are echoed by Thun Saray, an indigenous NGO coordinator, who suggested in the Phnom Penh Post:

> Our emerging civil society is very dependent on outside funding. We hope such dependency is only temporary . . . however; there are certain donors who impose models of development on their partners and control their growth and development. This has led to donors setting up their own local structures instead of entrusting tasks to existing, genuine local organisations.[125]

The problems of corruption and the precarious nature of civil society are further compounded by the inadequacy and subsequent lack of confidence in the rule of law. As the former UNTAC force commander commented,

> Laws in Cambodia are made at the whim of the controlling elite rather than the legislature and justice does not exist for the large majority of Cambodians. The opposition exercises its privileges at the discretion of the executive rather than by the law as it does in liberal democracies.[126]

The rule of law survives mainly on the whim of almost feudal local custodians who deploy it as a tool to sustain a more traditional socio-political hierarchy, and the existence of a vibrant civil society is mainly derived from international perspectives coloured by an almost non-secular faith in the virtuosity of the liberal peacebuilding project.

Human Rights

The construction of Cambodian political society and the central role of corruption within this also cause difficulties for furthering human rights. Cambodia has little or no history of human rights, nor a tradition of the individual as a rights-bearing agent intrinsically worthy of protection and representation. It has rather a culture predominantly centred on patronage-based networks and pyramid hierarchies that are underwritten by Brahamic and Buddhist ideologies. These beliefs create a structure in which the individual is not an actor empowered with rights and liberties but is a link in a chain that is subsumed by the power generated within the network. These hierarchical networks are intended to provide the protection and security that could otherwise be understood as forms of human rights.

The difficulty with imposing human rights, as they are understood in the liberal peace thesis, is again due to the nature of the Cambodian socio-political system. Therefore, the problem is not just the inability of the government to provide for human rights but also the lack of demand for rights. This is due in part to education but also to cultural mistrust of the role of the individual. Since the DK (Democratic Kampuchea, i.e. Khmer Rouge) period eroded the Buddhist principle of respect for life and dignity of the individual,[127] and effectively destroyed the Cambodian rural community,[128] Cambodians are as increasingly wary of attempts to empower and politicise the individual as they are of creating 'new' political systems and of social conditioning. This supports the contradictory belief often inherent in liberal peacebuilding projects that individuals lack the agency for reform even though they have the capacity for 'self-help': 'Cambodian society at the grassroots appears to lack established traditional organisational forms which might channel demands to the state'.[129]

Nevertheless, both the international and local actors are involved in extensive human rights programmes. However, as Heininger pessimistically points out, 'whether human rights efforts succeed in changing the attitudes of Cambodian people towards their own rights is a question that will not be answered for many years to come'.[130] This pessimism about success in changing the Cambodian 'system' to one of liberal democracy is also shared by Hinton. In his anthropological study of the Cambodian genocide, he clearly expresses his doubts as to whether Cambodia can support western liberal democratic egalitarian ideals. He believes that hierarchy is so deeply engrained that it is a mistake to assume, as the western-centric approach does, that it is a negative concept and one that suppresses a 'natural' desire for equality. He argues that formally hierarchy provides both protection and the possibility of improving status. But even in an informal context, 'people remain aware of status difference calculated on age, gender, family, ethnicity, birth order, occupation, political influence, power, education and personal character'.[131]

It is perhaps worth considering that the problems faced in another attempt to impose a different variant of peace on Cambodia – although it is perhaps impolitic to suggest a comparison – were also experienced by the Khmer Rouge. The DK period attempted to eliminate forms of inequality while creating an egalitarian, peasant-based communist society,[132] though the Khmer Rouge were brutal and extreme in doing so. But the point remains that despite the fundamental and clearly catastrophic demographic, socio-political and economic upheaval of the DK period, and despite the liberal peacebuilding project, Cambodian culture and society has, according to many observers, returned to embrace its own traditional mode of political and social organisation. The Khmer Rouge, far from revolutionising Cambodian sociopolitics, had engaged and manipulated traditional forms of Khmer society to suit its own ideology. This included a 'structural reversal' in society whereby the new elites of the revolution, namely the working – and mainly illiterate – 'peasant' classes in the countryside supplanted the old city educated elites on the social ladder.[133] This of course realised the Orwellian flaws of Communist utopias. Furthermore, the Khmer Rouge banned Buddhism, manipulated its epistemology of hierarchy, enlightenment and consciousness, to make them apply to DK officials, the party line and the indoctrination of the masses by Maoist ideology, all of which contributed to genocide.[134]

Clearly, local socio-political structures are not only in existence and operating but prove to be far more robust at repelling change than is often assumed. Such cultural dynamics have allowed a post-DK healing process in Cambodian society but also impede the introduction of the liberal peace. This is identified by Hughes and Conway, who point to 'persistent themes of a discourse of power which is profoundly incompatible with the principles of democracy and human rights'.[135] If the international peacebuilding community becomes complicit with these processes and dynamics, the liberal peace may maintain its virtuality, and this will not only be because of its socio-cultural incompatibility with the Cambodian polity, but also because it is expedient for the international community.

Economic Liberalisation

According to the World Bank, Cambodian society has no indigenous economic networks and fails to both provide and build economic capacity.[136] This is an inadequate assessment of the Cambodian economic situation, and one that fits the western economic liberalisation approach of the internationals who assume, as with the political system in Cambodia, that where no system apparently exists one needs to be provided. Certainly, the banking system mainly deals with elites, has had no lending facility beyond it, and the tax system favours the rich.[137] Capital flight affects most businesses, as does an archaic tariff system. Also, a large proportion of aid is spent on technical assistance[138] beside the fact that Cambodia has a subsistence economy, which accounts for the lack of government information on economic variables and unemployment figures.

The country does have a functioning informal economy that operates as the de facto economy. Although this provides no direct or accountable revenues to the government through taxation, it generates cash flows through corruption:

> the disparity between the importance and effectiveness of informal networks and the weakness and effectiveness of state institutions is mirrored, and to a great extent propelled, by the disparity in the level of rewards that can be reaped from rent-seeking and the levels of public salaries.[139]

Questions need to be asked whether the pessimism of international actors, donors and lenders regarding the inability of the Cambodian state to follow the path to economic liberalisation is misplaced. If, for example, an 'informal economy' exists cannot this form the basis for development?

There are also dangers with pursuing a process of economic liberalisation without establishing the proper institutions, against the background of a weak state that has a very limited range of government functions and a low capacity to achieve them.[140] Cambodia, by this rationale, is a weak state and lacks economic institutions. When Cambodia moved to embrace a free market in 1989, it 'opened the door to dramatic levels of corruption and a very low level of effective control over state officials by the centre'.[141] The implications of applying a liberal free market system to a state that lacked the capacity to coordinate it may in fact be responsible for the stagnating economy and be the reason for the growing disparity between socio-economic groups. It seems as if a different economic system – a localised Cambodian system – is being forced to operate within a structure where it does not have tools to function. Other Asian economies such as the so-called 'Asian Tigers' have, for a time at least, operated very successfully but not necessarily within the principles provided by liberal democracy.

Fukuyama, in addressing institutional capacity, suggests that there are four nested aspects of stateness: '(1) organisational design and management, (2) political system design, (3) basis of legitimisation, and (4) cultural and structural factors'.[142] Perhaps if these factors were examined a little more closely a different understanding of the nature of the Cambodian economy might emerge. At the moment, what seems to have developed is a thin version of a capitalist liberal economy through which corrupt elites 'asset strip' the foreign resources brought in to support the building of the liberal peace. As with many other examples, the economic interaction between, development of and prospects of Cambodian people at the grassroots level have barely developed since the early 1990s. What is even more notable about the failure of international efforts to develop the Cambodian economy is a general resistance on the part of international actors against admitting deficiencies in their approach. The World Bank does not deem it necessary to publish unemployment figures because Cambodia is a subsistence economy, despite the fact that their role is to produce a capitalist economy. Yet subsistence is also seen as gainful, even though the liberal peace model specifically demands a move towards a modern capitalist system of exchange as inherent to the development of peace, both promoting development and opportunity, profit and revenue, and creating an economically sustainable state. Though there is of course much discussion of the enormous corruption problem, there is little discussion of whether this should impact on capital inflows to the country from donors, raising the question of whether some level of corruption is tolerated as the price of a transition towards a liberal peace. A capitalist-style free market is very much a chimera, as is a sustainable labour market and widespread economic opportunity, given that without these elements and the ability to raise significant taxes, the government remains dependent upon the international community and donors. As a compromise, it is likely to resort to a partial reform-type syndrome.[143] Understanding this as the cost of reform and a future peace, the international community turns a blind eye, arguing that illiberalism can lead eventually to liberalism when the terms of the liberal peace are internalised. In Cambodia, after a decade and more of international economic engagement, such a transformation still looks unlikely, considering that the economic aspect of the liberal peacebuilding model emphasises its hybrid nature. At least partially, the liberal peace is a virtual model, directed externally from the top down. Where local cooperation is limited, for reasons of culture or disagreement, little can be done by the international community other than continuing to develop conditionality, occasionally turning a blind eye to deviation, and awaiting the 'inevitability' of the internalisation of the liberal peace that international actors crave. Where this does not occur, even after a decade or more, the liberal peace model offers little other than hope.

A square peg for a round hole?

Fundamental problems exist in reconciling Cambodia to the liberal peace model. This stems essentially from an incompatibility between the tenets of the liberal peace thesis and the nature of the political, socio-economic and cultural system in Cambodia. Historical and cultural indigenous structures are often contrary to the belief of internationals. These frameworks centre on the notion of political power as a zero sum game and on the importance of community. The discourse of power is profoundly incompatible with the principles of democracy, capitalism and human rights, and also contradicts the basis for indigenous political and cultural society. Most

44

importantly, perhaps, this 'system' maintains the chronic cycle of corruption upon which Cambodian society functions. The vast majority of our interviewees amongst both local and international actors remarked, for example, upon the incompatibility of local and external norms, and upon the failure to provide social welfare as fundamental flaws in the peacebuilding process.

Far from adopting a 'new system', Cambodia is actually already operating within a distinctive approach: 'whilst the international community claimed to have settled war in Cambodia in 1991, Cambodians appeared to have settled it themselves in 1997'.[144] Lizee suggests, 'The traditional Cambodian concept of peace and the one of the international community is untenable because it does not coincide with any identifiable socio-institutional complex.'[145] The question is whether Cambodia is 'on the road' to liberal peace or is it developing its own indigenous 'system(s)'? Clearly, both processes are occurring at once, though some commentators argue that the indigenous model is currently moving towards that of Burma[146] and others argue that a more authoritarian model of governance might benefit the country.[147] In this context, the question is whether an indigenous peace can coexist within the liberal peace and what effect one will have on the other? Does this suggest that the Hun Sen government is playing the internationals at their own game and free-riding on the liberal peace discourse? Are the internationals therefore wasting their time and money in Cambodia?

The liberal/virtual peace hybrid has the great advantage that it allows for international intervention, conditionality and dependency creation to be deployed to establish the governance frameworks of a recognisably liberal state. At the same time it imposes external norms and defers executive and administrative functions, as well as focusing on top-down institutions that have limited short- and medium-term impact on citizens' lives. It equally provides space for local actors to negotiate their own version of peace according to indigenous norms of governance. However, such an approach is deeply problematic because this hybrid allows for the coexistence of democracy and semi-feudalism, free market reform, corruption, and a subsistence economy, the establishment of human rights and the rule of law processes, and what appears to be the unaccountability of elites. The liberal/virtual peace hybrid indicates a superficial overlay of the liberal governance of politics, economy and society controlled by internationally induced conditionality and dependency, and at the same time a reassertion of the local indigenous norms, culture and tradition in both negative and positive forms. But its negative aspects indicate devious objectives, a partial reform syndrome, and the continuation of political, social and economic practices which led to the conflict in the first place, now camouflaged by international acquiescence as the price of the virtual/ liberal peace.[148]

What alternative to this liberal/virtual hybrid is there, given that the Cambodian example represents probably the longest-running attempt at constructing the liberal peace? The success of the liberal peace thesis in transforming conflict and statebuilding is a highly politicised endeavour and an approach on which world order is perceived to rest: can it be seen to fail? As we argued above, Cambodia is perceived by most as an orthodox liberal peace; yet it is probably not even a conservative liberal peace and may not even fit on the liberal peace axis at all. Indeed a transitional 'illiberal peace'[149] – a square peg into a round hole – exists where the emphasis should probably be on supporting and building an indigenous system that combines the principles of liberal peace with more localised approaches.

The liberal peace has a strong virtual component that allows space for local continuities and developments. Cambodia has held elections; it has established a government that operates in accordance with the traditional Cambodian political system, though neither operates in the manner expected by internationals. Civil society is also developing, albeit greatly aided by the internationals and the NGO community. Human rights, perhaps not protected and guaranteed in a format recognised by the liberal peace, do appear to exist in a particularly Cambodian hierarchical and religious form. Similarly, the informal economy is a functioning free market and the germ of capitalism is flourishing on Phnom Penh's streets. There is not much evidence to suggest that these developments are because of, or in spite of, international involvement. Ultimately, a form of peace exists – a local Khmer/Cambodian peace that includes an end to armed conflict and a semblance of personal security – and incorporates components of the liberal peace heavily modified by local cultural practices (see Figure 1.1). This is the virtual/liberal peace.

Figure 1.1 Cultural specificity and the virtual/liberal peace hybrid

Notes

1. A short version of this chapter was published as 'Liberal hubris: virtual peace in Cambodia', *Security Dialogue*, 38: 1, 2007.
2. Chuang Tzu was a Chinese Philosopher in the fourth century BCE and one of the founders of Taoism. See, M. Palmerand E. Breuilly (trans.), *The Book of Chuang Tzu* (London: Penguin, 1996), p. 13.
3. See UN doc S/26531.
4. Indeed, according to one prominent NGO, Cambodia is 'almost lawless'. Chen Vannath: Director of Centre for Social Development (CSD), *Personal Interview*, Phnom Penh, 7 November 2005.
5. See UN doc S/23613.
6. Important tasks within these components were human rights (education and protection) and civil administration, which included five fields: defence, foreign affairs, finance, public security and information. See

W. J. Durch (ed.) *UN Peacekeeping, American Politics and the Uncivil Wars of the 1990s* (London: Macmillan, 1996).

7. These missions have been termed 'post-settlement peacebuilding'. See H. Miall, O. Ramsbotham and T. Woodhouse, *Contemporary Conflict Resolution* (Cambridge: Polity, 1999), p. 186.

8. See B. Boutros-Ghali, *An Agenda for Peace: Preventative Diplomacy, Peacemaking and Peacekeeping* (New York: United Nations, 1992).

9. Ibid. p. 11.

10. See F, Fukuyama, *The End of History and the Last Man* (London: Penguin, 1992).

11. B. Boutros-Ghali, 'Supplement to an Agenda for Peace', UN doc A/50/60, S.1995/ 1.

12. The Millennium Development Goals are: eradication of extreme poverty and hunger, achievement of universal primary education, promotion of gender equality, reduction of child mortality, improvement of maternal health, combat of HIV/AIDS, environmental stability, development of a global partnership for development. See http://www. un.org/millenniumgoals/.

13. UN, 'A more secure world: our shared responsibility', Report of the Secretary-General's High Level Panel on Threats, Challenges and Change, UN doc A/59/565, 2 December; www.un.org/secureworld/.

14. M. W. Doyle, *United Nations Peacekeeping in Cambodia: UNTAC's Civil Mandate* (London: Lynne Rienner, 1995), p. 13.

15. UN doc A/46/608.

16. For a comprehensive assessment of UNTAC, see Doyle, *UN Peacekeeping.*

17. See J. Heininger, *Peacekeeping in Transition* (London: Fund Press, 1994); D. Chandler, *History of Cambodia*, 3rd edn (London: Westview Press, 1998).

18. D. Chandler, 'Three visions of politics in Cambodia', in M. W. Doyle, I. Johnstone and R. C. Orr (eds), *Keeping the Peace: Multidimensional Operations in Cambodia and El Salvador* (Cambridge: Cambridge University Press, 1997), p. 25.

19. R. Paris, *At War's End* (Cambridge: Cambridge University Press, 2004), p. 79.

20. Doyle, *UN Peacekeeping*, p. 26.

21. C. Hughes and T. Conway, *Cambodia* (London: Overseas Development Institute, 2005), p. 7.

22. This included $116 million for repatriation, $82.2 million for resettlement, $44.8 million for food security and agriculture, $40 million for health and sanitation, $33.6 million for education and training, $150.3 million for public infrastructure restoration and $111.8 million for programme support. Personnel to run this operation were provided by forty countries and totalled in excess of 22,000 people, comprising approxi-

mately 16,000 peacekeeping troops, 3,600 civilian police and an almost equal number of administration officials. P. P. Lizee, *Peace, Power and Resistance in Cambodia: Global Governance and the Failure of International Conflict Resolution* (London: Macmillan, 2000), p. 102.

23. Lizee, *Peace, Power*, p. 103. See also World Bank Officials, *Personal Interviews*, Phnom Penh, 7 & 8 November 2005.
24. Heininger, *Peacekeeping in Transition*, p. 35.
25. UNDP Official, *Personal Interview*, Phnom Penh, 8 November 2005.
26. Lizee, *Peace, Power*, p. 105.
27. Ibid. p. 103.
28. Ibid. p. 103.
29. Ibid. p. 103.
30. World Bank Officials, *Personal Interviews*, Phnom Penh, 7 & 8 November 2005.
31. G. Curtis, *Cambodia Reborn? The Transition to Democracy and Development* (Washington, DC: Brookings Institution Press, 1998), p. 119.
32. T. Saray, 'The way ahead to a civil society', *Phnom Penh Post*, January 26–Febuary 8 1996, p. 7. Quoted in Curtis, *Cambodia Reborn?* p. 121.
33. Curtis, *Cambodia Reborn?* p. 142. See in particular, Emma Leslie: Alliance for Conflict Transformation, *Personal Interview*, Phnom Penh, 11 November 2005.
34. www.pactworld.org/programs/country/cambodia.
35. Council for the Development of Cambodia Development Cooperation Report 2000, Phnom Penh, May 2001, p. 2.
36. See, Doyle *et al.*, *Keeping the Peace*; J. Mayall (ed), *The New Interventionism 1991–94* (Cambridge: Cambridge University Press, 1996).
37. M. W. Doyle, I. Johnstone and R. C. Orr, 'Strategies for peace: conclusions and lessons', in Doyle *et al.*, *Keeping the Peace*, p. 371.
38. Ibid. p. 382.
39. As Ham Samnang argued, the elections were free but not fair. *Personal Interview*, Phnom Penh, 10 November 2005.
40. Australia, Belgium, Canada, China, Denmark, France, Finland, Germany, Japan, Netherlands, New Zealand, Norway, South Korea, Thailand, Russia, Sweden, UK and US.
41. S. Peou, 'Collaborative human security? The UN and other actors in Cambodia', *International Peacekeeping*, 12: 1, Spring 2005, pp. 112.
42. UN, *An Inventory of Post Conflict Peace-Building Activities* (New York: UN, 1996).
43. Sok Hach and Sarthi Acharya, *Cambodia's Annual Economic Review*, Issue 2 (Phnom Penh: Cambodia Development Resource Institute, August 2002), pp. 14–15, quoted in Peou, 'Collaborative human security?', p. 115.

44. Lizee, *Peace, Power*, p. 108.
45. E. U. Kato, 'Quick impacts, slow rehabilitation in Cambodia', in Doyle *et al.*, *Keeping the Peace*, p. 202.
46. Doyle, *UN Peacekeeping*, p. 40.
47. Ibid. p. 46.
48. Economic Institute of Cambodia (EIC), *Cambodia Economic Watch*, Issue 3, October 2005, p. 34.
49. Aid is delivered in different forms: bilateral, multilateral, grants or loans. EIC, *Cambodia Economic Watch*, p. 35.
50. J. Sanderson, 'The Cambodian experience: a success story still?', in R. Thakur and A. Schnabel (eds), *United Nations Peacekeeping Operations: Ad Hoc Missions, Permanent Engagement* (New York: UN University Press, 2001), p. 155.
51. See M. Berdal and M. Leifer, 'Cambodia', in Mayall, *The New Interventionism*, pp. 25–58. Also, see J. A. Schear, 'Riding the Tiger: the United Nations and Cambodia's struggle for peace', in W. J. Durch, *UN Peacekeeping*; Kato, 'Quick impacts', in Doyle, *Keeping the Peace*, p. 200.
52. Doyle, *UN Peacekeeping*, p. 34.
53. Mayall, *The New Interventionism*, p. 40.
54. Doyle, *UN Peacekeeping*, p. 35.
55. Ibid. p. 44.
56. Ibid. p. 44.
57. FUNCINPEC won 45.5 per cent, Hun Sen's CPP 38.2 per cent, the Khmer Rouge abstained. Doyle *et al.*, *Keeping the Peace*, p. 9.
58. SOC is the term given to the provisional government established during the UNTAC period immediately preceding the election. It was comprised predominantly of the CCP under Prime Minister Hun Sen and therefore represented a continuation of the monopoly of power by the autocratic regime that had been installed by the Vietnamese following the civil war. See Chandler, *History of Cambodia*, pp. 236–8.
59. Mayall, *The New Interventionism*, p. 43.
60. C. Hughes and T. Conway, *Understanding Pro-Poor Political Change: the Policy Process, Cambodia* (London: Overseas Development Institute, second draft August 2003), pp. viii–ix, quoted in S. Heder and Hun Sen, 'Consolidation death or beginning of reform?', *Southeast Asian Affairs*, 2005, p. 114.
61. See Heder and Sen, 'Consolidation death or beginning of reform?', pp. 114–27.
62. *Phnom Penh Post*, 4–18 November 2005, p. 7.
63. United States Agency for International Development, *Anti-corruption* (Phnom Penh: USAID, 2005). Also, see www.usaid.gov.
64. C. J. Nissen, *Living Under the Rule of Corruption: an Analysis of Everyday Forms of Corrupt Practices in Cambodia* (Phnom Penh:

Centre for Social Development, 2005).

65. Governance indicators are: voice and accountability, political stability, government effectiveness, regulatory quality, rule of law, control of corruption. D. Kaufmann, A. Kraay and M. Mastruzzi, Governance Matters III: Governance Indicators for 1996–2002. www.worldbank. org/wbi/governance/pubs/govmatters3.

66. The ADB do not support public administrate reform and legal and judicial reform; see Asian Development Bank, *Country Strategy and Program, Cambodia 2005–9* (Philippines: ADB); www.adb. org/Documants/CSPs/CAM/2005. Also, an ADB representative in Cambodia suggested that it [the liberal state] felt like a failed plan for Cambodia, it was therefore a waste of money trying to impose it.

67. See UN, *Development Assistance Framework for Cambodia* (Phnom Penh: Office of the UN resident coordinator in Cambodia, 2004). Also, see www.un.org.kh.

68. UN doc S/23177 Paris Accord, part 3, article 15 and annex 1, section E.

69. www.hrw.org/english/docs/2006/01/18/cambod12269. Human rights overview, Cambodia 2005.

70. Ibid.

71. Ibid.

72. Nissen, *Living Under the Rule of Corruption*, p. 101.

73. Human rights overview, Cambodia 2005.

74. UNDP, *Investing in Cambodia's Future* (UNDP, 2005), p. 5.

75. Heininger, *Peacekeeping in Transition*, p. 39.

76. Economic Institute of Cambodia, *Cambodia Economic Watch*, p. ix.

77. HPI focuses on the proportion of people below a threshold level in basic dimensions of human development – living a long and healthy life, having access to education, and a decent standard of living. www.hdr.undp.org.

78. www.unicef.org/infobycountry/cambodia_statistics.

79. UNDP, 'Investing in Cambodia's future', Annual Report, 2004.

80. HDI measures average achievements in a country; UNDP Human Development Report, 2003: www.hdr.undp.org.

81. EIC, *Cambodia Economic Watch*, p. 34.

82. See EIC, *Cambodia Economic Watch*, p. 35; ADB, *Country Strategy and Program, Cambodia 2005–9*; 'Cambodia at the Crossroads', World Bank and IMF, 2004: www.worldbank.org.kh.

83. EIC, *Cambodia Economic Watch*, p. 35.

84. Ibid. p. 35.

85. Mayall, *The New Interventionism*, p. 53.

86. Kato, 'Quick impacts, slow rehabilitation in Cambodia', in Doyle *et al.*, *Keeping the Peace*, p. 202.

87. Mayall, *The New Interventionism*, p. 53.

88. HIV Sentinel Surveillance Dissemination, National Centre for HIV/ AIDS, 2004.
89. See Economic Institute of Cambodia, *Economic Review*, 2: 4, October– December 2005, p. 15.
90. Peou, 'Collaborative human security?' p. 116.
91. UNDP Official, *Personal Interview*, Phnom Penh, 8 November 2005.
92. World Bank Officials, *Personal Interviews*, Phnom Penh, 7 & 8 November 2005.
93. F. Fukuyama, *State Building: Governance and World Order in the Twenty-First Century* (London: Profile Books, 2004), p. 56.
94. See Chandler, *History of Cambodia*. Also, see D. W. Roberts, *Political Transition in Cambodia 1991–99* (Richmond: Curzon, 2001), p. 45.
95. Roberts, *Political Transition in Cambodia*, p. 32.
96. Ibid. p. 32.
97. Lizee, *Peace, Power*, pp. 124–37.
98. Fukuyama, *State Building*, p. 13.
99. Senior Advisor, Asian Development Bank, *Personal Interview*, 8 November 2005. Because of poor governance ratings, the ABD has reduced its commitment to Cambodia.
100. Curtis, *Cambodia Reborn?* p. 131.
101. Cooperation Committee for Cambodia, *Annual Report 1995* (Phnom Penh: CCC, 1995). Quoted in Curtis, *Cambodia Reborn?* p. 135.
102. Emma Leslie: ACT, *Personal Interview*, Phnom Penh, 11 November 2005.
103. Fukuyama, *State Building*, p. 55.
104. See the governance indicators in Kaufmann *et al.*, Governance Matters III.
105. Fukuyama, *State Building*, p. 49.
106. See ADB, *Country Strategy and Program, Cambodia 2005–9*; World Bank, *Cambodia Country Assistance Strategy of the World Bank Group*.
107. Senior Advisor, ADB, *Personal Interview*, 8 November 2005.
108. Roberts, *Political Transitions in Cambodia*, p. 213.
109. Hughes and Conway, *Cambodia*, p. 9.
110. Senior Advisor, ADB, *Personal Interview*, 8 November 2005.
111. Quoted in Curtis, *Cambodia Reborn?* p. 146.
112. L. French, quoted in Curtis, *Cambodia Reborn?*, p. 111.
113. A. L. Hinton, *Why did they Kill? Cambodia in the Shadow of Genocide* (Berkeley, CA: University of California Press, 2005), p. 98.
114. Ibid. p. 104.
115. Ibid. p. 105.
116 P. Lizee, 'Peacekeeping, peace building and the challenges of conflict resolution in Cambodia', in D. Charters, *Peacekeeping and the Challenge of Civil Conflict Resolution* (Fredericton, NB: University of

New Brunswick, 1994), p. 142.

117. See also Emma Leslie: ACT, *Personal Interview*, Phnom Penh, 11 November 2005.
118. Lizee, 'Peacekeeping, peace building', p. 142.
119. Hinton, *Why did they kill?* p. 107.
120. See Hinton, *Why did they kill?*
121. Roberts, *Political Transitions in Cambodia*, p. 33.
122. See Curtis, *Cambodia Reborn?* pp. 110–49.
123. USAID Official Source, *Personal Interview*, Phnom Penh, 8 November 2005.
124. Quoted in Curtis, *Cambodia Reborn?* p. 122.
125. *Phnom Penh Post*, 16 January 1996, p. 7.
126. Sanderson, 'The Cambodian experience', in Thakur *et al.*, *United Nations Peacekeeping Operations*, p. 155.
127. Roberts, *Political Transitions in Cambodia*, p. 46.
128. Hughes and Conway, *Cambodia*, p. 28.
129. Ibid. p. 28.
130. J. E. Heininger, *Peacekeeping in Transition: the United Nations in Cambodia* (New York: Twentieth Century Fund Press, 1994).
131. Hinton, *Why did they kill?* p. 186.
132. Ibid. p. 188.
133. Ibid. p. 192.
134. For a more comprehensive explanation of the creation of the DK social order, see Hinton, *Why did they kill?*, pp. 182–210.
135. Hughes and Conway, *Cambodia*, p. vii.
136. World Bank Officials, *Personal Interviews*, Phnom Penh, 7 & 8 November 2005.
137. Sok Hach: EIC, *Personal Interview*, Phnom Penh, 11 November 2005.
138. Ibid.
139. Hughes and Conway, *Cambodia*, p. 42.
140. Fukuyama, *State Building*.
141. Hughes and Conway, *Cambodia*, p. viii.
142. Fukuyama, *State Building*, p. 31.
143. See, for example, Nicholas Van der Walle, Nicole Ball and Vijaya Ramachandran (eds), *Beyond Structural Adjustment: the Institutional Context of African Development* (Basingstoke: Palgrave, 2003).
144. Roberts, *Political Transitions in Cambodia*, p. 5.
145. Lizee, 'Peacekeeping, peace building', p. 142.
146. UNDP Official, *Personal Interview*, Phnom Penh, 8 November 2005.
147. Senior Advisor, ADB, *Personal Interview*, 8 November 2005.
148. See Chen Vannath: Director of CSD, *Personal Interview*, Phnom Penh, 7 November 2005; World Bank Officials, *Personal Interviews*, Phnom Penh, 7 and 8 November 2005.
149. Paris, *At War's End*.

2

Bosnia: Between Partition and Pluralism[1]

Introduction

Ten years after the Dayton Peace Accords effectively ended the war in Bosnia and Herzegovina (BiH),[2] the prospects for a self-sustaining liberal democratic state in Bosnia seem still to face significant problems. The state remains ethnically and democratically polarised. Being subject to separatist political agendas, the government is constantly deadlocked and unable to move forward, ethnic and religious chauvinism are still relatively common, and development and marketisation have not produced a significant peace dividend for the people on the ground. Even civil society projects are marred by 'forum shopping' and a project mentality, while local politicians are dependent on the international community, whose members are forced to substitute for local stalemates even though they know that this undermines local capacity.[3] This deadlock has in turn allowed Republika Srpska (RS) to move forward with its own separate – and probably separatist – agendas while Bosnia remains politically deadlocked.

Indeed, some local commentators go as far as to say that there still is not a state in existence, given that there is little official documentation in local languages on the state and that there has not been a local ratification process to make the current situation accountable to the Bosnian citizens.[4] The view is commonly held that Dayton was a formula to end the war, for conflict management rather than creating a self-sustaining form of peace.[5] The General Framework Agreement for Peace in Bosnia and Herzegovina (Dayton Accords) was signed in November 1995 and effectively ended violence by creating two ethno-nationalist geo-political entities, the Bosniak-Croat federation, which controls 51 per cent of the of the single geographical region of the state of Bosnia, and the Republic Srpska, which controls the other 49 per cent. Looking beyond the terms of this agreement, its legacy appears to be dependent on a weak and decentralised state given that power is not only divided between the two main entities but is also dispersed across ten federation cantons, 149 municipalities

and the autonomous district of Brčko.[6] This has divided the governance of Bosnia three ways. For example, the Peoples' House in the
Parliamentary Assembly has fifteen delegates, two-thirds from the
federation and one third from Republic Srpska, but this de facto
means five Bosniaks, five Croats and five Serbs.[7] This constitutional
arrangement is then replicated from the national to municipal level
and reflects the entrenched ethnic positions adopted during the war
and persisting in the post-war environment.

The Bosnian war has its roots mainly in the fall of communism
and the ethno-nationalistic fracturing of Yugoslavia.[8] Between 1991
and 1995 Serbia fought bitter wars with the breakaway republics of
Slovenia and Croatia. However, shortly after the European Union
recognised BiH in 1992, a bloody civil war ensued that drew Serbia
and Croatia into the maelstrom and led to bitter fighting between
all the factions, provoking, among other horrors, the emergence of
ethnic cleansing. By 1994, over 200,000 soldiers and civilians were
dead or missing, and an estimated 2 million became refugees or
displaced persons.[9] Formal war subsided after the Croatian army,
following the relaxation of an arms embargo, drove Serb forces
out of their territory. The army then combined with Bosniak forces
in a joint offensive against the Serbs, which, coupled with NATO
air strikes, led the warring parties to a negotiated ceasefire and the
Dayton Accords.[10] However, as the fog of war lifted, what remained
was the deeply traumatised, war ravaged, ethnically divided and
economically broken territory and populations of Bosnia.

The clear aim of the international community through the Dayton
Accords and the associated United Nations Mission in Bosnia and
Herzegovina (UNMIBH) was to reconstruct Bosnia as a western
liberal democratic state. The UNMIBH mandate (initially focusing
on security)[11] and the General Framework Agreement (which was
designed to promote both peace and security)[12] both contained extensive remits to provide for the reconstruction of the Bosnian state.
Although Bosnia is an independent state (and member of the UN)
and therefore was not subject to a Kosovo or East Timor-type UN
protectorate, Dayton did bestow on the internationals significant and,
as Chandler points out, unaccountable[13] latitude to shape the post-
war agenda through the Office of the High Representative (OHR).
However, as Bose remarks, this was to be no easy undertaking:

The task for would-be state-builders and democratizers is daunting.
Bosnia is not just a society divided but a society polarized on the most

basic of issues –the question of legitimacy of state, its common institutions and its borders.[14]

It is widely accepted that the international mission in BiH, now over ten years after the Dayton Accords, has not successfully created a functioning liberal state, though, according to the OHR, some progress has been made particularly in the context of the recent elections, limited job creation, the rule of law and civil society. However, it is also clear that while Dayton ended the war, it could not 'normalise' society in terms of re-establishing peaceful social relations.[15] Much criticism has been directed at the Dayton Accords, which, it is argued, institutionalised the ethnic divisions of the war and created a divided and consequently weak and ineffective state, instead of a multi-ethnic and pluralist one.[16] Conversely, Chandler argues that the governance of the international community has held back the development of Bosnia, not to mention self-governance and self-determination;[17] Bose suggests that although the international involvement has done more good than harm the applicability of both the consociational and confederal paradigm established by Dayton, and the international control of this process, are to be questioned.[18] Many internationals are now hoping that the lure of the EU will assist in advancing the liberal peace project as multi-ethnic in character,[19] while others are of the opinion that constitutional reform is vital if any progress is to be made. Yet, local actors use the threat of 'backsliding' against the international community to prevent such change where it impinges on their interests.

This chapter seeks to draw on these arguments by unpacking the components of liberal peace – democracy, human rights, rule of law, civil society and liberal economics – thus questioning if the current stalemate is a failure of liberal peace praxis. In particular, it explores the nature of the relationship between international (sovereign) governance and the national/local political leadership, as well as the Bosnian peoples. Specifically this relationship has created interrelated and noteworthy aspects: a clear disconnect exists to the point where the polarised and nationalistic local political elites are opting out of the internationals liberal statebuilding process. This lack of cooperation is derailing liberal peacebuilding and the construction of a multi-ethnic and democratic state in Bosnia, perhaps because a liberal democratic state would ultimately undermine the internationals' political, social and cultural power base. The resultant political stalemate between nationalist groups, particularly in parliament, has led to a stagnation of the liberal statebuilding process whereby Bosnia is left to fester in a virtual and conservative form of liberal peace with the causes of the conflict remaining unresolved amidst a chronic socio-economic crisis and fragile security situation. This raises the questions of why the liberal peace has not been taken up, why it remains in the executive sphere of international peacebuilders, and what might be done about this.

This case study, as a critique of post-conflict liberal statebuilding, illustrates the paradox of local versus international ownership of the statebuilding process. Indeed, it has been argued that the agenda of international peacebuilding actors is partly responsible for the local inaction and political foot-dragging.[20] The paradox of this is the apparent desire by the internationals, in the light of neocolonial criticism, to relinquish direct control and ownership of the peacebuilding process (and indeed governance of Bosnia) to the local actors while ensuring at the same time that their liberal agenda is complied with. This is coupled with the locals' demand for national sovereignty over the unaccountable rule of the OHR,[21] which is perhaps incompatible with the aims of local political elites to increase their grip on power. This paradox, and perhaps the genuine reluctance of some internationals to let go of power, is aptly demonstrated by the apparent degradation of the powers of the OHR (and the push for constitutional reforms), which is now to be replaced by the expanding remit of the EU.[22] In the light of this contradiction we consider how liberal peace can be built with greater consensus between the local and the international, thus confronting the very nature of liberal peace in Bosnia, which as one seasoned observer noted, represents international ambivalence rather than liberal values.[23] As in Kosovo, and with the moves afoot in RS, there is a danger that despite all of these efforts to create a multi-ethnic, pluralist and liberal state, a shift towards partition may still occur, reverting back to the spectre of nationalist, ethnically homogenous 'liberal states'.

The following section examines the vision of peace that the internationals perceived and attempted to build from the Dayton Peace Accords.

Dayton: the Imaginary of a Liberal Peace

The praxis of liberal peacebuilding rests on a number of central tenets as outlined in the Introduction to this study, and these are clearly expressed in the constitution of BiH within the Dayton Accords as 'democratic principles – the rule of law and free and democratic elections, human rights and the promotion of general welfare, economic growth . . . and the promotion of a market economy'.[24] The suggestion is that these concepts, which together with the promotion of civil society are the main pillars of liberal peace praxis, would, under the guidance of the international community, transform the unstable post-conflict Bosnia into a multi-ethnic, pluralist and liberal democracy – hence a single liberal, pluralist, liberal state. The assumption is that whilst the Dayton Accords divided the territory of Bosnia between ethnic groups, this would be an interim arrangement, as the liberal statebuilding process would heal the ethnic differences and eventually recreate a multi-ethnic state through democracy, human rights and a liberal economic system. This linear process is clearly dependent upon local involvement and whilst the international community takes a leading role – certainly in the early stages of these post-conflict statebuilding projects – the end result is supposed to be a form of emancipatory liberal peace in which the local communities have ownership of the process. Indeed, as Chandler has pointed out, rather than an external imposition Dayton formally appears to be a treaty made by the local powers – BiH, Croatia and the remains of the Federal Republic of Yugoslavia – and notably was not instituted by a UN Security Council resolution.[25] Nevertheless, whether this arrangement that implied local ownership actually meant this is debatable, especially as the OHR was introduced to oversee the process, with the Dayton settlement establishing a conservative version of the liberal peace in the hope that it may eventually develop further. Indeed the imposition of a peace process and the close cooperation, or in fact supervision, by the international community, rested upon the military intervention of external actors to enforce it. Indications of an emerging orthodox liberal peace came from the presence of donors, organisations and NGOs, usually under the auspices of a UN mission, imposing top-down peacebuilding methods. As a result, the Dayton peace and development process was monopolised by international actors.

Unlike other examples of post-conflict statebuilding, such as Cambodia, Kosovo and East Timor, the final negotiations and completion of the Dayton Accords were facilitated by the Contact Group, consisting of the United States, United Kingdom, France, Germany and Russia, and not by the UN (due perhaps to the inadequacies of the UN during the war) – although it did have a significant supporting role. The constitutional arrangement for control of Dayton rested with the Peace Implementation Council (PIC), which was formed after Dayton and was responsible for directing and sponsoring the peace implementation. The PIC itself consists of a group of fifty five countries and international organisations.

However, the PIC steering committee entrusted the day-to-day supervision of Dayton to perhaps the most contentious international actor in the Bosnia peacebuilding process – the OHR. This position was created as a prerequisite of the Dayton Accords as an *'ad hoc* international institution responsible for overseeing the implementation of civilian aspects of the accord ending the war in Bosnia and Herzegovina'.[26] In effect, the OHR, far from being an advisory body, actually became the de facto executive and legislative of Bosnia. Indeed, so wide-ranging and flexible were the powers of the OHR, that Paddy Ashdown in his tenure was accused of 'running Bosnia like a Raj'.[27] Although the OHR reports to the PIC steering board, the Secretary General of the UN and to the European Parliament, the office ultimately empowered by the Dayton constitution and under Annex 10 is 'the final authority in theatre regarding interpretation of this (Dayton) agreement on the civilian implementation of the peace settlement'.[28]

The position of the OHR was further enhanced by what became known as the 'Bonn Powers', following an agreement made by the PIC in the German city in 1997 that elaborated on Annex 10 of the Dayton Accords and authorised the High Representative to 'remove from office public officials who violate legal commitments and the Dayton agreement, and to impose laws as he sees fit if Bosnia and Herzegovina's legislative bodies fail to do so'.[29] The OHR was created to carry out the will of the international community in Bosnia over and above that of local political institutions where they did not conform to the parameters of the liberal peace. The unrepresentative power of the OHR is often the focus of criticism and blamed for the lack of progress in the development of Bosnia. Nevertheless, the existence, and indeed employment, of the OHR is an example of how the international community visualises the nature of peace that it intends to create, how it understands the problems in Bosnia and ultimately how it intends to deal with them. In other words, the international community decided that peace should be imposed on the region by employing a robust and powerful international institution, perhaps not least because of the nature of the conflict, but also because of the perceived weakness and indecision of the local actors.

Another major actor in the peacebuilding process and particularly in the actual implementation of Dayton is the Organisation for

Security and Cooperation in Europe (OSCE), which was ascribed a particularly important role in the reconstruction process. Although Bosnia was not configured via pillars of responsibility as Kosovo or East Timor, the OSCE mission was assigned responsibility for elections, democracy building, human rights and regional military stabilisation. This was divided in the mandate into education, democratisation, human rights and security cooperation.[30] As to be expected, the language of the OSCE mission was centred on liberal peacebuilding, enshrined in the framework agreement. Hence, the task for democratisation was to 'lay the foundation for representative government and ensure the progressive achievement of democratic goals throughout BiH'. With regard to human rights and the rule of law a special department was introduced that developed a comprehensive programme including the enhancement of economic and social rights, judicial and legal reform, dealing with war crimes, trafficking and the rights of national minorities.

The OSCE mission in Bosnia is particularly comprehensive: it has a head office in Sarajevo and four regional centres based in Sarajevo, Tuzla, Mostar and Banja Luka, and twenty field offices, covering the entire country. Furthermore, the mission has helped to establish six political resource centres, which provide political parties, independent candidates and citizens groups with the necessary resources to participate in the creation of a pluralistic and multi-ethnic political environment.[31] This wide-ranging role for the OSCE left little doubt that the post-conflict vision of peace in BiH was based on the principle that a democratic society underpinned by the rule of law is the best guarantor of durable peace and security.

Although much reduced, the UN also derived an important role from the Dayton Accords. Established under Security Council Resolution 1035, UNMIBH was essentially tasked to provide security. In effect it transferred authority from the UN Protection Force (UNPROFOR) to NATO, led the multinational peace Implementation Force (IFOR) of 60,000 soldiers (reduced to 35,000 by 1998), instigated a UN civilian police force (the International Police Task Force – IPTF), and installed a U N civilian office headed by a Special Representative of the Secretary General. Alongside security and law enforcement, the task force was also charged with elections, rehabilitation of infrastructure and economic reconstruction.[32]

This closely supervised peacebuilding process in Bosnia was also assisted by other political actors such as the Council of Europe, as well as the 'usual' development institutions, such as the IMF and the World

Bank, as well as other UN institutions and a multitude of development NGOs. As a result, Bosnia has been described as 'the world capital of interventionism'.[33] However, the statebuilding project, no matter how comprehensive and inspiring, could not be achieved without local consent and indeed active participation – an element internationals often take for granted given the benefits they believe local communities gain. This is perhaps the failing of liberal peace: that it assumes all actors, no matter how diverse, will ultimately share the same vision, which has proved to be a serious flaw in the statebuilding mission in Bosnia, still not having laid to rest the possibility of partition in the name of liberalism. Herein lies its ambivalence, along with its relative lack of concern with the local experience of everyday life, and emphasis of institutionalisation over the local everyday life, and indeed, over pluralism.

Really Existing Liberal Peace

In 1995, the Dayton Accords divided Bosnia between the three ethnic parties in the conflict, Serb, Bosniak and Croat, thereby effectively institutionalising the ethnic divisions created by the civil war and reinforcing the political position and ascendancy of ethnonationalists. This is clearly apparent at the political level of government (national and local) as well as in the actual physical territorial divisions. It is also reflected at the local level where the fabric of society is torn three ways by the replication of public institutions. Indeed, the International Crisis Group (ICG) has identified five main 'dysfunctional' areas in Bosnian life – the constitution, judiciary, police, education and the military[34] – all of which suffer the same three-way ethnic split. Education, for example, has incompatible curricula, syllabi and textbooks for each of the constituent peoples, often influenced by the political elites.[35] Even though it is assumed that the liberal peace process will break down these barriers and create a single homogenous national entity, especially after more than ten years and over EUR 5.1 million[36] spent in funding for the priority reconstruction and recovery programme since Dayton, implementation has been very slow, if it has occurred at all. Indeed, according to the 2007 UNDP report,

> the impact of ethnic division – or 'ethnicization' – in BiH is more pervasive, in that it works to weaken social solidarity and retard progressive social processes . . . despite increasing growth rates, around a fifth of the population finds itself below the general poverty line and a still larger proportion (approaching a third) is poor in relativistic terms.[37]

The socio-economic situation in Bosnia is indeed worrying. BiH has an aggregate unemployment rate of 30 per cent, whereby 57 per cent of this – the labour-capable population – is inactive in the formal labour market and categorised as 'long-term unemployed' (though there are discrepancies between the different estimates available).[38] In health, the country is notably lagging behind EU standards: life expectancy is 74 years (EU average is 78 years), BiH loses an average of ten years per person to illness (the EU average is six years) and the child mortality rate has not yet dropped to EU levels. Whilst the EU average estimate of child mortality (under 5 years of age) is 4.6 deaths per 1,000 live births, the BiH estimate reaches 18 deaths per 1,000 live births.[39] Although a population and living conditions survey shows that there seems to be the basic supply to homes of water (96.6 per cent) and electricity (98.5 per cent), a significant number have no heating (53.6 per cent), sewerage (17.2 per cent) or telephone (15.6 per cent).[40]

The generally ascribed reason for this stagnation is the Dayton agreement, which has been described as 'a terrible way to end a terrible war'.[41] As Paddy Ashdown stated, it was a treaty 'designed to end a war, not build a state'.[42] Nevertheless, it has indeed succeeded in ending the violence and creating the semblance of a stable security situation in the region, which is a necessary and important achievement. However, critics of Dayton suggest that the agreement merely transformed the war into politics and the ethno-nationalist stalemate that exists now is a direct representation of the conflict aims because, although the war ended, the separate ethnic armies remained to consolidate their respective political power. This is supported by a RAND report that suggests that the fundamental problem of Dayton was that it did not settle the subject of the war, namely the identity of the Bosnian state. Instead, it created a very weak central government, highly autonomous entity-level governments, and powerful regional political units that allowed opposing groups to opt out.[43] Hence, the political and institutional structure created by Dayton clearly had serious consequences for ethnic discrimination and division. As the UNDP reports,

> The system promotes ethnic domination by territory . . . the whole system – state-level institutions, entities, cantons, municipalities, even Brčko District – is structured in such a way that the sole precondition for the functioning of these institutions, and for the protection of human rights, is based upon ethnic affiliation.[44]

Although Dayton was not negotiated directly by the parties within Bosnia – instead the nationalist war leaders of Serbia and Croatia,

Milosevic and Tudjman, and the Bosnian president Izetbegovic were accepted as the leaders of the three constituent peoples – they did represent the ethnic groups in Bosnia and sought to maintain their influence through local proxies. Responsibility for Dayton should be shared between these actors, regional states and the international community, all of whom had an agenda at Dayton. Indeed, it can be argued that the external interference of the states around Bosnia, whose war aims were to pull the country apart, has prevented attempts to bring the country together. In this context, Chandler refutes the argument that Dayton stunted the growth of Bosnia by securing the power of the ethnic elites, thus preventing external regulation. He suggests, in a criticism directed as much at the international community as at Dayton, that the flexibility of the Dayton agreement actually provided for external regulation and the derogation of rights. Hence, responsibility, he suggests, for the lack of development in Bosnia should be directed at the international community:

> The framework created at Dayton was an extremely flexible one, which has enabled international actors, unaccountable to the people of BiH, to shape and reshape the agenda of post-war transition. Dayton's flexibility has been the key factor enabling external powers to permanently postpone any transition to Bosnian 'ownership'.[45]

In contrast, Bose defends the Dayton agreement and claims that it is 'the most feasible and most democratic form of government for Bosnia's precarious existence as a multi-national state'. This is due to its construct as a consociational and confederal paradigm with layered sovereignties, porous borders and multiple citizenships.[46] Bose's consociationalist argument[47] is useful as it gives 'primacy to collectives rather than individual citizens'. His belief is that the war, and indeed Dayton, created 'ethno-territorial autonomy', so that 'BiH is, as it was before the war, a demographic microcosm of what was Yugoslavia'.[48] Many would dispute this suggestion not least because before the conflict Bosnia was much more of an integrated, multi-ethnic and pluralist society with far less ethno-territorial divisions than Yugoslavia. Indeed, the considered aim of liberal peace (and perhaps the more optimistic internationals) is to 'return' Bosnia to this pre-war integrated and multi-ethnic configuration. Bose, however, dismisses 'nation-building' integration as a 'fantasy' and suggests it is 'hopelessly naive and mindlessly arrogant', having no faith in segregation either and believing that the Dayton compromise was the only way forward;[49] though, as pointed out above, it may well lead to partition and in the short term has failed to offer the socio-economic resources for a discourse shifting away from petty ethno-nationalism. Indeed, RS appears at present to be profiting from ethno-nationalist strategies.

This may well be the future for Bosnia as the international community attempts to inch towards a solution. Bose's belief, however, in the primacy of the ethnic group over the individual as enshrined in Dayton, is exactly the structural problem that the UNDP have identified as particularly damaging for the development of Bosnia. A recent comprehensive report on social inclusion suggests that the ethnic institutions created by Dayton as the constitution of BiH are a serious barrier to overcoming the social exclusion and multiple deprivations that plague Bosnia. Indeed the root of the problem is the fact that numerous peacebuilding actors tend to view society through an ethnic prism (which is, of course, hard to avoid given the circumstances):

> The basis of change should be that of considering the citizen as an individual rather than belonging to any particular group. BiH institutions should be structured in such a way as to provide freedom both at individual and collective level.[50]

Indeed, the EU's Venice Commission ruled in 2004 that the constitution in parts violates human rights and must be changed as part of the BiH accession process.[51] Although the constitution has been identified as a primary area for reform and all-party talks (under EU and US pressure) have been held on the adoption of constitutional change, the amendments were rejected by the upper peoples' house of the state parliament in April 2006.[52] As a result, progress on constitutional change, although now an accepted priority, is making little headway. Not only have the ethnic tripartite ramifications of Dayton had a deep, and in some cases lasting, effect on the development of society in Bosnia, but the conceptualisation and subsequent construction of the liberal peace is also problematic. The application of the liberal peace itself thus needs to be critiqued especially in regard to the role of the local elites in derailing the liberal statebuilding process, and the paradoxical impulse towards both pluralism and separation that it entails.

The polarised and entrenched ethnic positions created by Dayton are recreated at almost all levels in society and are a particularly obstructive barrier to the development of a liberal democratic and pluralist Bosnia. Nevertheless, they should not necessarily represent an insurmountable obstacle. Indeed, it is acknowledged that peacebuilders have accepted that the Dayton Accords created this interim situation in order to end the conflict and establish a secure environment for liberal democracy. However, despite the existence of ethnic divisions – and perhaps the inherent assumptions of liberal peacebuilding – the actors attempting to assemble this Bosnia jigsaw do not necessarily share a common vision. The international community, despite the label, is far from cohesive and revolves around the agendas of the reconstruction institutions – particularly the OHR, OSCE, UN, EU, World Bank and other donors. Also, regionally the (re)construction of Bosnia is greatly affected by the interests of Serbia and Croatia, and internationally by Russia and the United States as well as the interests of actors from the Islamic world. Thrown into this mix are the hundreds of multifarious NGOs whose agendas are uncoordinated and in some instances even counterproductive.

The types of problems associated with liberal peacebuilding are familiar. The situation in Bosnia requires closer examination because, alongside the usual problems associated with foreign involvement, the reconstruction of Bosnia (or any post-conflict state) is ineffective without local participation. It is the lack of cooperation – deliberate or otherwise – by local actors within the liberal statebuilding project that is derailing liberal peacebuilding efforts and causing the stagnation of sustainable development in the region, provoking a contest between centripetal ethnic and centrifugal liberal impulses. Clearly, the structural problems created by the Dayton Accords are part of the problem and certainly are exploited by the local actors. Indeed, Chandler and others have argued that the international community does not want to relinquish control of the peacebuilding process and in fact has designed the structure (of Dayton) with enough flexibility to prevent local ownership and consolidate international management.[53] These emerging issues with the liberal peace framework and its application suggest that, as a one-size-fits-all paradigm, it provokes and disguises partition over pluralism and thus in its present form may not be suitable for the Bosnia jigsaw – a blasphemous suggestion in the current theology of liberal peace.[54]

Democratisation

The democratic process, is failing for a number of reasons. The Dayton Accords, widely considered responsible for institutionalising ethnic divisions, created a constitution that became a 'straitjacket'[55] that effectively further reinforced the divisions within the political infrastructure. The resultant three-person presidency and the division of national sovereignty along ethno-nationalist lines naturally made it possible that 'many of Bosnia's political elite continue to pursue narrow ethnic agendas that are fundamentally incompatible with the development of an inclusive, pluralistic state'.[56] Early democratic elections certainly solidified this situation and 'largely resulted in returning to office the nationalist parties that helped spark the civil war'.[57] Although constitutional change is supposedly a negotiation process,[58] the international community has made little discernable progress in altering this party system. Consequently, Bosnia is predominantly led by political leaders who represent one of its three main ethnic groups because no significant political parties exist (at least until recently) that cross ethnic lines or are from more than one of the three nations that comprise BiH society.[59]

Criticism for this ongoing situation has been levelled at the international community who, it is often suggested, should have done far more to forge and maintain a single civic and national identity based on the concept of multi-ethnicity.[60] However, the (Dayton) democratic process provides for free choice in elections and certainly the local ethno-nationalist leaders are in no hurry to relinquish their powerful and easily motivated support base. Indeed many nationalist party leaders are particularly defensive of their assumed remit to 'protect diversity' and 'historical legacies' particularly in the face of democracy, which, it was suggested to us, 'does not like differences'.[61] As a result, the nationalist parties, in rhetoric reminiscent of the conflict, justify the reason for maintaining a separate ethno-nationalist identity and employ the historical narrative of a falsely constructed and artificial Yugoslav state that during the last fifty years suppressed their national and cultural identity.[62] What is concerning is that ten years after Dayton and the best efforts of the international community to create a liberal peace that incorporates these differences and (re)creates a sense of unified national multi-cultural identity – as supposedly existed before the conflict – this peace is no closer to becoming sustainable.

The nationalist rhetoric of the ethnic parties remains and indicates that a sense of a multi-ethnic community is a myth or a utopian dream. Indeed, pluralism is seen by some nationalists as a way of eliminating differences rather than accommodating them.[63] There is also a suspicion that these problems have arisen out of a contempt for the internationals' liberal agenda.[64] This in turn questions the very nature of liberal peace, its universal claims, and if it is up to the international community to make decisions on who should be in government, at the same time overriding election results. Certainly the OHR, on a number of occasions (particularly under Paddy Ashdown), employed the full range of the Bonn Powers by dismissing elected representatives that were considered unsuitable. On the other hand, there have also been continued demands, the loudest unsurprisingly from opposition parties within the federation, for the OHR to remove Milorad Dodik, Prime Minister of the RS. This illustrates how the democratic process is potentially being undermined by the internationals on the one hand, as they use unrepresentative and unelected powers to remove elected politicians, and by opposition parties on the other hand, which try to manipulate the OHR for their own political gain.

This point illustrates a further problem of democratisation in the context of such international trusteeship systems. Whilst the international focus is on the democraticisation process and sustainability in accountability and representation, the international authority in Bosnia is on the receiving end of its own democratisation rhetoric: specifically that the OHR is undemocratic and is stifling democratisation because it is both unrepresentative and unaccountable to the people. It is clear, as Caplan points out, that 'international administrators are not elected by the citizens of BiH and cannot be removed by them'.[65] The dilemma here is whether internationals abide by (their own) rules and delegate political power to the local institutions and their electorates and risk surrendering Bosnia to ethno-nationalism, or continue to undermine their own rules, position and moral authority. Indeed, Chandler suggests that internationals use these dilemmas to legitimate their institutional guidance, by casting aspersions on local capability to consolidate democratisation by themselves.[66] What is unclear here is whether this is a rejection of democracy or just a general refusal to be externally ruled.

This friction over ownership of the democratic process is also clearly felt at the local level, where indeed many local actors feel that they are 'disillusioned with the internationals', 'not consulted' and thus marginalised in the decision-making process. However, this is counterbalanced, and indeed contradicted, by demands from the same local actors for the internationals to 'take responsibility for the problems the (Dayton) constitution caused'.[67] This sums up the problems of democratisation and accounts for much of the stagnation in development. Local communities want ownership of the process, at least in rhetorical terms, and they want the internationals to change the system. However, when the opportunity for constitutional change is available, local actors tend to opt out citing the ethnic difficulties of making a compromise on ethnic issues. Consequently, the OHR is left to make the difficult decisions, which naturally leads to accusations ranging from undemocratic and unrepresentative practices to colonialism. Either way, the end result has created a culture of dependency and ambivalence whilst also undermining the capacity of BiH's political institutions.[68] Those who benefit from this stalemate are nationalist leaders.

Human Rights and Rule of Law

Although the human rights situation is deeply affected by the structures created at Dayton, the Peace Accords actually promised respect for human rights and the creation of a human rights culture.[69] This is viewed by the international community as denoting an acceptance of the spirit of Dayton,[70] and the restoration of the pre-war multi-ethnic society clearly requires the removal of the ethnic barriers and the reunification of the different communities. These difficult steps are linked to the two main human rights issues – the trial of war criminals and the right of return for refugees and the displaced. Both are regarded as vital for creating a climate of confidence in Bosnian society.[71]

Even before tackling the practical problems associated with the application of human rights issues, there exists a conceptual problem with building the single human rights culture inherent within the internationals' understanding of liberal peace. This entails a (re)construction of a multi-ethnic society, which implies bringing back together the different ethnic 'sides' of Bosnian society, as well as a change in identity consciousness.[72] The assumption that before the conflict there *were* ethnic 'sides' that represented multi-ethnicity[73] is a serious cultural misunderstanding on the part of the western liberal peace project in Bosnia. Pre-war Bosnian society was a largely homogenous culture based on interwoven ethnicity, a level in institutional coercion and persuasion, and was not necessarily explicitly defined by a number of different communities living together.[74] Furthermore, it also ignores the pre-war emphasis on collective rather than individual rights. This has important implications for the statebuilding project as it affects not only the estimation of the damage done to the society by the conflict but also the international vision of how to rebuild it.

The Dayton Agreement set out to repair this traumatised society by initially separating the warring ethnic factions with the long-term aim of bringing them back together again. However, the concern of this approach is the extent to which Bosnian society has been torn apart by the conflict and the underestimation of the irreparable damage this may have done to the fabric of the former Bosnian society, which was so deeply ethnically interwoven. Clearly, there was a deep lack of understanding by the internationals of both the region and its genuine traditions of multi-ethnicity,[75] as opposed to its traditions of violence – towards which most attention focuses.[76] It would thus be possible to separate these communities, albeit temporarily, in order to achieve an end to the fighting. This was based on the assumption that the communities would then, under Dayton, be restored to their single 'multi-cultural' but divided entity. Multi-ethnicity was very deeply enmeshed at the lowest level and commonly existed within families. Indeed, in developments similar to the current situation in Iraq (where the difference between Sunni and Shi'a was never particularly alluded to before or even considered within a family) the Bosnia conflict emphasised ethnic difference – which was problematised during that conflict for the first time and thus created serious difficulties within families. The implications of this for the entire fabric of society were very serious as mixed marriage was a very common occurrence between all three ethnic groups. The conflict not only turned neighbours against each other but also divided families under the same roof, while individuals with parents from different ethnic groups were forced to choose allegiances and families were irreparably divided. In this light, the implications of the ethnic divisions created by Dayton suggest a fundamental misunderstanding of Bosnian society and make it particularly difficult for the liberal peacebuilders to promote multi-ethnicity as this involves more than just allowing separate communities to live in peace together[77] or indeed controlling them by divide and rule.[78] As a result of this situation the main barrier to progress in human rights is the discrimination inherent within the society based on ethnicity, which is of course reinforced by the structure of Dayton. This is despite efforts by the international community to develop a curriculum on human rights – 'difference', according to a local human rights NGO, is primarily identified through race, origin and nationality as no single national identity, even one including dual or triple nationality, has been encouraged.[79] Human rights are hence viewed subjectively by each ethnic nationality and divided three ways throughout society, with little acknowledgement of the different culture of human rights that exists in a post-communist setting.

These fundamental problems experienced in the realm of human rights indicate the absence of a common, self-sustaining state and the obstacles to the construction of a common community.[80] Although efforts to develop a shared identity have been introduced to offset the effect of ethno-nationalism, such as a state flag, a national anthem and national currency, ethnic difference still prevails and ethnic flags are still visible in divided cities.[81] The central problem is the absence of a shared *superordinate* identity that does not threaten local identities, and the fact that the most politically salient identification remains anchored in ethnically defined communities,[82] reinforced by the structures and institutions created at Dayton.

Further difficulties relate not just to implementing those structures as a universal understanding to all ethnic groups but also to their conceptual understanding. Human rights as a western liberal discourse have been applied via Dayton to a post-war, former communist state whose conception of individual and neoliberal rights requires the necessity for a large conceptual leap from the socialist, and indeed multi-ethnic, understanding to one based solely on the importance of the individual. Indeed, the local understanding of human rights is enmeshed in the notion of the ethnic community. This situation demonstrates the cultural inflexibility of liberal peace with respect to the social complexity of Bosnian society, or post-conflict societies more generally. It demonstrates how the local elites may derail the liberal peace by opting out of the process, forcing it down a path towards either illiberalism or the partition of the polity into mono-ethnic units.

The rule of law in Bosnia is equally affected by these chronic problems. According to a local human rights NGO, the rule of law has failed primarily due to the division of the judicial system into three parallel systems presided over by the unaccountable internationals 'who terrify the local judiciary and seek to introduce a form of Anglo-Saxon law that not even associated with the six different legal systems in existence in Bosnia':[83]

> Bosnia is divided into, three, four, or fourteen territorial-hierarchical jurisdictions (depending on how the one state, two entities, one autonomous district and ten cantons are counted); it also has four separate sets of laws, two of which are replete with contradictory provisions . . . and some jurists suggest war crimes should be tried under old Yugoslav law.[84]

The problems caused by the absence of a national legal system are also reflected in the civil courts where there is no state level Supreme Court but instead six high courts (constitutional and supreme) shared between the ethnic entities.[85] Unsurprisingly there are also three police forces, Bosniak, Croat and Serb, each with its own jurisdiction.[86]

Fundamental problems clearly exist in the realm of human rights and rule of law in Bosnia. Above all, the actors are reluctant to comply with the internationals' liberal agenda or their mantras of human rights (which are often felt to be expedient and inconsistent anyway), due to their own ethnic agendas. The compatibility of liberal peace with the pre-conflict cultural past of weak religion, nationalism and an emphasis on the socialist idea of equality can be questioned.[87] These 'soft' relationships have clearly been hardened by the trauma of conflict into differences, which as a result of Dayton and of the subsequent statebuilding framework have become so institutionalised that they have irreconcilably changed the nature of Bosnian society.

Civil Society

The development of a sustainable civil society is an indicator of the progress of liberal peacebuilding. Other statebuilding projects, often focused on the political level, have floundered at this level.[88] Indeed, during the past ten years, a focus on building civil society from the grass roots has increased as a way to circumvent the political stagnation in Bosnia.[89] Yet, recent reports of the UNDP indicate that the existing institutional matrix has stunted the growth of civil society. The development of Bosnian civil society, and in particular institutions such as the electoral process, political parties and the media, have been unable to move beyond political exclusion as caused by Dayton.[90] However, this does suggest that civil society can be improved by discussion and consensus between interest groups, greater independence in the media and cultural and institutional change of the formal political process.[91] These are familiar problems affecting all the components of the liberal peace along with the common difficulty of overcoming the reticence of the ethnic actors in Bosnia to engage with the liberal agenda.

Responsibility for the arrested development of civil society in Bosnia is due, at least in part, to the non-participation by political elites who are once again opting out of the liberal peace. Should the structures imposed by Dayton, so often the bête noire of liberal peace in Bosnia, be held responsible for this non-compliance? Certainly, Dayton is responsible for creating the political environment in which individuals are identified by their ethnic group. However, liberal-civil society is designed to avoid this and has been identified as a way to undermine the stranglehold of ethnic politics groups as well as a potential area outside of political, cultural and economic strategies in which progress could be made to break down identity and ethno-nationalist boundaries. Problems with developing a sustainable civil society at the grass-roots level suggest that derailing the liberal peace is not just the preserve of the political elites and that individuals are opting out of the process too.

Civil society as a concept is generally considered as the space between the people and the political elite. In liberal thinking it is an area in which civil relationships naturally develop as a society liberalises, albeit with financial and NGO assistance. Civil society therefore can also mean civility.[92] Active civil society requires, above all, participation, and this is clearly a problem if the sub-text for involvement is creating civility. Belloni suggests opposition to civil society is found at specific contextual and historical levels. Civil society programmes that pre-suppose a lack of civility in a society and contain hegemonic discourses are naturally going to arouse opposition.[93] Furthermore, even though the internationals may open this channel to further their liberal agendas this does not preclude the use of the route by ethno-nationalists to maintain their own monopolising agendas. Individuals generally cannot be condemned for being suspicious of civil organisations.

Civil society, although presumed to be an indigenous socio-political organism, is paradoxically driven by the international community, who provide the political and social agendas derived from their own liberal perspectives and, more importantly, the finances. Thus, 'civil society building has been conceived as an externally driven process that is dependent upon external resources'[94] with little connection to local indigenous and cultural practices. As a result, NGOs in this area are increasingly regarded as builders of a 'new elite' or 'new sector'[95] that draw funding from the internationals by speaking their language and playing their game.[96] The donors are as much at fault here as, whilst they might employ the rhetoric of statebuilding, their emphasis is often focused on tangible and prompt returns on their investment. This generates competition for resources and creates a highly exclusive and specialised environment that probably excludes exactly the individuals and groups that it was designed to include, whilst erecting even more barriers to social inclusion. It also creates a short-term NGO community that lurches between in-vogue funding projects, where donors, instead of the actors on the ground, set the agenda.[97] This undermines permanent projects as it disorientates NGOs, which are unable to run their own agendas and long-term strategies, and ultimately degrades the local self-sustainability of civil society, inducing a difficult mix of disillusionment and dependence. It is also notable that the economic project of liberalisation affected pensions, social welfare and healthcare; all have a negative impact at this level.

This also has a wider effect on the accountability of peace and the structure of peacebuilding as actors and agendas are centrally uncoordinated, often unaware of each other's programmes or indeed of their place in the big picture of statebuilding.[98] All the more concerning is that these problems are not unrecognised. The Swedish International Development Cooperation Agency (SIDA), for example, cooperate with three Swedish NGOs that work in the field; they are not project funded and are in long-term partnerships with local NGOs, often deploying long-term ethnographic expertise rather than solely acting as managers, administrators and officials. SIDA also works in parallel with the state government to alleviate the difficulties of working with a partner that lacks capacity.[99]

Nevertheless, the international community has been quick to blame the NGO community for these problems by suggesting that the availability of funding streams promotes 'forum shopping', which demonstrates 'the mentality of the NGOs as self-serving'.[100] It also clearly displays the inherent confusion in liberal statebuilding and the divergence between the agendas of the internationals and the NGOs; it is little wonder that civil society is slow to develop, especially when international organisations suggest 'civil society in Bosnia does not work'.[101] Academics on the other hand, have been quick to blame the international community – and not the lack of democracy – for the problems stemming from the international regulation of Bosnian life, the denial of self-government and the lack of accountability by political representatives.[102] Indeed, it has also been controversially argued that the preconditions for creating a sustainable civil society, such as functioning state institutions and a stable social order, do not exist in countries where international agencies deploy their civil-society building efforts.[103] From this perspective, the creation of civil society is undermined because the space for independent (from state politics) development of individuals is reduced by the intrusion of political elites, both local and international:

The nationalist parties oppose any form of universalistic values, the OHR tries to combat any from of ethnic-particularistic values. Hence, individual redefinition of identity has become extremely difficult . . . the individual is forced to retreat to even smaller communities.[104]

Although the rhetoric from the internationals is mostly positive about the development of civil society,[105] it is clear that a number of fundamental problems exist with it. Not least among these is the lack of committed participation from both the political elites and individuals and the subversion of international assistance to create new local elites.[106] The NGOs and international community blame each other for the shortcomings of civil society. What is clear in this context is the absence of a sustainable civil society.

Economic Liberalisation

According to the UNDP since the end of the conflict there has been

> economic growth, macroeconomic stability, low inflation and the revenue budget in balance. The central monetary institutions (chiefly the Central Bank of BiH) are strong and the transition to the market is well advanced. Growth in the current period, at around 5.5%, is in line with policy projections and GDP per capita is finally approaching pre-war levels.[107]

Indeed, the World Bank suggested that its successful reconstruction projects mean that Bosnia is now back to the pre-war level. Since the government introduced a new (and particularly harsh) value-added-tax scheme (VAT) it is 'swimming in money' and no longer interested in World Bank assistance.[108] However, this economic growth is fragile and is occurring at a time of immense transition from a highly structured, former-communist to a neoliberal model, and key reforms have been blocked mainly at the political level where capacity is deemed to be very low.[109] The transition is also taking place following a particularly destructive conflict that has created an ethno-politically fragmented state infrastructure in an environment where internationals and locals vie for leadership. Pugh terms this process the 'political economy of transformation' and suggests that this economic change, particularly in such a difficult political environment, is 'adversely affecting economically vulnerable sectors of society' because the process of emancipation is susceptible to distortion by local and international social engineering.[110] Thereby, the economic space provided by the new freedom of capitalism and the individual empowerment provided by neoliberalism has led to the hijacking and monopoly of economic resources by war elites to the detriment of the economic development of the individual. Perhaps worse has been the undermining of the previous systems of social welfare, for pensions and healthcare, which in a post-conflict setting would have played a valuable role in stabilising social relations. Generally speaking, internationals have seen it as too costly to invest in these areas even though their absence forces people into the grey market, which in turn undermines Bosnia's attempts to develop a viable economy.

There is a growing gap between the rich and the poor, with the (known) unemployment rate in 2006 being estimated at 30 per cent[111] and, according to the World Bank, 40 per cent of the economy unregulated.[112] Half of the population are also living on a minimum wage in order to avoid 68 per cent income tax, hence opting out of economic development.[113] In formal terms, there is an unemployment rate of about 42 per cent (though World Bank personnel were quick to point out that this was only 18 per cent if one took into account the grey economy). This raises questions regarding the suitability of a model that introduces a neoliberal economic system in such a fragile socio-political environment and the attraction for individuals to participate in the new economy given the financial tax penalties. Indeed, international financial actors have asked if such a model 'would work in Texas'.[114] Pugh suggests that the internationals would not be able to support such models and also highlights the contradictions in economic policy:

> The United Sates and EU subsidize agriculture, steel works, arms manufactures and dealers, technological development and the airline industry. The US has a public deficit running into trillions of dollars. No US farmer would tolerate BIH interest rates.[115]

Local economic advisors have recognised exactly the effects of neoliberalism by suggesting that international investment has opened up economic competition but without protecting the local economy and business.[116] International investment has also created a false economy. However, the central problem with the economy in Bosnia is that it requires consensus from three national governments.[117] These problems relate not just to the suitability of a neoliberal economy but also to the difficulties of political progress. The relatively strong economic growth of RS compared to the Bosniak-Croat federation is an example of how the deregulation and liberalisation is really only benefiting the ethno-nationalist grip on political power. The growth of the BiH economy, so important for the welfare of the people, is clearly affected by the Dayton structures but more worryingly by the imposition of such an advanced economic system – one that not only expects poor unemployed individuals to survive on their own but also to make extensive contributions to the growth of the economy without having a stake in it. In this context, the absence of a welfare system that gives the people a stake in the economy, and so in democracy and the state, is a serious problem. This disconnection between the development of pluralism and the impact of a lack of jobs or a safety net again underlines the ambivalence of the liberal peacebuilding project in Bosnia.

Conclusion

Over a decade after the Dayton Accords, an ambivalent form of peace exists in BiH. There is a semblance of security as daily life is returning to a level of normality without direct violence and the economy is slowly developing. However, the liberal statebuilding project, in relation to the theoretical model of liberal peace, is very conservative and is sowing the seeds of its own failure by not being able to actualise the benefits of the liberal state in social and economic terms, as well as in the political sphere. On first sight, the main structural barrier to the development of liberal peace are the Dayton Accords, which in an attempt to make peace have institutionalised ethnic difference at all levels in society. However, deeper questions arise from examining the liberal peace in Bosnia. Some of those emanate from the general post-conflict statebuilding realm, relating to the compatibility of the liberal peace as a model for western statebuilding that is applied to a culturally and historically, not to mention ideologically, different society. Others relate to the overbearing paternal influence of the internationals in ensuring their agenda is followed irrespective of the cultural differences and welfare gaps, as well as the multifarious NGOs whose diverse, and in many cases, uncoordinated attempts to provide development often impede their progression.

The clearest problem in BiH is the resistance of many local political actors to the liberal peace. Despite the rhetoric, they have been particularly reluctant to move beyond the constraints of Dayton, by for example, endorsing constitutional reform or even working together for (Bosnian) national unity. This development has important ramifications for the imposition of liberal peace, not least for the recognition, perhaps naively, that the local actors not only reject the model but also actually discourage it by opting out of its requirements despite the concerted efforts of the internationals to encourage participation and in some cases even enforce it. As a result, the internationals are unable to co-opt local cooperation unless it suits a local elite agenda that is potentially based on ethnic exclusive identity.

There is little doubt that in many instances the local elites are exploiting the problems of Dayton and seek to maintain the political stagnation that has arisen from the Accords as this clearly benefits their parochial nationalist agendas. Many difficult decisions are avoided by the national governments, which instead put the onus on the OHR to adjudicate, thus absolving themselves from responsibility whilst allowing blame to be apportioned to the OHR for unpopular decisions. The situation in BiH clearly highlights the difficulty of enforcing liberal peace and perhaps questions the need some commentators have pointed to for more substantial mechanisms that can be employed to enforce compliance by local actors to internationals agendas. Although the OHR has made many arbitrary, and as locals would contend, undemocratic and unrepresentative-decisions it has still not been particularly successful in overcoming local resistance to change. Nevertheless, in order to induce compliance with the liberal peace agenda, the internationals are currently attempting to induce cooperation through promises of EU accession. Unsurprisingly, the entry requirement's conditionalities bear a close similarity to the principles of liberal peace, namely, democracy, human rights, rule of law, civil society and liberal economic development without much prioritisation between these frameworks. This ambivalence has so far failed to connect the grass roots to the post-Dayton polity, reflecting a virtual peace and 'bare life' for many Bosnians.

Notes

1. A shorter version of this chapter was published as 'Between partition and pluralism: the Bosnia jigsaw and an "ambivalent peace"', *Journal of Southeast Europe and Black Sea Studies*, 9: 1, 2009.
2. Bosnia is correctly termed Bosnia and Herzegovina or BiH but will be referred to in this chapter as Bosnia or BiH.
3. Tim Cartwright: Special Representative of Council of Europe, *Personal Interview*, Sarajevo, 1 February 2007.
4. Confidential Source, Centre for Human Rights, *Personal Interview*, Sarajevo, 30 January 2007.
5. Many of our interviewees expressed this view.
6. M. Cox, *State Building and Post-Conflict Reconstruction: Lessons from Bosnia* (Geneva: Centre for Applied Studies in International Negotiations, 2001), p. 6.

7. For the composition of the Parliamentary Assembly, see www.ohr.int/dpa.
8. For a history of Bosnia, see N. Malcolm, *Bosnia: a Short History* (London: Macmillan, 2002).
9. Estimate of the UN Special Humanitarian Operation in the former Yugoslavia. Jolene Kay Jesse, *Humanitarian Relief in the Midst of Conflict: the UN High Commissioner for Refugees*, Pew Case Studies in International Affairs no. 471 (Washington, DC: Georgetown University, 1996), p. 1.
10. J. Dobbins *et al.*, *America's Role in Nation-Building from Germany to Iraq* (Santa Monica, CA: RAND, 2003), p. 88.
11. www.un.org/Depts/dpko/missions/unmibh/mandate.
12. www.ohr.int/dpa/.
13. D. Chandler, 'From Dayton to Europe', *International Peacekeeping*, 12: 3, Autumn 2005, pp. 337.
14. S. Bose, *Bosnia After Dayton: Nationalist Partition and International Intervention* (London: Hurst, 2002), p. 3.
15. Diplomatic Source, OHR, Sarajevo, 29 January 2007.
16. R. Paris, *At War's End: Building Peace After Civil Conflict* (Cambridge: Cambridge University Press, 2004), p. 106.
17. Chandler, 'From Dayton to Europe', pp. 336–49.
18. S. Bose, 'The Bosnian state a decade after Dayton', *International Peacekeeping*, 12: 3, Autumn 2005, pp. 336–49.
19. Diplomatic Source, OHR, Sarajevo, 29 January 2007.
20. Confidential Source, LDS Party, *Personal Interview*, Sarajevo, 30 January 2007.
21. See R. Caplan, 'Who guards the guardians? International accountability in Bosnia', *International Peacekeeping*, 12: 3, Autumn 2005, pp. 463–76.
22. See, Chandler, 'From Dayton to Europe', pp. 336–49.
23. Peacebuilding Workshop, University of Sarajevo, March 2007.
24. Annex 4 of the General Framework Agreement/constitution of BiH; see www.ohr.int/dpa/default.
25. Chandler, 'From Dayton to Europe', p. 337.
26. www.ohr.int/. The mandate of the OHR is broadly outlined in Annex 10 of the Dayton Peace Agreement. Article II of Annex 10: www.ohr.int/dpa/.
27. I. Traynor, 'Ashdown running Bosnia like a Raj', *The Guardian*, 5 July 2003.
28. www.ohr.int/dpa/.
29. An example of this sweeping power were the events of November 1999, when the High Representative dismissed twenty two popularly elected Bosnian public officials – nine Serb, seven Muslim and six Croat – from their posts. Bose, *Bosnia After Dayton*, p. 92.

30. www.oscebih.org/overview/mandate.
31. Ibid.
32. See www.un.org/Depts/dpko/missions/unmibh/mandate.
33. S. Jenkins, 'Ulster of the Balkans: British Troops have been sent on a Mission Impossible in Bosnia', *The Times*, 17 December 1997, quoted in D. Chandler, *Bosnia: Faking Democracy After Dayton*, 2nd edn (London: Pluto Press, 2000), p. 2.
34. ICG, 'Ensuring Bosnia's future: a new international engagement strategy', Europe Report 180, 25 February 2007, p. 9.
35. UNDP, National Human Development Report: Social Inclusion in Bosnia Herzegovina, 2007, p. 50.
36. Swedish Ministry of Foreign Affairs, *Country Strategy for Development Cooperation, Bosnia and Herzegovina* (Stockholm, 2005), p. 2.
37. The estimated Human Poverty Index (HPI) in 2004 was 13.88 (13.88% of BiH's population is poor); the poverty line is considered to be approximately EUR 3 per day. UNDP, National Human Development Report: Social Inclusion in Bosnia Herzegovina, 2007, pp. 33–43.
38. BHAS, Labour Force Survey (preliminary data), Press Release No. 1, 27 July 2006, Sarajevo.
39. UNDP, National Human Development Report, pp. 111–12.
40. Ibid. pp. 203–4.
41. Ibid. p. 48.
42. P. Ashdown, 'International humanitarian law, justice and reconciliation in a changing world', The Eighth Hauser Lecture on International Humanitarian Law, New York, 3 March 2004: www.nyuhr.org/docs/lordpaddyashdown.
43. Dobbins *et al.*, *America's Role in Nation-Building*, p. 89.
44. UNDP, National Human Development Report, p. 49.
45. Chandler, 'From Dayton to Europe', p. 336.
46. Bose, 'The Bosnian state a decade after Dayton', p. 323.
47. See A. Lijphart, *Democracies: Patterns of Majoritarian and Consensus Government in Twenty-One Countries* (New Haven, CT: Yale University Press, 1984), chaps 1, 2.
48. Bose, 'The Bosnian state a decade after Dayton', p. 327.
49. Ibid. p. 328.
50. UNDP, National Human Development Report, p. 53.
51. Ibid. pp. 48–9.
52. ICG, 'Ensuring Bosnia's future', p. 10.
53. Chandler, 'From Dayton to Europe', pp. 336–49.
54. See Richmond and Franks, 'Liberal hubris', 'Co-opting the Liberal Peace', 'Liberal peace in East Timor'.
55. ICG, 'Ensuring Bosnia's future', p. 9.
56. R. Caplan, 'International authority and state building: the case of Bosnia and Herzegovina', *Global Governance*, 10: 1, 2004, p. 57.

57. Dobbins *et al.*, '*America's Role in Nation-Building*, p. 103.
58. Deputy SRSG, Bosnia, *Personal Interview*, Sarajevo, 29 January 2007.
59. Bose, *Bosnia After Dayton*, p. 206.
60. Confidential Source, Centre for Interdisciplinary Postgraduate Studies (ACIPS), *Personal Interview*, Sarajevo, 29 January 2007.
61. Confidential Source, Party of Democratic Progress (PDP) representative, *Personal Interview*, Sarajevo, 1 February 2007.
62. Confidential Source, Croatian Democratic Union of Bosnia and Herzegovina (HDZ) representative, *Personal Interview*, Mostar, 2 February 2007.
63. It was explained in this meeting that the international community in Bosnia were attempting to 'eliminate diversity'; Confidential Source, PDP representative, *Personal Interview*, Sarajevo, 1 February 2007.
64. Confidential Source, Liberal Democratic Party (LDS) representative, *Personal Interview*, Sarajevo, 30 January 2007.
65. Caplan, 'Who guards the guardians?', p. 464.
66. Chandler, *Bosnia*.
67. Confidential Source, LDS representative, *Personal Interview*, Sarajevo, 30 January 2007.
68. Chandler, 'From Dayton to Europe', p. 337.
69. Annex 6 of the General Framework Agreement.
70. Chandler, *Bosnia*, p. 110.
71. Chandler, *Bosnia*, pp. 99–109.
72. Confidential Source, OSCE, *Personal Interview*, Sarajevo, 1 February 2007.
73. Srdjan Dizdarevic: President, Helsinki Committee for Human Rights, *Personal Interview*, Sarajevo, 31 January 2007.
74. Ibid.
75. Ibid.
76. Ibid.
77. Some Bosnians we spoke to explained that mixed families had split with parents (and children) leaving Bosnia for their respective ethnic homelands such as Serbia and Croatia.
78. Srdjan Dizdarevic: President, Helsinki Committee for Human Rights, *Personal Interview*, Sarajevo, 31 January 2007.
79. Confidential Source, Centre for Human Rights, *Personal Interview*, Sarajevo, 30 January 2007.
80. See A. K. Talentino, 'The two faces of nation-building: developing function and identity', *Cambridge Review of International Affairs*, 17: 3, October 2004.
81. This was particularly noticeable in Mostar on either side of the bridge.
82. A. Jakobsson Hatay, *Peacebuilding and Reconciliation in Bosnia*

and Herzegovina, Kosovo and Macedonia 1995–2004 (Uppsala: Department of Peace and Conflict Research, 2005), p. 81.

83. Confidential Source, Centre for Human Rights, *Personal Interview*, Sarajevo, 30 January 2007.
84. ICG, 'Ensuring Bosnia's future, p. 11.
85. Ibid. p. 14.
86. Ibid. p. 14.
87. Srdjan Dizdarevic: President Helsinki Committee for Human Rights, *Personal Interview*, Sarajevo, 31 January 2007.
88. See Richmond and Franks, 'Liberal hubris', Co-opting the liberal peace' and 'Liberal peace in East Timor'.
89. See A. Fagan, 'Civil society in Bosnia ten years after Dayton', *International Peacekeeping*, 12: 3, Autumn 2005, pp. 406–19.
90. UNDP, National Human Development Report, pp. 133–45.
91. Ibid. p. 145.
92. R. Belloni, 'Civil society and peacebuilding in Bosnia and Herzegovina', *Journal of Peace Research*, 38: 2, 2001, p. 169.
93. Ibid. p. 170.
94. Ibid. p. 175.
95. Confidential Source, Centre for Human Rights, *Personal Interview*, Sarajevo, 30 January 2007.
96. Ibid.
97. Confidential Source, National Dialogue Centre, *Personal Interview*, Mostar, 2 February 2007. This is something that we have observed ourselves during the various case studies for this project, particularly in the case of local peacebuilding, conflict resolution and related NGOs. In an area where one would expect local analysts to understand their situation and how to develop areas of cooperation best, international models take precedence with generally poor results.
98. Confidential Source, National Dialogue Centre, *Personal Interview*, Mostar, 2 February 2007.
99. Confidential Source, SIDA, *Personal Interview,* Sarajevo, 01 February 2007.
100. Confidential Source, Council of Europe, *Personal Interview*, Sarajevo, 1 February 2007.
101. Ibid.
102. Chandler, *Bosnia*, p. 152.
103. C. Gotze, 'Civil society organisations in failing states: the Red Cross in Bosnia and Albania', *International Peacekeeping*, 11: 4, Winter 2004, p. 664.
104. Gotze, 'Civil society', p. 679.
105. Deputy SRSG, *Personal Interview*, Sarajevo, 29 January 2007; Ambassador Davidson, OSCE, *Personal Interview*, Sarajevo, 1 February 2007.

106. Confidential Source, Centre for Human Rights, *Personal Interview*, Sarajevo, 30 January 2007.
107. UNDP, National Human Development Report, p. 70.
108. Confidential Source, World Bank, *Personal Interview*, Sarajevo, 27 January 2007.
109. Ibid.
110. M. Pugh, 'Transformation in the political economy of Bosnia since Dayton', *International Peacekeeping*, 12: 3, Autumn 2005, pp. 448–62.
111. BHAS, Labour Force Survey (preliminary data), Press Release No. 1, 27 July 2006, Sarajevo.
112. Confidential Source, World Bank, *Personal Interview*, Sarajevo, 27 January 2007.
113. Confidential Source, Independent Economic Advisor, *Personal Interview*, Sarajevo, 30 January 2007.
114. Confidential Source, World Bank, *Personal Interview*, Sarajevo, 27 January 2007.
115. Pugh, 'Transformation in the political economy', p. 458.
116. Confidential Source, Independent Economic Advisor, *Personal Interview*, Sarajevo, 30 January 2007.
117. Ibid.

3

Liberal Peace in East Timor: the Emperors' New Clothes?[1]

Introduction

At midnight on 19 May 2002, in the presence of Kofi Annan, the United Nations General Secretary, East Timor[2] became a democratic republic. This auspicious event saw the creation of one of the world's newest states and represented an important marker in the liberal statebuilding process that hoped to end a period of 'western duplicity and self-interest with a brutal Third World dictatorship that had consigned East Timor to almost twenty-five years of systematic killing, gratuitous violence and primitive plunder'.[3] Indeed the events driving foreign occupation of East Timorese history have been far from constructive for the nascent state and its population. The period following colonial occupation has consisted primarily of a succession of occupations and civil war that have impoverished and traumatised the tiny population of this tropical island.

A Portuguese colony from the eighteenth century, East Timor suffered Japanese occupation in the Second World War and then, from 1975, Indonesian domination and a civil war that culminated in eventual intervention of the UN in 1999 and InterFET (International Force East Timor) during and after the violent withdrawal of pro-Indonesian militias.[4] The UN missions in East Timor; UNAMET (1999), UNTAET (1999–2002), UNMISET (2002–5) and UNOTIL (2005–6) were peacekeeping and statebuilding projects, variously described as 'governance or national-building missions',[5] intended to end the civil war and years of foreign oppression through the creation of liberal peace and the construction of an independent liberal democratic state in East Timor.

UNAMET was an initial short mission to oversee the ballot for secession from Indonesia and, as it transpired, the destructive withdrawal from the region,[6] leading to the swift intervention of InterFET. This was followed by the statebuilding mission,

UNTAET, which, although considered a test case for national building missions, had serious structural problems. According to Suhrke, from its inception the mission suffered from an underlying contradiction between its structure – based on peacekeeping tools – and its mandate, which was to prepare the Timorese for independence.[7] Nevertheless, in May 2002, the mission had succeeded in creating independence for East Timor and became UNMISET – which was intended to assist the development of the new state. This mission was also deemed a success in 'attaining self-sufficiency for East Timor'[8] and was scaled down in 2005 to a smaller mission, UNOTIL, ahead of the proposed completion of the mandate in August 2006. However, less than a year later, East Timor, and in particular Dili, the capital, exploded into gang violence, the type of which had not been seen since the Indonesian withdrawal in 1999. This violent uprising left twenty dead, hundreds of homes burnt and tens of thousands of people displaced into IDP camps, in and around Dili.[9] Although small in scale, these events led the UN Security Council to hastily launch a 'new' UN mission in East Timor, namely UNMIT, which was to follow the redeployment of an Australian-led 2,500-man-strong peacekeeping force that restored an uneasy calm to the streets of Dili. This was because these events were deemed to be a threat to the stability of the new state – and most of all to the credibility of various UN and World Bank officials who had only recently been praising East Timor's success with respect to the peace process.[10]

Although the catalyst to the events in the spring of 2006 has been portrayed as disgruntled members of the Timorese armed forces (F-FDTL) claiming discrimination in the upper echelons of the organisation (almost 600 members were dismissed from service in March 2006), this discrimination is linked to deep divisions and political struggles within the ruling party, Fretilin.[11] As a result of the crisis, this situation has been recognised, albeit belatedly, not as a short-term political crisis but as an indicator of chronic and deep-rooted problems. This was pointed out in the report of the Secretary-General on Timor-Leste in August 2006, '[i]t is now evident that those events (of April 2006) were only the precursor to a political, humanitarian and security crisis of major dimensions with serious consequences for the young state of Timor-Leste.'[12] Although this was recognised by the UN *after* the outbreak of violence and the virtual implosion of the state, it begs the question why the UN mission was scaled down and why international security forces departed in the first place.

Indeed, worryingly for the state of East Timor, the events led to factioning within the armed forces. This was followed by conflict with the Timorese National Police (PNTL) and led directly to their rapid disintegration, as well as causing the complete break down of law and order and the rise of criminal and youth gangs – which committed widespread looting and arson while displacing tens of thousands of Dili residents.[13]

This situation came as no surprise to many observers of political affairs in East Timor, who had been predicting serious problems in the statebuilding project even before independence – contrary to the official UN view. Indeed, Jarat Chopra, the head of district administration in UNTAET, was particularly pessimistic and suggested as early as 2002 that there would be a 'next round of State failure in East Timor'[14] at much the same time that the UN Deputy Special Representative was proclaiming the mission an 'undeniable success'.[15]

Needless to say, this collapse of the mechanics of state has had particularly serious implications for the statebuilding project. The violence, far from reopening old wounds, actually represents a 'new' conflict in the turbulent history of East Timor and a further division within society – this time between easterners and westerners.[16] Some argue that the political situation is even more complicated and view the supposed east-west division as political entrepreneurship, suggesting that the uncoordinated and random violence of youth street gangs is being politically exploited.[17] Irrespective of these arguments, but perhaps linked to them all, are chronic socio-economic problems. Indeed the recent UN report (August 2006) points to the 'underlying causes' of the crisis as 'political and institutional' but suggests that

> poverty and its associated deprivations including high urban unemployment and the absence of any prospect of meaningful involvement and employment opportunities in the foreseeable future, especially for young people have also contributed to the crisis.[18]

Without doubt, a functioning liberal state is struggling to survive and has been teetering on the edge of chaos. Even though the immediate causes of the recent crisis might be debatable post-conflict peacebuilding and liberal state construction are fragile and even basic security is unsustainable without an international peacekeeping and policing force, let alone a retreating UN mission to shore it up.

Was the proclamation of a democratic republic in the world's newest state in May 2002 a charade? Did the UN and the internationals, desperate for a success in liberal statebuilding, unveil and parade to the world a state dressed in the invisible new clothes of a functioning liberal democratic state? Thus, far from failing does East Timor even qualify as a functioning liberal state with the working facets of democracy, human rights, civil society, rule of law and liberal economics? In this chapter, we seek to address these questions and assess the nature of liberal peace in East Timor by examining the statebuilding project and its sustainability through an examination of the facets generally believed to be part of a functioning liberal state.

Although much of the blame for the current problems has been levelled at the inadequacies and incompetence of the political system and to a certain extent the liberal statebuilding process, there is without a doubt a serious problem at the grass-roots level where the needs of the East Timorese people are ignored and constantly over-shadowed by political power struggles. As the violence of 2006 demonstrated, the liberal peacebuilding process neglects these individuals at its own peril. Therefore, we will be questioning in this chapter not only if East Timor has failed in the creation of liberal peace but also if the liberal peace and the internationals have failed the East Timorese people. There are two aspects to this that we want to note. The first is the construction through liberal peacebuilding of a social contract between society and institutions of governance, and the broader issue of the legitimacy of, and contract with, international actors in the eyes of local societies and its complex groupings. The second is a key weakness of liberal peacebuilding, which does not, at least in the transitional period, deal with the experience of everyday life and welfare requirements for citizens. Without engaging in these areas, liberal peacebuilding cannot lead to a self-sustaining situation which is at the same time contextually responsive to a society's needs.

Before moving on to examine the liberal peace in depth, we will consider briefly the vision of liberal peace the internationals are trying to build in East Timor.

Envisioning Peace

The argument that the liberal peace is mainly institutionally oriented, neoliberally aimed, and constructed around the need for elite governance thus leading to a virtual peace, liberal hubris and the problems of local co-option have been outlined in previous chapters. It is clear that the liberal peace is based upon Enlightenment thinking, on rational ontologies and methods, presenting the peacebuilding project as a problem-solving device in which people and societies are incidental.

This means that they are defined by the institutions of governance, rather than by their own agency, leading to a lack of attention to the indigenous, welfare and culture. This is particularly problematic in contexts where there may be resistance to the goals of the liberal peace. However, in contexts where there is broad support, consensus and legitimacy on the ground for the liberal state, one would expect the process to be smooth. Yet this has not been the case in East Timor.

Post-conflict peacebuilding is carried out by various actors, often with very different agendas and visions of peace. According to the liberal peace framework,[19] the type of peace that is being constructed in East Timor is between the conservative and orthodox formulations. It is conservative because it required force and military intervention by external actors to enforce, and orthodox because donors and organisations, usually under the auspices of a UN mission, impose top-down peacebuilding methods. The immediate problem with this type of imposed peace is the lack of bottom-up approaches, which might include social justice and welfare programmes, as well as the actual involvement and inclusion of locals in their own peace-building and ultimately statebuilding process.

The UN in East Timor, like UNTAC in Cambodia and UNMIK in Kosovo, encapsulated both conservative and orthodox approaches by assuming authority for the region during the transition period – that is until such a time as it could self-govern. This raises questions about when and how local actors are deemed ready to assume a national government. In fact, the UN mission in East Timor went further than in both Cambodia and Kosovo and actually assumed sovereignty over the region, because in UN terms it was regarded as a 'non-self-governing territory'.[20] The UN rationale of post-conflict liberal peacebuilding in this instance was to assume full control in order to build a sustainable liberal state and indeed prepare national government for independence. This was based on the assumption that local actors, due to a lack of capacity, were unable to do this for themselves.[21] This task, a particularly difficult undertaking by itself, was not assisted by the time and financial constraints imposed on the UN mission from New York. For this reason, the UN involvement in East Timor was viewed as a relatively short-term process that required quick and positive results.[22]

UNTAET, established on 25 October 1999, was deployed as the key UN mission in East Timor. According to UNSC Resolution 1272, it was endowed with 'overall responsibility for the administration of East Timor and was empowered to exercise legislative and executive authority, including the administration of justice'.[23] Further elements of the mission included the provision of security and the maintenance of law and order, the requirement to establish an effective administration, to assist in the development of civil and social services, provide humanitarian assistance, support capacity building for self-government, and create sustainable development.[24] The UNTAET mission, with a budget of over $520 million, was headed by SRSG Sergio Vieira de Mello and had a total strength of over 10,000 personnel. This number included uniformed troops, civilian police, international civilian personnel and local staff.[25] It was organised in a similar way to that of the Kosovo mission, except that it had only three pillars – peacekeeping (military), governance and public administration, and humanitarian and rehabilitation.[26] By far the biggest pillar was the peacekeeping component, which totalled over 6,000 troops. This replaced InterFET in peacekeeping duties in 2000 and was responsible for the provision of basic security.

The second pillar was Humanitarian Assistance and Emergency Rehabilitation (HAER). It was led by the UN Office for the Coordination of Humanitarian Affairs (OCHA) and, together with the World Food Programme (WFP), set about delivering emergency food relief to the refugees and displaced persons in the aftermath of the ballot for independence and the destructive Indonesian withdrawal that followed (in 1999 around 70 per cent of the population – 500,000 people – were displaced).[27] This involved resettlement of displaced persons within East Timor and the return of refugees from West Timor.

The third pillar, Governance and Public Administration (GPA), had the responsibility of re-establishing governance at the central and district levels including the management of the civilian police, regenerating public and social utilities, and establishing the rule of law, as well as encouraging and regulating investment in the private sector.[28]

The mission itself was a very ambitious project considering the complex nature of the task, especially as it should not be forgotten that East Timor was a new state in which local actors had so far had little experience of democracy. According to the World Bank, which took an unprecedented role in development, capacity and institution building, 'public administration needed to be built from scratch because eighty per cent (until 1999) had been Indonesian'.[29] A huge gap existed not only in the actual institutions themselves but also in their capacity to operate and the experience of those operating in them. The mission lasted less than three years, and East Timor became an independent state in May 2002.

Upon the declaration of independence, UNTAET was succeeded by UNMISET and was granted a mandate for one year. This new mission was intended to offer assistance to core administrative structures critical to the viability and political stability of East Timor, and to provide interim law enforcement and public security while contributing to the maintenance of the external and internal security.[30] It also had responsibility to support three key programmes: stability, democracy and justice; public security and law enforcement; and external security and border control.[31]

Independence for East Timor was without doubt an important and positive result, not just for the Timorese people who had realised their dream of self-rule but also for the UN and the liberal statebuilding project. However, as the recent violence demonstrated, the veneer of the state is very thin and scarcely conceals serious societal problems.

In the next section, we discuss the nature of the peace constructed in the last six years, in particular critiquing the UNTAET mission. We examine the effect and current state of the liberal statebuilding project in the region and ask if the deep-rooted problems that have been creating conflict in Timorese society are being addressed.

The Realisation of a Particular Form of Peace

The roots of the conflict are widely perceived to be political.[32] This telling focus of attention is to the detriment of the socio-economic situation. The reason for the focus on the political are the number of layers that exist in the conflict, with the surface layer to which the internationals responded in 1999 relating to the Indonesian withdrawal and the rise in violence after the ballot for independence. This was a particularly brutal period, as the Indonesian military (ABRI) carried out a scorched earth operation, the aim of which was to leave East Timor in ruins and largely depopulated.[33] However, even before the ballot result was proclaimed, violence had erupted between pro-autonomy and pro-independence armed factions and militias. Following the result (78.5 per cent for independence), the fighting became more widespread, characterised by a number of systematic and brutal massacres by the ABRI.[34] These events, from which the population is still largely traumatised,[35] concluded active Indonesian involvement and effectively ended the war of resistance by Fretilin and Falintil who had been conducting this guerrilla war since the Indonesian invasion in 1975.

It also supposedly ended the ongoing civil war between pro-autonomy and pro-independence forces that had begun in 1975 when the attempted coup of the pro-Indonesian UDT party was defeated by Fretilin and led directly to the Indonesian invasion. Although this conflict seems to have come to an end with the departure of the Indonesian military, administration and West Timorese militias, as well as the arrival of the UN statebuilding mission, the influence of the Indonesian period on the East Timorese should not be underestimated. An entire generation has been educated under this system, speaking the Indonesian language, with many having governmental or administrative jobs in the Indonesian administration. As a result of this influx of Indonesian language, culture and administrative structures, the East Timorese suffer an identity crisis,[36] which is exacerbated by the destabilising influence of East Timorese refugees and ex-militias just across the border in West Timor.[37]

A second layer of conflict exists both within and between Fretilin and Falintil. These ideological and political disputes that date back to the 1980s[38] are particularly damaging for democratic development given that Fretilin is the dominant political party[39] and Falintil comprises the core of F-FDTL, the new defence force. These political disputes are regularly exploited and can lead, as happened in April 2006, to open violence. Fretilin is the major holder of political power so it is within this organisation that the major contests for resources take place. Although the party is divided in many ways, a deep central division exists between those who left East Timor during the occupation and those who remained to fight the guerrilla war. The F-FDTL is similarly divided between ex-members of Falintil and new recruits: this division has manifested itself into a rough east-west divide, with the old guard from the east (*lorosae*) discriminating against new comers from the west (*loromonu*).[40] Such sensitive divisions are easily politically exploited, as the events in the spring of 2006 showed.

A further layer of the conflict is between the East Timorese people and the government over the country's desperate socio-economic condition. This deeply unstable situation manifests itself in street riots and marauding armed gangs, such as those that terrorised Dili in April 2006. Regardless of the political situation there has been little or no improvement in the socio-economic situation since the promises of independence. East Timor has a particularly low Human Development Index (HDI) due to the high level of poverty, which currently stands at 41 per cent of the population or one in five (on or below the poverty line of $0.55 per day).[41] Life expectancy is 55.5 years, infant mortality is 90 per thousand births, half of the population are illiterate, only 30 per cent have their own drinking water facilities and 73 per cent have no access to electricity.[42] Unemployment figures are considered to be about 20 per cent in urban areas such as Dili,[43] while this is believed to be verging on 44 per cent for urban youth.[44] The economy meanwhile is weak, GDP in 2004 grew only modestly at under 2 per cent and with a population growth of 3 per cent this has probably increased poverty.[45] Although East Timor has enormous revenue-generating potential in gas and petroleum reserves, little of this has filtered back.

In order to deal with these layers of conflict the internationals and UNTAET embarked on a liberal statebuilding project in 1999. The first and perhaps most important achievement of this process was the geographical creation of the state. This was achieved through the UNAMET mission, which organised and executed the ballot for independence. This was an enormous task in the presence of mounting violence but as Martin points out it was 'international humanitarian intervention . . . had the future of East Timor remained unresolved within Indonesia . . . how many more might still have died before a better opportunity for self-determination been created?'[46] The subsequent InterFET mission was also widely acclaimed as an outstanding success as it 'provided an interim administration, urgent humanitarian assistance and won the hearts and minds of the Timorese by driving away the Indonesian army and militias'.[47]

UNTAET, the following UN mission, suffered harsher criticism and is held by some to be responsible for the current problems. According to the literature on UNTAET,[48] there is agreement that at its inception it enjoyed two developments that are rarely available in peace missions: firstly, the belligerent power had completely withdrawn and secondly, there was a single interlocutor with which to negotiate – the National Council of Timorese Resistance (CNRT).[49] These developments allowed the UN to operate in conditions that should have been conducive to a successful outcome according to some.[50] However, according to Chopra, 'it still went wrong'.[51]

The main thrust of Chopra's bitter criticism of UNTAET is directed against its arbitrary and authoritarian exercise of political authority and failure to include local people in the political process

(Timorisation) as well as be accountable to them.[52] As already dis-
cussed, UNTAET was in the unprecedented position of exercising
sovereignty over East Timor so the SRSG held both legislative and
administrate powers. Chopra argues that this situation damaged the
development of democracy, which paradoxically the UN mission was
there to create. He suggests its centralised approach was reminiscent
of colonial administrations in their reluctance to share power.[53] This
approach, it seems, greatly impeded the transition (and preparation)
to independent statehood in East Timor. Equally, it generated mistrust and the development of parallel institutions, particularly affecting much needed capacity building, especially in governance and civil
service where gaps in knowledge and experience persisted upon the
Indonesians' departure. The paradox here is that in order for local
actors to build capacity they need the time to be included (and trusted)
by internationals to perform the roles and tasks, and if necessary to
make mistakes from which to learn.[54] Yet, 'UNTAET was established as an exclusively UN-staffed entity, and political mechanisms
for local consultation were only gradually added as the Timorese
and donor governments pressed for greater "Timorisation"'.[55] From
the beginning of international involvement in the building of liberal
peace, local involvement was noticeably excluded.

The central problem with UNTAET, according to Suhrke, was its
configuration as a peacekeeping not statebuilding operation. It was
therefore ill equipped to institution- and capacity-build.[56] Indeed, as
a result of this gap, and in notable departure from its usual hands off
approach, the World Bank latterly undertook this role.[57] In a critical
appraisal of UNTAET, and in particular the GPA, Smith suggests that
it faced three challenges, namely 'creating a sustainable budget, developing a larger and more experienced staff and winning the confidence
of the East Timorese'.[58] In fiscal matters, Smith points out that both the
GPA and the SRSG were constrained by the bureaucracy and complications of UN budget procedures, which greatly slowed reconstruction.
Also, the lack of civil servants and the appointment of under-qualified
internationals hampered the efficiency of the civil administration.[59]
Overall, however, Smith's main criticism of UNTAET was its lack
of strategic planning. He concludes, 'the mission continued to feel its
way in a rather uncomfortable manner . . . in an environment where
"today's survival" sapped all its energies and resources.'[60]

Indeed, Chopra suggests that 'UNTAET's inability to deliver basic
services or tangible reconstruction and its failure to reduce unemployment cost the confidence of its people'.[61] Certainly UNTAET has

received severe criticism for its insensitive approach and neglect of the Timorese people. Suhrke goes as far in her criticism of the mission to suggest that 'the mission was a purely UN operation, with no recognised local counterpart. It had an internationally recruited civil administration, staffed by people with no expertise of the country or knowledge of locally understood languages.'[62] Those inside the mission also shared this pessimistic view. As Anthony Goldstone, a senior political affairs officer in UNTAET suggests, 'the mission was a success for the UN but not for the East Timorese, who have inherited a failed state.'[63] Political institutions had been created but socio-economic needs were far from being appropriately addressed.

The next section examines the nature of the liberal peace that currently exists in East Timor and explores its components in order to discover what kind of peace – if any – has actually taken root. We will take as our navigation points for this exercise the principal tenets of liberal peace – democratisation, the rule of law, human rights and civil society, as well as economic liberalisation and development. This section investigates why local culture dynamics and issues relating to welfare and development have not been properly addressed in the liberal quest to develop a self-sustaining peace.

The Emperors' New Clothes?

There seems little doubt that when the international community paraded its newest state in May 2002 serious problems existed. Indeed the argument can be made that the state existed only in name and the substance of the newly created liberal state was indeed fantasy. The tailors of this new suit, in this case the UN and the internationals, have a vested interest in making it believable.

Certainly the UN intervention, the withdrawal of Indonesia and the renewed support and interest of regional actors such as Australia, and to a lesser extent Portugal, helped placate the interstate conflict with Indonesia and created the potential for a form of peace in the newly formed state, which had the requisite components of a fixed population in a bounded territory, albeit without an internationally legitimised political system or being economically capable of sustaining itself. In this respect, East Timor bears some relation to a post-colonial state from which the imperial power has withdrawn to leave the local elites to establish a political system in the remaining vacuum (or, from a Fanonian perspective, to employ the same colonial violence to maintain power and dominate the spoils).[64] Indeed, the uniqueness of this situation in which the aggressor state has departed and the nation remains aided by the international community should present a relatively straightforward statebuilding prospect. However, the political divisions created during the Indonesian occupation and ensuing civil war soon resurfaced after the 'honeymoon' period of independence and have morphed into a form of intrastate conflict between the elites.[65] They compete for power in the shell of a barely formed state.

Nevertheless, as we have argued above, in spite of attempts to solve the difficulties, the country's current problems seem to have been created or certainly exacerbated in part by the international community and the successive UN missions. In the light of the recent implosion of the state security apparatus and the paralysis of the political leadership, especially after seven years and millions of dollars in funds, the efforts of the international community to create an orthodox version of the liberal peace and build a self-sustaining liberal democratic state in East Timor looks precarious. Indeed, a conservative version of the liberal peace plagued by political divisions and security and welfare problems is a more accurate description of the state entity. The result has been a state destabilised by the effect of the continued existence of the roots of the political conflict that have not been properly addressed; the creation and legitimisation of a monopolising single-party government paralysed by a lack of capacity and political division; and dire socio-economic conditions which are still deteriorating. The way out of these problems is supposed to be provided by the liberal peace and its army of supporters and engineers. Just why this has not occurred is the subject of the following sections.

Democratisation and Governance

The democratic process has provided defining moments for the development of East Timor. The plebiscite on autonomy – in August 1999 – produced an incredible turnout of almost 98 per cent of registered voters.[66] In the ballot, overseen by the UN, 78.5 per cent voted against autonomy (effectively endorsing independence). However, this event caused the implosion of the Indonesian-dominated political infrastructure and sparked the violence and destruction that shattered the country, leaving many hundreds dead and many more thousands displaced. In this context, Paris suggests that the UN deserves criticism for this early introduction of democracy into a volatile and dangerous environment and he suggests that the UN never recovered from this setback.[67] Indeed, the same can also be said of the Timorese people. Paris' argument is that liberalisation occurred too soon, before the necessary institutions had been cemented. Yet this argument does not offer a response to the linkage between poverty, welfare and the uptake of liberal institutions by the population, or for the problems caused by a lack of understanding of local cultural and identity dynamics (though it may well chaperone the political elites more 'effectively' through the development of liberal governance).

During the fragile post-ballot period, Fretilin maintained dominance of the CNRT, which in the aftermath of the Indonesian withdrawal and preceding independence, acted for national unity. Even Xanana Gusmano, the heroic Falintil resistance leader who maintained an agenda for national unity, put aside his differences to allow himself to be elected leader. More importantly, between 1998 and 2000 the CNRT included leaders associated with the pro-Indonesian UDT and APODETI parties.[68] This was a particularly important development because the post-ballot CRNT was configured for national unity and thus was integral to the development and formation of Timorese governance and these parties were the driving forces behind the pro-independence movement, being largely comprised of the former resistance movement. For this reason, the CNRT enjoyed a certain de facto legitimacy and in many areas became the effective governmental authority.[69] However, this was not effectively recognised by the UN transitional authority,[70] and as a result the latter failed to capitalise on this nascent, but short-lived political unity. Indeed, this lack of recognition of CNRT as a local partner for development was a failure for the development of democracy because it led to a contest of authority between the CRNT and the UN instead of building on potential synergies. The failure to politically engage the CRNT allowed the UN to capitalise on the extent of their own support and create the space to develop their own parallel structures. 'A gap therefore developed between the UN's *de jure* authority on paper, and the CNRT's *de facto* control in the field.'[71]

However, the sense of authority and national legitimacy generated by the CRNT was hijacked by Fretilin which in a development reminiscent of Hun Sen in Cambodia, exploited the democratic process and national euphoria of approaching independence to effectively stage a palace coup, albeit under the auspices of a democratic election, to ensure their sole domination of political power. Thus, in 2000, Fretilin orchestrated a public split from the CRNT and took with it the political organisation and powerful party infrastructure that had been created, and preceded to monopolise national politics.

On their defection from the CRNT, Fretilin fully exploited the de facto legitimacy enjoyed by the CRNT to secure an overwhelming victory in the Constituent Assembly elections in 2001, (they gained 57 per cent of the vote). This produced a fully Timorese cabinet; however, of the eighty-eight seats, fifty-five were taken by Fretilin, thus reflecting its large electoral victory and ensuring political domination. This development 'tilted the balance of power between UNAET and the emerging East Timorese institutions of governance firmly in favour of the latter'.[72] By securing this mandate the constituent assembly was able to introduce the 'Fretilin Constitution', which effectively subordinated the president (the popular Xanana Gusmao)[73] to the government – the implications of this for the effective operation of separation of powers are clear. It sowed the seeds for future power struggles between the president and government. The constitution also stipulated, quite controversially for the democratic process, that the established constituent assembly should transform into the national parliament without a second election.[74] This development allowed Fretilin to transform democracy into dictatorship as the transformation allowed for the consolidation of their sole ownership of political power. This was even more apparent on the creation of the national parliament as 'the Fretilin central committee gave itself a stranglehold on the state by assigning most key cabinet positions to party members'.[75] As a result, the national parliament is considered by many to be both illegitimate and unrepresentative.[76] Fretilin's consolidation of power was even felt at the village level where local *Suco* elections for leadership positions were politicised and individual candidates were pushed out by representatives of the political party.[77]

There is a growing body of literature that highlights the dangers of early elections before effective political institutions are created, simply for this reason: it allows the democratic process to be abused in the legitimisation of elites and causes the institutionalisation of competition and violence.[78] It is difficult to guess how far UNTAET and the internationals were aware of these developments. But mindful perhaps of the pressure from New York to establish a functioning democratic liberal state with a working government in line with pressing financial and time constraints, the UN needed democratic progress. However, this need for progress effectively stunted the growth of democracy as it established Fretilin in an unrivalled

position of power, a development that had profound and indeed particularly damaging effects.

The current political situation of governmental collapse and the
armed conflict that erupted in April 2006 can be seen as a direct
result of this. However, it also appears that even within Fretilin
itself, who are monopolising power in the national assembly, old
divisions and rivalries within the organisation are being brought
to the surface, leading to open violence. For example, Rogerio
Lobato, a Fretilin central committee member, exploited divisions
and resentment among ex-Falintil members to construct an independent power base, which after a brief show of force earned
him a position in government.[79] Although these political divisions
draw on old resistance-period rivalry within Fretilin they also
exploited recent 'Indonesian period' animosity against those who
had worked within the Indonesian government.[80] This clearly
demonstrates that the wound preventing reconciliation is far from
healed by liberal peacebuilding and in reality is continually opened
by political entrepreneurs.

A further personification of the failure of democratisation and the
chronic condition of the political infrastructure was Major Alfredo
Reinado, who, unusually for a *loromonu* – someone from the west
of the country – was head of the military police and former head of
the navy. He deserted, however, from the security forces in protest at
the suggested discrimination and violence against *loromonu* and was
instrumental in establishing a rebel force that fought pitched battles
with F-FDTL during the April 2006 crisis. The result of this was to
further divide loyalties within the political and security infrastructure
and led directly to the formation of similar armed gangs which felt
themselves threatened and whose sympathies varied between east
and west as well as between for and against the government. Reinado
was eventually killed during attacks on the prime minister and president in February 2008.

Much has been made of these events in recent analyses in the
media. Although this is important, surely the point is not necessarily the details of these events but that they have occurred at all,
especially within a supposedly democratic state. The fact that actors
from *within* the government and security apparatus are prepared to
take such violent actions, to augment their own claim to power, vent
their frustrations or indeed protect themselves, clearly illustrates the
weakness of the current political system and the dysfunctionality of
the state. It is particularly worrying that political actors are prepared

to act outside of politics and resort to violence, easily harnessing the aggrieved Timorese people who are quick to join in. Remedies of arrest and imprisonment for individuals, although clearly deserved, might not necessarily stop this happening again if the 'natural' recourse for political dissatisfaction or opposition politics is violence.

This argument can also be made about the dictatorial style and micro-management of the former Prime Minister, Mari Alkatiri, who monopolised political power and effectively stagnated government. Government advisors explained that his style is such that ministers are afraid to make decisions without his direct authority; this not only obstructs the process of governance but also fails to build much needed capacity in the government ministries. As a result, the process of government is in paralysis.[81] Although it is necessary in this analysis to consider the role of the individual (Alkatiri was forced to resign following a battle of political wills with Gusmano), it is perhaps more important to consider why this consolidation of power in one individual was allowed, as this clearly problematises once again the nature of democracy in the government. Questions relating to the correct function of constitutionally enshrined governmental checks and balances and the separation of powers, especially via an independent role for the president and the judiciary, are perhaps important here. Related to this problem is the position of the elected president, who under the conditions of the constitution had been rendered virtually powerless.

To compound these political problems, or perhaps because of them, the socio-economic situation of the Timorese people has worsened. The undercurrent of unrest and dissatisfaction with the government (and in particular the east-west situation) is fertile ground on which unrest and violence are sown and indeed exploited by political elites with their own agendas for power. As a result of the problems of democracy there has been a political backlash against the dominance of Fretilin, standing for the old guard – the elitist families favoured during the Portuguese colonial period but perhaps more importantly representing the revolution and independence movement, which grants them a powerful mandate. Nevertheless, smaller opposition parties such as the Democratic Party and Social Democratic Party are attempting to provide opposition movements. These movements are run mostly by the young (disaffected) generation who grew up under the Indonesians and have since studied abroad. However, the Democratic Party in the 2001 election won only 8.7 per cent of the popular vote (seven out of eighty-eight seats), making it the second biggest party, and the Social Democratic Party 8.2 per cent (six seats), so compared to the power of Fretilin (fifty-five seats) providing democratic opposition has not been an easy undertaking.

These developments suggest that democracy, even under the guidance of the UN, has failed to take root and become self-sustaining. The political process and the open contention for power that democracy provides have been exploited, following the results of the initial preparatory elections. But this is not a new development for post-conflict statebuilding projects, given that similar dynamics have been identified in Cambodia and Kosovo. The outcome of this is a monopolised and exclusive, unrepresentative and dictatorial state government. Is this all too familiar occurrence a failure of the internationals who, desperate for a positive result and early exit, have not ensured that the democratisation process is correctly implemented? Or is it a failure of the locals to understand and implement the technical political processes of democracy, which is supposed to be inclusive and based on power sharing? Or is it, more worryingly, a failing of democracy itself, where a sufficient majority attained in an election provides the authority to circumvent democracy by marginalising other actors and instituting a one-party regime? This last question implies that the rush to democratise a post-conflict state on the part of the internationals, together with the understanding of democracy of the locals, has created a structure which paradoxically has had a contradictory outcome, or even represents a localised hybrid form.

The problems of democratisation and governance in East Timor are perhaps not necessarily new, as Alexis de Tocqueville's observations of mid-nineteenth-century Europe aptly illustrate, 'It is difficult to induce the people to take part in [democratic] government; it is still more difficult to supply them with the experience and the beliefs which they lack, but need in order to govern well.'[82] To this we might add the difficulties caused by the assumption that all of this will be achieved within a liberal paradigm which does not reflect the cultural experience of local societies or take the form of a locally legitimate social contract.

Civil Society and Rule of Law

The focus of attention in statebuilding has been at the political elite and institutional level. However, there has been support of NGO activity in the attempt to develop East Timor at the grass-roots level. Indeed UNDP has identified the development of civil society as one of the Millennium Development Goals to reduce poverty.[83] It must be remembered, however, that East Timor is one of the poorest counties in South-East Asia. The emergence of local civil society is therefore painfully slow. In an effort to alleviate this situation, the UNDP development report has identified capacity building as the route out of poverty. The report suggests that

> all the institutions share a common weakness the lack of skilled people ... one of the most urgent priorities is to raise levels of education, skill and capacity in the public service, NGOs and civil society and the private sector.[84]

Indeed 'capacity building' rapidly became the mantra for development agencies in East Timor.[85] The problem, however, according to many locally based NGOs, seems to be that East Timor started out on the road to a liberal democratic state from 'ground zero'.[86] This can be criticised as an orientalist and rather arrogant, western, understanding of the situation (supported by some of our interviews with development agencies). The East Timorese, of course, had been living their lives and running their country from the village level up upwards long before the UN and its retinue arrived. On reflection, however, perhaps the point being made by development agencies is that whilst there is little doubt that the East Timorese their own subsistence systems, western intervention and indeed the liberal peace has introduced a completely new system of which they have no heritage or experience. Indeed it was explained in an 'off the record' statement that the development agencies need to 'break' the traditional cultural system and replace it with a new (liberal) one. An example of this would be generating a system whereby all family members are encouraged to work in the formal economy instead of sharing, bartering, networking and subsistence living as they have practised for generations. The extent of change partly explains why this neoliberal approach has often faced resistance.

It should come as no surprise that the main problem for building a sustainable civil society is the lack of local 'capacity' pertaining to the operation of a liberal state. The obvious question is how to create capacity and develop civil society in a legitimate way. The chronic lack of capacity is due to a number of factors. Firstly, many of those who were in positions of responsibility left with the Indonesians – those who stayed lost their jobs and currently experience prejudice. Secondly, the demands of the job market require education so, without this, applicants tend to be viewed as under-qualified and inexperienced. This is compounded by the fact that the internationals introduced advanced standards, some enforced by the conditionality on loans from donors,[87] others of their own making,[88] which are simply unattainable (and indeed might also be unrealistic in their own country).[89] So, in an effort to achieve some tangible results, particularly desired by donors, the internationals at their own admission often carry out the tasks themselves, citing reasoning such as, 'they (locals) are just simply not capable'.[90] The situation is therefore absurdly self-defeating as the locals cannot gain education, capacity or indeed the financial rewards which they desperately need. One NGO member explained that the difficulty of working with local NGO partners was that they had such a low level of education and management capacity that they were a low priority compared to achieving the tasks required.[91] This myopic approach will hardly create the foundations for a sustainable state. It was suggested that 'lip service was paid to capacity building because they [internations] were too busy: capacity building was therefore approached on an ad hoc basis'.[92] The statebuilding process (and in particular, civil society) is consequently sustained by internationals so when they begin to leave naturally the state collapses. This less a failing of individual NGOs who are trying under very difficult cir-cumstances to make a difference albeit with their own agendas and need to continually secure funding. Rather it is due to the lack of management and coordination by donors, international community and the UN, which take little responsibility for what the sharp end of the statebuilding project is, except perhaps to make capital avail-able. One way of reframing this argument about a lack of capacity is to explore the possibility that the liberal-state solution is unsuited to the specific context, and that local capacity might best be generated to reproduce a polity more reflective of this context. This may reflect a locally mediated liberal state. This might ameliorate the chronic lack of contextualised and localised understanding and capacity that international actors engaged in East Timor have had.

The growth of civil society is also affected by the 'usual' criticism of civil society practices found in most liberal statebuilding projects, such as NGOs employing mainly internationals. This effectively channels the funding out of the country to no financial or capac-ity benefit. Indeed development missions have created a type of 'alternative' environment. Similarly, the all too prevalent 'us and them' culture, typified by the daily route of air-conditioned house to air-conditioned car to air-conditioned office to 'help the locals' is worryingly reminiscent of colonial attitudes.

These problems are also particularly apparent in the development of the rule of law. The rule of law and judicial system reinstituted were based on Indonesian law, with the necessary modifications to ensure UN conventions on human rights were observed.[93] Implementation means the difficult task of finding and training qualified judicial and correctional staff. In the initial period, some East Timorese judges had only secondary education and less than two years of training and experience.[94] The problem was not just at the upper level, according to one judicial NGO, because 'the rule of law does not even exist for many Timorese'.[95] Instituting a 'new' rule of law and judicial system that is acceptable to the internationals (not necessarily to the East Timorese) requires an engagement with *suco* (village) and tribal law. The international assumption is that a formal centralised justice system is superior to the more traditional village system. In order to institutionalise this change a massive public education programme is required, but as one judicial NGO explained, 'there is limited contact and communication with the government in these issues and we are left to do our own thing.'[96] The difficulty is that internationals are acting primarily on their own to introduce a fundamentally new legal (and indeed social) system that will undermine the institutional and political fabric of Timorese society, from the *suco* level up.[97]

It might be asked who is driving the construction of the liberal peace in East Timor? The international agencies have one vision – albeit supporting different agendas – but then so does the national government and the myriad of international and local NGOs. An example of this confusion is the development of the police force. They have no centralised training college (as in Kosovo) but instead are trained in different areas by different national governments (primarily Australia and Portugal).[98] Yet this is expected to create a unified national police force with the same operating procedures.

Human Rights

The initial problems encountered by UNTAET in introducing the rule of law to East Timor were also experienced in the realm of human rights: 'The human rights co-ordinator arrived in the mission

(UNTAET) without a budget or adequate staff. There was no human rights concept of operations or a detailed plan.'[99] The development community also experienced difficulties at the grass-roots level. It was widely thought that there was such a low level of capacity in local, district and national governance that complicated and alien concepts like human rights needed to be introduced slowly because local actors simply did not have the ability to process the implications let alone implement them. As an international governance advisor explained,

> The government (East Timor) is being overloaded with complicated new systems and is unable to cope: new ideas need to be applied by the very basic principles in small amounts to allow the concepts to trickle down.[100]

In fact, it was pointed out on a number of occasions that the need for human security should be fulfilled before human rights are even considered. As Curtain explains, 'this relates not just to personal safety in all its forms but also to concerns about food supplies in many rural areas and meagre incomes in urban areas.'[101] Notably, the UNDP human development report stressed the priority for provision of such basic needs as health, education, and poverty and food security.[102]

Human rights and human security require an understanding of the self and position in society. This is also an area of difficulty for the East Timorese as they were experiencing growing insecurity in their sense of identity. It was expressed a number of times that the new state of East Timor (and consequently the people in it) are struggling to find an identity largely because the statebuilding mission lacks 'a vision of a nation'.[103] Since the Timorese people have very little rooting in a 'national society', there is little sense of ownership in the new state.[104]

The UN mission adopted the identity provided by Fretilin and took the existence of a national identity as a given. However, this was a unifying identity created by post anti-colonial feeling and independence euphoria. In the light of the problems in government, chronic socio-economic conditions and the violent divisions on the streets, this social cohesion soon unravelled and the East Timorese began questioning their sense of belonging as well as the substance of the state.[105] This situation is clearly illustrated by the language question. Fretilin are the remnants of the colonial period and are the old guard of the Portuguese-speaking educated urban elite. They do not necessarily represent the majority of East Timorese who are substantially poorer, rural and who speak any one of East Timor's sixteen indigenous languages – of which Tetum is the most widely used.[106] This is compounded by the question of the Indonesian educated – mainly young people. Approximately 90 per cent of East Timorese speak Indonesian whilst only 17 per cent speak Portuguese.[107] In in an attempt to placate the masses and maintain control, Fretilin announced Tetum and Portuguese were to be East Timor's official languages.[108] However this created the curious situation of Portuguese being the official language with Tetum as the national language and preferred language of conversation and meetings, and with Indonesian as a working language.[109] The official use of Portuguese created animosity and was increasingly seen not as the language of the resistance[110] but rather as the language of oppression. Even the most basic concept for state- and nation building – a sense of identity – proved difficult to create or even maintain. It is unsurprising that more complicated and technical concepts such as human rights and rule of law are proving difficult to implement. A state structure certainly exists but its liberal substance seems like rhetoric and exists only in name. Indeed, it has been somewhat aptly described as a 'Hollywood film set'.[111]

Economic Liberalisation

Paradoxically, although East Timor has been described on a number of occasions as a rich country,[112] this is not obvious. These statements relate to the extensive oil and gas reserves that exist in the 'Timor gap'. Needless to say, the newly formed East Timor government was able to negotiate lucrative deals with Australian and international energy organisations to exploit these natural resources.[113] The result of this development was regarded as a 'success story' and the potentially destabilising oil wealth was to be managed like a 'Norwegian pension fund and as a result generates $6–700 million per year'.[114] This is a staggering amount considering donor funding is $10 million. The East Timor government has subsequently been described as 'awash with oil money'.[15] If this is the case, why is the government in paralysis and on the edge of civil war with a declining national economy and desperately poor population? The account the government established to manage the oil funds is run through the United States central bank in order to prevent corruption (although some suggest it actually allows the Fretilin government to monopolise control)[116] because this prevents direct access to the funds. The annual budget is allocated to the government from these funds. The problem is that the government cannot spend it because 'it has no capacity to execute the budget',[117] while, according to the ADB, the government's capital expenditure programme is less than 5 per cent.[118] This is due to a number of reasons. The first relates to a genuine lack of capacity in the government, which has also caused a lack of trust by government ministers in the capacity of the public administration to distribute funds. This outcome seems attributable to either a governmental fear of corruption or grip on power – or indeed both. Either way funds are not flowing from the highly centralised government, so development programmes are not being implemented, capacity is not being built and progress is not being made.

Although a number of schemes have been introduced to alleviate the extreme problems, such as a World Bank social security net strategy that encourages people to work for cash and food[119] and the pensions plan for veterans, there is very little in the realm of direct financial assistance to the people who most need it. As Curtain argues, direct cash transfers, for instance, could be used to improve economic security and help cushion the immediate adverse effects of shocks.[120] After all, the introduction of a neoliberal economy requires participants in that economy to inject cash into it in order for it to be self-sustaining. The dismal performance of the economy is unsurprising as there is no cash to sustain it.[121]

The progress of economic liberalisation, like the other areas of liberal peacebuilding, has been hampered by the problems in government and this is not helped by the fact that the government appears to have plenty of funds available. The lack of welfare programmes to alleviate poverty, an aim the UNDP have identified as central to development,[122] is a continuing structural problem that requires more than political change to alleviate; in fact, it needs direct assistance from the grass-roots level. Alongside this particular difficulty is the immense challenge of introducing liberal economic development in a country that has little experience of an advanced capitalist system. The current culture of a subsistence and informal economy, according to the aims of the World Bank, needs to be transformed into a 'new' culture that develops capitalism, creates opportunity and ultimately formalises the economy.[123] Given that the former represents the vast bulk of the population, the latter aim appears to be unrealistic in the short to medium term. This shortcoming has the indirect effect of undermining the transitional status of democracy, human rights and the rule of law, because the lack of material benefits provided by the state for its citizens means that the social contract appears to be little more than an empty motif of a virtually liberal state.

Conclusion

The liberal peace has failed the people of East Timor because the project started in 1999 has succeeded only in creating only a virtual peace and a state that has all the appearances of a liberal democratic institution but has little substance – the Emperor's new clothes. Although criticisms of the UN missions help explain why this situation has arisen, the deeper reasons relate to the roots of the conflict and the neglect of the Timorese's welfare. This relates to a number of unresolved issues, first being local people's exclusion from the international statebuilding project and the failure of the Timorisation of local and national government, and civil society. This is by now a well-known story across many statebuilding operations. The failure has meant that government ministers applied their own understanding'.[124] Also, the overemphasis of the project on political solutions had the unwelcome result of the monopoly of the political situation by Fretilin. This led to the consolidation of power and an interpretation of democratic politics as a zero-sum political game in which traditional patronage systems were used to create power and consolidate positions.[125] Clearly, the freedom created by democracy is based on the assumption that once established, democratic politics and liberal principles will filter down to the people and not be monopolised. The question for the future stability was whether Fretilin will be able and willing to share power.

Lastly, however, and perhaps most damagingly of all, has been the disregard of the social contract and the socio-economic situation of the population as well as the neglect of bottom-up welfare and social justice. This has left a mass of discontent, and a situation that can be, and is, manipulated for political infighting, thus destabilising the country. East Timorese society – from the generations under occupation – is a 'society of activists who have a culture of protest'.[126] It should be remembered that they won in the struggle against Indonesia and have a stake in the construction of their future; continued neglect can only lead to greater problems.

Liberal peacebuilding has become a neoliberal process in which citizens are seen as empty vessels waiting to be directed once they have been provided with political rights. Yet, a social contract and its connection with welfare has been shown to be a key oversight of the peacebuilding process in East Timor, despite the fact that the resources and expertise are available to address this area. Thus, a contract between the liberal peacebuilders' much vaunted institutions and the broader population has not emerged. Indeed, it might be fair to say that the new state does not yet carry legitimacy amongst its people other than as a 'national' idea. Yet this nationalist notion is anachronistic and itself now a source of conflict. The state's institutional capacity has failed because of the focus of internationals on creating empty institutions rather than dealing with the pressing problems of everyday life, which might then create a social contract between citizens and institutions that citizens would perceive as legitimate. In the eyes of local societies and their complex groupings, the state is merely a vehicle for local elites and international interests, while liberalism (read neoliberalism) has resulted in an illiberal and ineffective state in the most important area of its facilitation of a secure and prosperous everyday life. Perhaps more problematic has been its failure to engage with the cultural traditions and customary forms of governance of Timor.

There is little doubt that the construction of a liberal democratic state is a Sisyphean task. The technical requirements of democratisation, rule of law, civil society and liberal economisation require what amounts to fundamental political and socio-economic change. It is also clear that the gap between conception and reality is very large and is revealed by the low level of capability of the internationally engineered state to deal with these issues.[127] To achieve these objectives requires huge long-term commitment on the part of internationals and a deep sensitivity to the bottom-up nature of the social contract rather than merely to its top-down requirements engendered in the 'panopticon' style regime of liberal governance. A self-sustaining liberal state should put the individual first, with welfare requirements being the building blocks of democracy, human rights, the rule of law, and development, as well as of cultural pluralism and diversity. The Timorese people, in the wake of independence, are still creating, and thus perhaps are unsure of, their new state and new sense of identity, which in a multi-ethnic/linguistic culture with a traumatic background of political upheaval is particularly challenging. They are in a difficult situation from the perspective of everyday life.[128] The most telling question, that does not seem to have been asked, is what do *they* need and want? Until this is answered and the conditions of the Timorese people are improved, we may not see an end to the cycles of conflict in East Timor.

East Timor's situation is indicative of a very basic problem with liberal peacebuilding more generally. Its focus on institution building at the expense of local experience of everyday life is counter-productive and does not produce a self-sustaining situation. Instead, it panders to elites who continue to contest the privileges they believe to be naturally theirs. Dealing with everyday life and welfare, we argue, would begin to deliver a much more sustainable form of peace. This would be predicated upon a social contract and a local hybrid of the liberal peace model. This would be in place of the unfortunate liberal democratic model neoliberal which in post-conflict zones such as East Timor is little more than fantasy. In the short to medium term at least this has produced a very conservative, even virtual, version of the liberal peace.

Notes

1. A short version of this chapter was published as 'Liberal peace in East Timor: the emperors' new clothes?', *International Peacekeeping*, 15: 2, 2008.
2. East Timor is officially known in Portuguese as Timor-Leste – in this chapter, to avoid the debate over the national language, we have chosen to refer to it in English.
3. J. Taylor, 'East Timor: the silence and the betrayal', *The New Internationalist*, 253, 1994, p. 6. Quoted in P. Hainsworth and S. McCloskey (eds), *The Question of East Timor: the Struggle for Independence from Indonesia* (London: I. B. Tauris, 2000), p. 1.
4. For an excellent history of East Timor, see J. Dunn, *East Timor: a Rough Passage to Independence* (Sydney: Longueville, 2003).
5. A. Suhrke, 'Peacekeepers as nation-builders: dilemmas of the UN in East Timor', *International Peacekeeping*, 8: 4, Winter 2001, p. 1.
6. For an interesting and in depth examination of this period, see I. Martin, *Self-Determination in East Timor: the United Nations, the Ballot and International Intervention* (Boulder, CO: Lynne Rienner, 2001).
7. Ibid. p. 1.
8. UNMISET, www.un.org/Depts/dpko/missions/unmiset.
9. *The Economist*, 3 June 2006.
10. Ian Bannon: Manager of the Conflict Prevention and Reconstruction Unit Conflict Unit, World Bank, *Personal Interview*, Washington, 23 February 2007.
11. International Crisis Group, 'Resolving Timor-Leste's crisis', Asia Report 120, October 2006, p. 1.

12. United Nations, 'Report of the Secretary-General on Timor-Leste pursuant to Security Council resolution 1690', August 2006, p. 1. Undocs, S/2006/628.

13. Ibid. p. 7.

14. J. Chopra, 'Building state-failure in East Timor', *Development and Change*, 33: 5, Autumn 2002, p. 996.

15. Jean-Christian Cady, quoted in A. Goldstone, 'UNTAET with hindsight: the peculiarities of politics in an incomplete state', *Global Governance*, 10.1, January–March 2004, p. 83.

16. Confidential Source, Australian Government Official, *Personal Interview*, Dili, 25 September 2006.

17. Confidential Source, International Governmental Advisor, *Personal Interview*, Dili, 27 September 2006.

18. United Nations, 'Report of the Secretary-General on Timor-Leste pursuant to Security Council resolution 1690', August 2006, p. 9. Undocs, S/2006/628.

19. Oliver P. Richmond, *The Transformation of Peace* (London: Palgrave, 2005), p. 217.

20. Suhrke, 'Peacekeepers as nation-builders', p. 2.

21. Confidential Source, International Governmental Advisor, *Personal Interview*, Dili, 27 September 2006.

22. Confidential Source, Executive Director of World Bank, *Personal Interview*, Dili, 27 September 2006.

23. UNSC Resolution 1272 (1999): www.un.org/docs/S/RES/1272.

24. Ibid.

25. www.un.org/peace/etimor/UntaetF.

26. Suhrke, 'Peacekeepers as nation-builders', p. 7.

27. M. Smith, *Peacekeeping in East Timor: the Path to Independence* (Boulder, CO: Lynne Rienner, 2003), p. 51.

28. Ibid. p. 63.

29. Confidential Source, Executive Director of World Bank, *Personal Interview*, Dili, 27 September 2006.

30. www.un.org/Depts/dpko/missions/unmiset/mandate.

31. www.un.org/doc/UNDOC/GEN/N02/327/74/IMG/N0232774.

32. ICG, 'Resolving Timor-Leste's crisis', p. 1.

33. Dunn, *East Timor*, p. 350.

34. Dunn estimates that the true death toll in this period was in excess of 1,000 people. Ibid. pp. 353–8.

35. Sophie Rougevin-Baville: Protection Delegate, International Committee for the Red Cross (ICRC), *Personal Interview*, Dili, 27 September 2006.

36. Joao Fonach: Director, The Foundation for Law, Human Rights and Justice (HAK), *Personal Interview*, Dili, 28 September 2006.

37. www.ec.europa.eu/comm/external_relations/east_timor/index.

38. In 1987, following a long dispute, Xanana Gusmao took Falintil out of the central command of Fretilin and made it a non-partisan army. ICG, 'Resolving Timor-Leste's crisis', p. 4.
39. Fretilin won 57per cent of the vote in the 2001 elections.
40. ICG, 'Resolving Timor-Leste's crisis', p. 1.
41. UNDP, Human Development Report, 2006.
42. Ibid.
43. World Bank, Country Assistance Strategy for Timor-Leste FY 06–08, p. 11.
44. United Nations, 'Report of the Secretary-General on Timor-Leste', p. 9.
45. World Bank, Country Assistance Strategy for Timor-Leste FY 06–08, p. 11.
46. Martin, *Self-Determination in East Timor*, p. 131.
47. Dunn, *East Timor*, p. 367.
48. See Chopra, 'Building state-failure'; Suhrke, 'Peacekeepers as nation-builders'; J. Steele, 'Nation building in East Timor', *World Policy Journal*, Summer 2002; Smith, *Peacekeeping in East Timor*.
49. Chopra, 'Building state-failure', p. 28.
50. Goldstone, 'UNTAET with hindsight', p. 83.
51. Chopra, 'Building state-failure', p. 29.
52. Ibid. pp. 27–39.
53. Ibid. p. 33.
54. Telibert Laoc: Country Director, National Democratic Institute (NDI), *Personal Interview*, Dili, 28 September 2006.
55. Suhrke, 'Peacekeepers as nation-builders', p. 4.
56. Ibid. p. 2.
57. Confidential Source, Executive Director of World Bank, *Personal Interview*, Dili, 27 September 2006.
58. Smith, *Peacekeeping in East Timor*, p. 63.
59. Ibid. p. 64.
60. Ibid. p. 64.
61. Chopra, 'Building state-failure', p. 34.
62. Suhrke, 'Peacekeepers as nation-builders', p. 11.
63. Goldstone, 'UNTAET with hindsight', p. 91.
64. See F. Fanon, *The Wretched of the Earth* (London: Penguin, 2001).
65. Confidential Source, Australian Government Official, *Personal Interview*, Dili, 25 September 2006.
66. Dunn, *East Timor*, p. 351.
67. Roland Paris, *At War's End* (Cambridge: Cambridge University Press, 2004), p. 220.
68. ICG, 'Resolving Timor-Leste's crisis', p. 4.
69. Goldstone, 'UNTAET with hindsight', p. 87.
70. The UN was particularly worried about legitimising a national authority particularly before an election and consequently regarded the CRNT

as a faction. See Suhrke, 'Peacekeepers as nation-builders', p. 11.

71. Chopra, 'Building state-failure', p. 32.

72. Goldstone, 'UNTAET with hindsight', p. 87.

73. He received 82 per cent of the vote in the 2002 presidential elections.

74. Goldstone, 'UNTAET with hindsight', p. 88.

75. ICG, 'Resolving Timor-Leste's crisis', p. 4.

76. Joao Fonach: Director, HAK, *Personal Interview*, Dili, 28 September 2006.

77. R. Curtain, 'Crisis in Timor Leste: looking beyond the surface reality for causes and solutions', SSGM Working Paper, Australian National University, Canberra, July 2006.

78. See Paris, *At War's End*; J. Snyder, *From Voting to Violence* (New York: Norton, 2000).

79. See ICG, 'Resolving Timor-Leste's crisis', p. 4.

80. For example, Lobato further exploited this position to dangerously divide the police force between former Indonesian employees and returning Falintil members. Ibid. p. 5.

81. Confidential Source, International Governmental Advisor, *Personal Interview*, Dili, 27 September 2006.

82. H. Brogan, *Alexis de Tocqueville: a Biography* (London: Profile, 2007), quoted in the *Guardian Weekly*, 16 February 2007, p. 27.

83. UNDP, Human Development Report, 2006, p. 3.

84. Ibid. p. 47.

85. This was explained on a number of occasions in interviews particularly with donors such the World Bank, Aus Aid and USAID.

86. Confidential Source, Executive Director of World Bank, *Personal Interview*, Dili, 27 September 2006. There seemed to be consensus among donors and agencies that East Timor was starting 'from scratch'.

87. See for example, World Bank Conditionality: www.worldbank.org/WBSITE/EXTERNAL/Projects.

88. It seems to us that many international organisations are imposing unrealistically high expectations on the Timorese, due perhaps top their own 'developed world' experience.

89. Such as the subjectivity of the understanding of corruption, for example.

90. In some cases, this is western arrogance speaking, while in others it is simply true when the requirements are pitched too high and the locals have not had the access to the necessary education or experience.

91. Confidential Source, Avocats sans Frontieres, *Personal Interview*, Dili, 25 September 2006.

92. Ibid.

93. Smith, *Peacekeeping in East Timor*, p. 75.

94. Ibid. p. 76.

95. Confidential Source, Avocats sans Frontieres, *Personal Interview*, Dili, 25 September 2006.
96. Ibid.
97. It was explained that the reason for government inaction is either political paralysis due to the domination of Alkatiri and Fretilin (and) or possibly the lack of support for the changes. Ibid.
98. Confidential Source, International Governmental Advisor, *Personal Interview*, Dili, 27 September 2006.
99. Smith, *Peacekeeping in East Timor*, p. 76.
100. Confidential Source, International Governmental Advisor, *Personal Interview*, Dili, 27 September 2006.
101. Curtain, 'Crisis in Timor Leste', p. 10.
102. See UNDP, Human Development Report, 2006.
103. Confidential Source, HAK NGO, *Personal Interview*, Dili, 28 September 2006.
104. Confidential Source, NDI, *Personal Interview*, Dili, 28 September 2006.
105. Confidential Source, HAK NGO, *Personal Interview*, Dili, 28 September 2006.
106. G. Hull, 'The languages of East Timor: 1772–1997: a literature review', in *Studies in Languages and Cultures of East Timor* (University of Western Sydney: Macarthur, 1999), pp. 1–38.
107. www.untl.labor.net.au/information_sources/language.
108. Australian Federal Police (AFP), 11 December 2001.
109. Twenty-six per cent speak English: www.untl.labor.net.au/information_sources/language.
110. Portuguese was used by Fretilin as the secret language of the resistance during the Indonesian occupation.
111. Confidential Source, International Governmental Advisor, *Personal Interview*, Dili, 27 September 2006.
112. Confidential Source, Executive Director of World Bank, *Personal Interview*, Dili, 27 September 2006; Confidential Source, Director of ADB, *Personal Interview*, Dili, 25 September 2006.
113. The Timor Sea Treaty signed in 2002 awarded East Timor 90 per cent of revenues and 10 per cent to Australia (this reversed the 50/50 deal Australia made with Portugal in 1989).
114. The argument is that the programme created to deal with the profits has avoided the destabilising political problems and corruption encountered in Nigeria and Angola for example. Confidential Source, Director of ADB, *Personal Interview*, Dili, 25 September 2006.
115. Ibid.
116. Confidential Source, Executive Director of World Bank, *Personal Interview*, Dili, 27 September 2006.
117. Ibid.

118. Confidential Source, Director of ADB, *Personal Interview*, Dili, 25 September 2006.
119. Confidential Source, World Bank, *Personal Interview*, Dili, 21 September 2006.
120. Curtain, 'Crisis in Timor Leste', p. 18.
121. Ibid. p. 10.
122. UNDP, Human Development Report, 2006.
123. Confidential Source, World Bank, *Personal Interview*, Dili, 21 September 2006.
124. Confidential Source, International Governmental Advisor, *Personal Interview*, Dili, 27 September 2006.
125. Curtain, 'Crisis in Timor Leste'.
126. Confidential Source, Australian Government Official, *Personal Interview*, Dili, 25 September 2006.
127. Confidential Source, NDI, *Personal Interview*, Dili, 28 September 2006.
128. Confidential Source, Director of ADB, *Personal Interview*, Dili, 25 September 2006.

4

Co-opting the Liberal Peace:
Untying the Gordian Knot in Kosovo[1]

Introduction

The liberal peace framework, when placed in the context of peacebuilding and statebuilding operations, aims to balance an empowerment of the individual with institutions of governance designed to guide the behaviour of that individual. Yet, as we show in the following chapter, liberal peacebuilding, even on the scale employed in Kosovo, is much more susceptible to local co-option than often thought, particularly where one group can adopt the language of the liberal peace and thereby gain strong support and credibility within and from the international community. Yet, the outcome of this process does not necessarily conform to the expectations of peacebuilders, as the process becomes one of marginalisation for other identity groups and their agendas. As a result, this may perpetuate the initial conflict that led to the arrival of the peace operation in the first place.

In June 1999, the United Nations Security Council (UNSC) adopted Resolution 1244, which authorised the creation of the UN Interim Administration in Kosovo (UNMIK).[2] Underwritten by the principal tenets of the liberal peace, the Kosovo 'trusteeship' was to be the most ambitious UN statebuilding project to date. It has so far received 2 billion euros in donor funding,[3] is comprised of personnel from the UN, OSCE and Civilian Police (CIVPOL), and is supported by KFOR, a NATO-led peacekeeping force of 50,000 troops.[4] For a geographical region of only ten thousand square kilometres and with a population of barely 1.9 million, it was an undertaking of impressive proportions. By mid-2006, senior KFOR personnel saw the situation in Kosovo as 'calm but tense', or alternatively, 'very fragile', pending the outcome of pending final status talks (for which contingency plans *had* been made if one side or the other was violently dissatisfied with the results).[5] By mid 2008, the situation still remained precarious but miraculously quiet despite the failure of the Ahtisaari plan, the deadlocked final status agreement and, more importantly, the unilateral declaration of independence on 19 February 2008. In response to this declaration, which effectively enacted the Kosovo constitution, the EU launched a new mission – EULEX (EU Rule of Law Mission to Kosovo) – to support the new constitution and begin the 'downsizing' and reconfiguration of UNMIK through the EU. How far this new mission will succeed in instituting the liberal peace remains to be seen, but what is apparent is that it must confront the deep divisions that exist within Kosovo at a time when international political will has waned.

Kosovo was the last region to be consumed by the brutal ethnic conflict that ravaged the Balkans after the break up of the Federal Republic of Yugoslavia (FRY). Unlike other former FRY states, Kosovo as never been an independent state.[6] The experiment in Kosovo was under a great deal of pressure to succeed as it offers an evolving model, which also pertains to the current situations in Afghanistan and Iraq. In 1999, when the UN mandate was issued it stated that under the interim administration the people of Kosovo would enjoy substantial autonomy within the FRY (Serbia) but would not form an independent state. However, years later the FRY is defunct[7] and Kosovo has declared independence. The 'fate' of Kosovo as a unified state is essentially in the hands of the national government but in reality it still falls to the statebuilding missions of UNMIK and EULEX underwritten by the principles of liberal peace to hold the region together. This has to be seen against the background that independence was not welcomed by the Kosovo Serbs and, of course, Serbia. Indeed, a recent ICG report suggests that the future of Kosovo could be a redrawing of borders along ethnic lines as the divisions between Albanian and Serb areas have increased and the prospects for a unitary state are diminishing as the de facto partition has hardened, particularly along the River Ibar division line.[8] The 'fate' of Kosovo has been 'decided' by the Kosovo Albanian Unilateral Declaration of Independence in 2008, despite the efforts of the contact group[9] to decide the final status of the province.[10] Needless to say, the Kosovo Albanians' demand for nothing less than full independence from Serbia continues to be opposed by Serbia and Kosovo Serbs.

The obvious paradox in Kosovo is that liberal statebuilding requires a state to house the institutions it requires, thus prejudging the outcome of UNMIK's mission, which is a priori contested by Serbs. It is contested not just because of the smouldering ethnic tensions of the region, but also because members of the wider international community, in particular China and Russia on the UN Security Council, are reticent about encouraging secessionist or irredentist claims. International actors expected a form of 'conditional independence' to emerge for Kosovo, despite the fact that many of the conditions of liberal peacebuilding have not been met, unemployment is rampant and ethnic divisions have been institutionalised.[11] This conditional form of independence would have meant that an international 'trustee' (probably the EU) would play a central role.[12] Even this now looks implausible.

Although progress has been made, Kosovo represents a polity that is far from an orthodox liberal peace.[13] The process of liberal peacebuilding in Kosovo prejudged the outcome of final status talks on a separate state, thus impinging early on key issues of the dispute. Kosovo Albanians were strongly supported in their tactic of constructing a state by co-opting the peacebuilding process itself. This raises a further question: can liberal peacebuilding operate in a non-state framework without prejudging its possible statehood? Kosovo Albanian officials and actors were provided with a state-in-waiting and used the resources they were provided with to co-opt the international community into accepting their claims, despite Serb opposition.[14] Hence, liberal peacebuilding, for all of its claims of top-down governance and institutionalisation, can be co-opted by those it is being applied to, utilising the limited agency they may have and even where their goals may not support a liberal polity. This indicates that liberal peacebuilding does not just consist of top-down international conditionality and local dependency, but also represents a local contest (or at least a negotiation process) over the shape of the new entity, who controls it, and whether this is a state or not. In these processes of contestation, the Kosovo peace project has struggled to find a liberal form. Indeed, like the example of Cambodia in a previous chapter, this is little more than a thin veneer concealing the roots of the conflict, despite the best intentions of internationals,[15] and has been co-opted by the shrewdly acquiescent and occasionally manipulative Kosovo Albanian elites. The strands of the liberal peace in Kosovo, namely democratisation, civil society, rule of law, human rights and economic liberalisation, are tangled lines drawn into a Gordian knot, which only tightens despite attempts to untie it. Far from expecting 'final status' to be the sword stroke of Alexander, unless the underlying roots of the conflict are dealt with only a fragile virtual liberal peace will be achieved which will not be able to sustain the institutions integral to the liberal peace without potentially coming into conflict with both the Serb minority and Serbia itself.

This chapter evaluates peacebuilding in Kosovo with respect to the arguments above.

Envisioning the Liberal Peace

In this section, we examine the nature of the peace that UNMIK intended to create in Kosovo. The mission was to deal with the roots of the conflict, principally between Serbs and Albanians. Even to the seasoned peacebuilding observer, the international efforts in 1999 were impressive. UNSC Resolution 1244 gave UNMIK, as the interim civilian administration, unprecedented scope and indeed capacity for statebuilding. UNMIK assumed control of central, regional and municipal government and performed almost every aspect of governance, including health and education, banking and finance, law and order, and even post and telecommunications.[16] Although this was supposed to be in cooperation with the leaders and people of Kosovo, UNMIK became the government of Kosovo. In its construction, the mission was linked to an unprecedented network of multinational organisations and comprised a four-pillar structured organisation under UN command that clearly reflected the cornerstones of liberal peace. Pillar one was initially responsible for humanitarian assistance under the UN High Commissioner for Refugees (UNHCR; this changed in 2001 to Police and Justice under UN direct control). Pillar two represented civil administration, also under UN command, while pillar three coordinated democratisation and institution building led by the OSCE. Pillar four ran reconstruction and economic development under the EU.[17] All of these pillars reported to the Special Representative for the Secretary-General (SRSG) for Kosovo, creating, it was hoped, a streamlined command structure, rationalising the functions of governance into a hierarchy which was determined by international personnel. KFOR remains outside this structure and, although responsible for security, reports directly to NATO headquarters in Belgium. It is generally thought that KFOR and UNMIK have been considerably more dynamic in managing the liberalisation process than earlier peacebuilding missions.[18]

Pillar one coordinated the vast amount of humanitarian assistance that was sent to Kosovo along with many humanitarian NGOs. According to a peacebuilding study, 400 international NGOs (INGOs) and 2,079 local NGOs (LNGOs) were operating in Kosovo by 2003.[19] Although most of the NGOs are concentrated in Pristina, a UNDP report suggests that many NGOs are led by minorities and are making a significant contribution to civil society through joint projects and by establishing inter-ethnic coalitions. This is particularly evident in youth and women's organisations.[20]

In the realm of governance (pillar two) quite the reverse was the case. Indeed the purpose of UNSCR 1244 was to provide provisional democratic self-governing institutions – quite literally statebuilding – but this had to be implemented in an awkward situation where it was still violently contested whether there would be a state at all. The way this issue was 'solved' was through the establishment of a UN trusteeship. That international actors regarded their role as comparable to running or representing a state is indicated by the fact that many diplomatic personnel in Kosovo regard themselves as exactly this – officials and diplomats. Under this remit, the UN had to provide the civil administration and governance.[21] The mission also required a huge amount of personnel in specialised and technical posts as well as the creation of basic political institutions, starting with the formulation of a constitution and the creation of the institutions of governance, as well as the organisation of elections to form both national and municipal governments.

Although acting initially as a transitional authority, UNMIK, in accordance with Resolution 1244, sought to establish a constitutional framework for a provisional self-government (this was drawn up in May 2001). In this document, Kosovo was represented as an undivided territory and was to be composed of local self-governing municipalities, which were to become its basic territorial units. It was to be governed democratically in accordance with the constitutional framework set out in (and overseen by) UNSCR 1244.[22] This effectively meant that, although a national government was elected and governance institutions created, it was to remain under UN/SRSG authority until such a time as it was deemed capable of running the country by itself or a final status had been decided (of course, the country's unilateral declaration of independence – UDI – has made this assumption meaningless). The Provisional Institutions of Self-Government (PISG) created by UNMIK in the constitutional framework included the assembly, president of Kosovo, government, courts and other bodies and institutions (set forth in the constitutional framework).[23]

In the realm of democratisation, October 2000 saw the first free and fair elections held, albeit at the municipal level. Over a million voters were registered, as were thirty-nine new political parties, coalitions, citizens' initiatives and independent candidates. The voter turnout was almost 80 per cent.[24] The following year, in November 2001, elections for the National Assembly were held, the results of which configured the PISG; subsequent successful elections were held in October 2004. Successful municipal elections were also held in 2002.[25] As a result and according to an OSCE democratisation employee, UNMIK has created 'functioning elected institutions'.[26] This was quite an achievement, especially at such an early stage, for such a complex project. Resolution 1244 was orientated towards a great deal of emphasis on the democratisation process, creating from the top down a constitutional allocation of twenty out of 120 seats in the Assembly for communities other than Kosovo Albanians (this included ten specifically for Kosovo Serbs).[27] In support of this, the UN/OSCE initiated, coordinated and monitored national and municipal/local elections. From the bottom up, the OSCE embarked on extensive education campaigns, sponsored democratisation NGOs and provided local education, assistance and advice through units operating in the local communities.

Pillar three encapsulated some of the main principles of the liberal peace project, notably democratisation, human rights and the rule of law, implemented by the OSCE through a democratisation unit that focused on building local capacity with political actors and NGOs. It established a police training school and provided divisions specialising in the rule of law and human rights.[28] In the field of democratisation, the OSCE supported active social involvement and the education of the various Kosovo communities on issues related to societal development, local government reform, teaching of democratic standards, budget formulation and electoral system development.[29] Within civil society it facilitated and fostered links between local, national and international NGOs and civic groups in order to 'empower Kosovo civil society actors'.[30] Moreover, through its extensive human rights and rule of law programmes, the OSCE sought to build capacity. The human rights expert programme is focused on government, judiciary and law enforcement, and aimed at 'developing institutions that ensure human rights are respected and that ensure people have effective remedies to human rights violations'.[31] In addition, a police school was formed, and the work carried out by the rule of law and human rights departments helped build judicial capacity as well as recognising and monitoring human rights abuses against minorities.[32]

Economic development is the focus of pillar four. Run by the EU, this has provided over 1.6 million euros in funding since 1999. The aim of pillar four is to create a neoliberal, 'robust, modern economy by modernising the economic framework of Kosovo, with a view to developing the structures and instruments that form the basis of a competitive, efficient market economy'.[33] According to the EU, economic development is to be achieved by the introduction of commercial and economic legislation conforming to European standards, the launch of privatisation processes,[34] the introduction of the euro as a single currency, the creation of a working banking system, free trade agreements[35] and the integration of Kosovo into various European structures.[36] Reconstruction of the economy in Kosovo is a complex statebuilding task, requiring deep structural reforms in order to overhaul the post-communist agricultural, and largely informal/grey economy, into a market-based formal one. According to a UNMIK economic advisor this means the 'construction of economic and social institutions from scratch'.[37]

The vision of liberal peace in Kosovo is clearly defined and it appears as if the international community – and the people of Kosovo – after a decade and a total of 2 billion euros in funding is making progress in building a sustainable liberal peace. However, the case of Kosovo also exposes significant flaws in the design and assumptions of liberal peacebuilding. Is this a 'really existing' peace, or are the tensions and divisions between Kosovo Serb and Albanian merely being embedded into its institutional frameworks (as recent events appear to suggest)? There has been much criticism of UNMIK by local actors: it has been seen as inefficient, endlessly deferring final status negotiations, distant, unaccountable and dysfunctional in that it sacrifices democracy and human rights for stability, and is both an executive and legislature rolled into one.[38] The division of Mitrovica is seen as indicative of its failure, especially in preventing the creation of parallel structures.[39] Indeed, it has been commonly argued that the 'Contact Group' was the key player, rather than UNMIK. Given that liberal peacebuilding prejudged the outcome of autonomy if not a new state for Kosovo, it seems unlikely that any party can accept that it is an unbiased, neutral and universal process.

Building the Liberal Peace

The roots of the Kosovo conflict are largely perceived to lie in the struggle for power between ethnicities (Albanian and Serb), represented by elites and states.[40] As an 'ethnic' conflict, it is characteristically fuelled by conflicting structures created by historical narratives, national discourses and opposing identities, territorialised and historicised in order to create implacable enmities between the two communities rather than harmonious linkages. These are compounded by familiar 'development' triggers, such as socio-economic needs, discrimination and marginalisation of minorities, underdevelopment, poverty and crime.[41] This situation was confirmed in a 2005 report covering socio-political and economic trends in Kosovo. The report stated that political pessimism had increased, with the blame for the worsening political situation focused on the shortcomings of the PISG, bodies that were supposed to be the embodiment of the process of restructuring governance. Not only was there a growing gap between the final status views of Kosovo Albanians and Serbs – which were exacerbating inter-ethnic tension – but dissatisfaction with the economy was also causing economic protests about rising unemployment. There was also a worrying increase in serious crime, organised crime and corruption. Perhaps as a result of this, the overall sense of security had fallen.[42]

Democratisation and governance were not fairing well either. According to a UNDP report, 'a democracy deficit exists that is undermining the legitimacy if its institutions'.[43] Kosovans, it suggested, have yet to properly embrace democracy given that confidence fell dramatically in the governance provided by UNMIK and the SRSG, as well as in the ability of the Kosovan government and Assembly.[44] As a result, voter turnout declined and individuals felt they cannot influence decision-making.[45] The problems with democracy relate to the lack of participation, particularly by Kosovo Serbs, who widely boycotted elections and their political parties refused to present candidates or take up their constitutionally allotted political posts in the Assembly. The lack of participation can be ascribed to the lack of a common identity and growing cleavages between communities. Kosovo Serbs withdrew their participation on instructions from Belgrade (which is funding them)[46] whilst Kosovo Albanians competed for a zero-sum monopoly of political power between themselves.[47] This is especially true of the two main parties, the Democratic League of Kosovo (LDK) – formerly led by former President Ibrahim Rugova –[48] and the Democratic Party of Kosovo (PDK) – the main successor to the Kosovo Liberation Army (KLA), led by Hashim Thaçi.[49] As the ICG pointed out, 'mutual distrust between the two leading parties is distracting politicians from seeking a consensus position for the approaching negotiations on final status'.[50] These problems with democratisation and governance created a 'political illusion' of democratic politics and an 'artificial functionality' of governance,[51] a condition exacerbated by the governance of UNMIK, which was both non-participatory and unrepresentative. Yet, as a transitional administration, albeit in cooperation with the institutions of self-government in Kosovo, it was expected that UNMIK would act to compensate for these problems in an attempt to preserve the liberal peacebuilding process. Blerim Reka, a UN human development consultant asked:

> How can democratic principles be exercised under conditions of asymmetrical governance by two different authorities with different legitimacy and power? How can accountability be applied to international authorities, and to whom are they accountable?[52]

Yet, in acting to develop democratic principles and accountability, UNMIK effectively reinforced the claim of the Kosovo Albanians for a separate state within which to locate democratic institutions, prejudicing the final outcome of status talks. At the same time, it was perceived by Kosovan Albanians that UNMIK reduced their capacity for self-determination. Their response was to accept UNMIK where it aided in the development of their own institutions and resist it where it seems to deny them self-rule. This is a key aspect of the Gordian knot that liberal peacebuilding in Kosovo became drawn into.

Despite these difficulties and the resultant limitations imposed on the Kosovo government and National Assembly, progress has been made in creating institutions of governance and building capacity. The World Bank has committed $80.4 million in grants since 1999[53] and was 'confident that funds are building capacity'.[54] However, a UNDP report found that 'many ministries lack a consistent structure and hierarchy for proper delegation, follow up, monitoring and intervention in relation to policy making'.[55]

Civil society has burgeoned due to the emergence of NGOs and is currently grappling with the difficulties of civic participation. In general, activity in this area has been greatly affected by the fickle nature of donor funding. Consequently, most NGOs are temporary, short-term projects without strong constituencies that tend to dissolve or become inactive after donor money has been spent.[56] This casts doubt on the sustainability of a 'Kosovan civil society' especially as donor funds were reduced due to ambiguity over final status.[57] The notion of a single civil society is unlikely to be realised in the short term, given the de facto partition of Albanian and Serb communities. This is compounded by the belief that many NGOs running multi-ethnic projects are actually exploiting funding streams and are only involved 'just to get funding'.[58] Even worse, the involvement of Serbs in NGO activities and the funding of Serb NGOs is relatively far less than for the Albanian community. If the liberal peace is predicated upon the existence of 'civil society', it is still doubtful to what extent this is sustainable in Kosovo. Indeed civil society in such contexts seems actually to exist only as an imagined community – a figment of aspiring international imaginations. Alongside this is the familiar criticism that NGOs 'lack coordination and a long-term strategy'.[59] Interestingly, a Kosovan LDK MP even went as far as to suggest that 'the internationals invest too much money in civil society and not enough in governance'.[60] Actors within the NGO community perhaps unsurprisingly are often seen as illegitimate interlopers who usurp governance from the 'established' government, officials and elites. This is particularly so in Kosovo, where the Kosovo Albanians are protective of governance and of their perceived ownership of it.

Difficulties have been experienced in the implementation of the rule of law. O'Neill points out that when KFOR troops entered Kosovo in 1999 the judiciary dissolved, the Serbs fled and Albanians left through fear of revenge attacks.[61] Hence, UNMIK's failure to declare martial law in this early period led to the institutionalisa-tion of lawlessness and organised crime, led by a post-KLA political class.[62] UNMIK has also been criticised for politicising the judicial system by choosing between Serb and Albanian law instead of imposing a generic penal code and code of criminal procedures with modern human rights guarantees,[63] as recommended in the Brahimi report.[64] Despite the creation of a working judiciary under the rule of law, the system has not provided for free and fair treatment for minorities. It has been suggested that it is heavily biased against Serbs who, it is argued, cannot get a fair trial.[65] Widespread system-atic problems such as intimidation and corruption are jeopardising judicial independence.[66] Furthermore, the Kosovo justice system has become an awkward hybrid of international and local systems, causing the local judiciary to be continually undermined by the deci-sions of international judges[67] thus demonstrating a failure in the growth of local capacity.[68]

In any liberal peacebuilding project international actors fund, coordinate and in some cases run the organisations of 'state' until such a time as those institutions have enough capacity to become self-sustaining. The 'success story' of UNMIK in this case is generally considered to be the Kosovo Police Service (KPS). UNMIK drafted 4,718 international police offers from forty-nine countries into its emergency police force, CIVPOL, making it the largest UN police force ever.[69] This organisation policed the peace whilst training a local equivalent (KPS). Now CIVPOL is rather secondary to the well-established and fully operational KPS, which is one of only two institutions (the other being the fire department) in Kosovo in which minorities work together. The latest statistics show a high per cent of overall minorities' participation (16 per cent) of which 9 per cent are Kosovo Serb (it also has a comparatively high 15 per cent proportion of female officers).[70] Nevertheless, despite this achievement, unfortunately, as O'Neill points out, KPS officers cannot yet patrol in ethnically mixed groups or operate in areas not of their own ethnicity.[71]

The development of human rights, despite the extensive programmes and political rhetoric (both international and local), has also proven a slow process and has been a central focus for criticism of both UNMIK and PISG leadership. As UNMIK admitted, their involvement from the start unintentionally affected the attempt to create a human rights equilibrium:

> UNMIK was brought to Kosovo to guarantee the freedom of all its inhabitants. However the arrival of UNMIK and KFOR automatically bestowed freedom on the Kosovo Albanian majority . . . and triggered significant reductions in the rights and freedoms of national communities, particularly the Kosovo Serbs.[72]

This is probably the principal barrier to the successful development of human rights in Kosovo. As O'Neill points out, this discrimination (and hatred) is very deep and has become almost institutionalised because in some situations, especially in the early period of UNMIK, the associated violence was regarded (by UNMIK) as 'understandable' and viewed as summary justice in the aftermath of conflicts.[73] So despite the pledge of Resolution 1244 to 'promote human rights' and the leadership and programmes of the OSCE to 'develop institutions that ensure human rights are respected and that ensure people have effective remedies to human rights violations'[74] the current situation remains far from encouraging. The Kosovo Serbs, once a substantial population in Pristina, are now all but non-existent and those who remain fear for their lives. They are virtual prisoners in their own enclaves scattered throughout the region and 'protected' by KFOR. They rarely make journeys outside of these communities, but when they do, they need KFOR military convoys. The Kosovo Serbs live in ethnically polarised enclaves, which are, even by Kosovo standards, particularly run down.[75] There is frequent racial/ethnic violence and

KFOR, CIVPOL and the KPS patrol, guard and monitor the dividing lines between the ethnic communities, thus reinforcing the ethnic divide. Ethnic discrimination is rife on both sides of the divide, but as the Kosovo Albanians now have greater access to resources and power, it appears more detrimental to the Kosovo Serb community and position. The dark undertone of discrimination and violence against Kosovo Serbs represent a 'reverse ethnic cleansing', which O'Neill argues needs to be recognised as such and can in no way be justified or excused in response to the earlier attempt (by Serbs) to cleanse Albanians from Kosovo.[76]

Both ethnic communities are still deeply scarred from the conflict in which neighbours destroyed each other's homes, property, businesses and livelihoods, and in some cases took them over. As is the case in ethnic conflict the distrust and fear of the 'other' as well as the hate and anger at the destruction of lives takes a long time to heal – if ever – thus undermining both human rights and multi-ethnic statebuilding. Perhaps the most serious open wound that remains is the problem of the 'missing' or the 'disappeared'. This includes members of both ethnic communities[77] that remain unaccounted for. Their faces stare blankly out from the lines of photographs, which represent a constant painful reminder, attached to the railings of the PISG complex in central Pristina. Ethnic fragmentation is no more apparent than in Mitrovica where the once mixed city is now starkly divided by the River Ibar that demarcates the boundary between ethnic communities. Frequently the bridge becomes a site of violence. It is 'guarded' by KFOR to separate the communities, thus creating a de facto partition between the populations of the city. This outcome 'visibly contradicts the international community's vision of a multi-ethnic, undivided Kosovo'[78] and indeed a coherent and successful human rights programme. As Booth suggests, 'the current human rights/security situation seems to be pointing to a complete failure, characterised as it is by violence, ethnic radicalisation, disenchantment, and incompetence'.[79]

An economic overview or current state of the progression of liberal economics in Kosovo also paints a bleak portrait. Economic growth, after an initial post-conflict spike has slowed to 5.4 per cent in 2004 (from 21.2 per cent in 2000). GDP is US $3.05 billion and GDP growth is 1.9 per cent.[80] But as UNMIK pointed out, six years after the conflict the economy was still dependent on external support, in the form of remittances (15 per cent of GDP), and donor assistance (23 per cent). Added to this was a current account deficit of 30 per cent.[81] Further worrying statistics are found in the labour market. UNDP calculated that the unemployment rate is 44.42 per cent but this is from a participation rate of only 52.47 per cent,[82] suggesting that a formal economy is only half operating. Since Kosovo has the highest birth rate in Europe and half the population are under 27, this delivers around 30,000 people onto the virtually non-existent job market every year.[83]

The result of high unemployment and low wages is of course a rising poverty rate and growing gap between rich and poor. Currently the poverty rate, according to the World Bank, is at 37 per cent of the population, who live on or below $2 per day (poverty) and 15 per cent below $1 per day (extreme poverty).[84] The UNDP HPI dropped from 17.6 per cent in 2001 to 9.6 per cent in 2004 (this includes a life expectancy of 68.8 and an infant mortality rate of 3.5 per cent). In terms of development, the HDI is 0.734, ranking it in the lower end of the mid level of the scale.[85]

The Gordian Knot

The liberal peacebuilding project's success is threatened by socio-economic failures and an apartheid system in government. This can be considered the main criticism of the UNMIK mission, which has so far failed to reconcile the Kosovo Albanians and Kosovo Serbs and to create, even in an embryonic from, any kind of nascent multi-ethnic state. As a result, the current situation in Kosovo is one of dual societies: the polarised communities have created parallel state institutions whose ethnic networks are linked to and funded by their ethnic motherlands.[86] What is equally worrying is that the Kosovo Albanian community has clearly managed to co-opt many of the internationals to some degree, receiving support even when their leadership followed ethnic agendas. This has certainly been demonstrated by the support Kosovo received after its declaration of independence.

The development of the Kosovo Albanian agenda as a defence mechanism against Serbian intervention has established historical roots. Following the Kosovo Albanian constitution of 1974 and the gradual disintegration of the Yugoslav republic, the survival of the Kosovo Albanians depended upon the construction and defence of parallel structures to counter the strength and dominance of Greater Serbia. As Vickers explains, 'all areas of life in Kosovo have subsequently remained divided into two parallel worlds, one belonging to the legal system of government and the other to an illegal system for organising all aspects of life.'[87] These worlds are mirror images of each other, fuelled by mistrust, anger, hatred and fear – boiling emotions that often spill over into violence. This situation was graphically illustrated in March 2004 when the province became immersed in anti-Serb and anti-UN rioting that culminated in 'ethnic cleansing'. The violence left nineteen dead and nearly 900 injured, over 700 Serb, Ashkali and Roma homes were destroyed along with Serbian churches and monasteries, and roughly 4,500 people were displaced.[88] These events demonstrated just how fragile is the peace in Kosovo and how thin the veneer of the achievements of the UNMIK mission. The roots of the 2004 violence were broadly those of the Kosovo conflict. After a decade of international political, social and financial investment, why does the vision of the liberal peace propagated by UNMIK and now EULEX not match the reality on the ground? In the next section, we examine the main aspects of the liberal peace and the problems that they have faced in Kosovo.

Democratisation and Governance

Liberal democracy, according to Held, is designed to create 'a system of rule embracing elected "officers" who undertake to represent the "interests" or views of citizens within delimited territories while upholding the "rule of law"'.[89] Yet the immediate difficulty in the context of Kosovo was that democratisation and governance were directed by unelected international and unrepresentative national bodies. This was in the context of the political apparatus of a state being externally constructed. There were enormous implications of this for not only the people of Kosovo but also for the actual geography of the region.[90] UDI has since threatened the attempt to create a multi-ethnic democratic state. The ethnic elements as the major stakeholders had diametrically opposed views of what they expected Kosovo's final status to look like. The internationals are suffering from 'Kosovo fatigue', and, some are frank about the unlikelihood of achieving multi-ethnic democratic governance, not just at national but also municipal level.[91] The reality of the situation meant promoting a 'compromise' or 'best solution'[92] that is the easiest to support, superficially conforms to the democratic cornerstone of the liberal peace and, more importantly, allows for the exit of the internationals. The unilateral declaration of independence by the Albanian majority in February 2008 followed this logic.

Some officials argued that liberal peace is an unrealistic 'theoretical approach' and that 'sometimes the best solution is not always the right one, but at least it works'.[93] This familiar argument about the 'art of the possible' is perfectly understandable but appears complacent when the peace promised to Kosovo claimed to be a liberal peace, not an undemocratic, ethnicised, virtual peace. Liberal democracy is intended to be inclusive and create a multi-ethnic society. Divergence from this, regardless of the ease of solution and the political necessity to 'succeed', will not deal with the central causes of the conflict. It was clear that the Kosovo Albanian, the Kosovo Serb and indeed Serbian leaderships were just playing the internationals' game as long as it suited them, in the hope that they would be rewarded with their desired objectives. This was particularly applicable to the Kosovo Albanians who created the pretence of democratic governance. Without the participation of the Kosovo Serbs, the PISG could hardly be considered representative and inclusive. Yet the PISG was considered a success by the internationals because it created institutions of governance and was building 'capacity'. The problem was that this was an exclusive Kosovo Albanian version based on the 1974 constitution that created the Kosovo Albanian national movement, laying the foundations for the creation of parallel institutions within the Yugoslav federation as a response to Serb dominance. As Vickers explains, the 1974 constitution 'allowed Kosovo to emerge as an independent factor . . . it led to the Albanisation of public life in Kosovo and the positive discrimination for Albanians.'[94] The demands from Kosovo Albanians for more governance, greater freedom and increased or total control of their 'own' institutions[95] has only marginalised the Serb communities further, moving them closer to Belgrade in response.

The Kosovo Albanian leadership had a clear agenda to create a viable state with working institutions in order to facilitate full independence and future EU accession. Yet, persecution and cleansing of the Kosovo Serbs by radical elements of the Kosovar community echoes the bleak Fanonian maxim that 'the native is the oppressed person whose permanent dream is to become the persecutor'.[96] The more the Kosovars dominated and monopolised democracy and governance to build a state without Serb participation the greater the likelihood that the Serbs would be 'sacrificed for a Kosovo Albanian state'[97] and supposed 'lasting settlement'. Attempting to overcome the obstacles to multi-culturalism and democracy seems to have become 'too difficult' (for the internationals – who appeared to have abandoned pluralism in all but rhetoric[98]). The main problem with building democracy and governance was the inability to create an inclusive notion of citizenship. In this context, UNDP pushed for reforms by calling for greater civic participation, representation and protection of minority rights in order to enable democratic governance:[99] 'Kosovo must effectively confront the Achilles' heel of majoritarian democracies: the exclusion and marginalisation of minorities'.[100] This, of course, was extremely difficult in an environment where a lack of final status meant that the political configuration was exactly what was contested, especially given that the complexities of democracy were new to a political cohort educated in a communist one-party structure: 'modern democratic governance is inevitably linked to stateness, without a state, there can be no citizenship; without citizenship there can be no democracy'.[101]

The Herculean task in Kosovo is to reconcile ethnicities with the notion of citizenship and the creation of a multi-ethnic state. The reality is one of de facto separation of the Kosovo Serb population and a demographic reality of a Kosovar majority (95 per cent) in a now widely – but not fully – recognised state. Yet ironically, Kosovo also possesses an ethnic uniformity that few states in Europe can claim.[102] Because of this the Kosovo Albanian majority monopolised political, social and economic institutions, beneath the eyes of the internationals. The Kosovo Albanians have free-ridden upon a majoritarian democratic discourse to serve the goal of an independent Kosovo Albanian-dominated state. The adoption of the Albanian flag which flutters on every government or official building in Pristina is representative of this and is hardly conducive to encouraging the participation of Kosovo Serbs in a new multi-cultural state. As Holohan points out, even though the UN forbade the use of the Albanian flag without the Serb flag being also present, this was ignored.[103] As a UN officer acknowledged, 'Because we didn't stop them, now it's too late . . .'[104]

The democratic process is not just a simple application – a technical problem – but rather a complex political and social process which requires a sophisticated political approach. The concern has been that the Kosovans – Serb or Albanian – were both unable and unwilling to show respect for their opposition or to trust in its ability to provide fair governance through power sharing. The majority of Albanians enjoy the privilege of representing a permanent ethnic majority while the Serbs perceive themselves as permanently marginalised. In this context, Snyder points out that the political freedom provided by democracy can also act as a catalyst for further ethnic conflict.[105] Political power is viewed as 'winner takes all', which has caused polarisation between the ethnic communities because the violence of the battlefield has simply been transferred to the political arena. As a local leader of the Serb National Party explained, 'We do not believe in power sharing, we do not believe they (Albanians) have legitimacy.'[106] This imbalance is also affecting state and institution building, leading to the politicisation of bureaucracy and the lack of ability of political parties to organise legislative activity.[107] The capacity of the Assembly to operate democratically has also been hampered by the large volume and politicisation of the civil service, which is mainly comprised of Kosovo Albanian employees.[108]

This is further complicated by the otherwise sensible habit of the employment by UNMIK of local civil servants in jobs formerly occupied by internationals, gradually leading to the 'Albanianisation' of governance as well as to a hijacking of the internationals' agenda. Though, it is crucial that such roles are returned to local actors, liberal peace is being undermined by local actors who have their own ethno-political agenda. In other words, returning governance has resulted in an ethnic majoritarianism that may be as problematic, if not more, as being ruled by supposedly benevolent internationals. Simply put, local Kosovo Albanian appointments to international organisations have had a vested interest in the creation of an independent Kosovar state.[109] These devious objectives undermined the success of the liberal peace project, which in turn illustrates another flaw of liberal peacebuilding, which is predicated upon the training of local actors in good governance before the return of governance to them. All levels of government are affected by the 'legacy of the past' and the division of party and government politics along ethnic lines. It seems that democracy has institutionalised these problems: 'UNMIK's structure and mandate are now exposed as inappropriate to prepare Kosovo for the transition from war to peace, from socialism to the market economy, and from international political limbo to final status.'[110]

Criticism has also been levelled at UNMIK is particularly fierce with regard to its legitimacy. In comparison to the UNTAC mission in Cambodia, which was established on the basis of a peace accord agreed upon by the conflict parties, UNMIK was established with the agreement of NATO, Russia and the FRY, excluding the Kosovo Albanians. This created problems for local acceptance of UN authority and allowed Kosovo Albanian officials to construct an argument supporting their strategy of co-option.[111] The arbitrary nature of UN governance had a detrimental effect on the democratic process by also encouraging its co-option. Local governance was hijacked, co-opted, dominated by one ethnic group, and its capacity was impeded by the governance of UNMIK.[112]

Civil Society and the Rule of Law

Similar problems also affect the development of a civil society and rule of law as envisaged by the liberal peace. Increasingly, civil society has been monopolised by internationals and NGOs, who have brought in their own agendas:

> NGOs found it difficult to cooperate with the other actors on the ground, and their impatience with other organisations and desire to carry out their centralised agreements ended up being a significant impediment to cooperation . . .[113]

Indeed a common view amongst internationals is that there is no real civil society present. The existing post-conflict civil society in Kosovo, whilst benefiting from the influx of aid and technical assistance, was overwhelmed by the cumbersome UNMIK structure and the hundreds of NGOs that arrived with it.[114] This has obvious implications, with the first relating to the sustainability of civil society once the internationals withdraw. Civil society artificially burgeons in post-conflict peacebuilding missions, and although the aim is to regenerate and in some cases create a civil society[115] it is difficult to assess what actually constitutes civil society, whether local people are actually involved and to what degree. What appears to have emerged is that the development of 'civil society' has been monopolised by foreign internationals and exploited by local entrepreneurs. The 'post-conflict' individual, who is supposed to form the substance of civil society and be the recipient of education, protection of rights and civic empowerment, is largely ignored or included only notionally – as is any collective notion of community which is not oriented around ethnic identity.

The second problem with international involvement in civil society is the issue of local ownership of the peacebuilding process. UNMIK controlled every aspect of the peacebuilding operation in Kosovo from the top down. This neo-colonial practice[116] was clearly illustrated by the imposition of the liberal peace as a 'process' onto the conflict actors. This raised questions about local involvement, the indigenous acceptability of the peacebuilding process, as well as the sustainability of the internationals' liberal vision. Holohan suggests that the internationals, in their bid to dominate the peacebuilding, failed to recognise the existence of the Kosovo Albanian 'parallel society', instead favouring their own NGOs and the creation of completely new institutions. This led to a flood of foreign relief workers and the marginalisation of local staff and indigenous NGOs. The UN argued that the reason for this was the politicised nature of the parallel society but Holohan argues it was more to do with the 'old' UN attitude of colonial superiority.[117] The haste of the internationals to completely dismantle and replace existing institutional frameworks was understandable when directed at the former Serb-controlled framework, but was more perplexing in the context of the informal Kosovan structures. This indicated a reluctance to accept the nationalist Serbian structures as well as the indigenous Albanian structures of governance. This is a common element of many peacebuilding processes, during which internationals want to build an institutional governance structure from a clean slate in order to bypass the perceived social, economic and political psychosis that may have lain hidden in existing frameworks. But in doing so they also undermine local agency – in this case on the part of both communities.

Local responses to such behaviour indicated more capacity than internationals supposed. Kosovo Albanians were soon infiltrating the peacebuilding process, while the so-called 'Albanisation' of the peace process was indicative of both local desire for custodianship and international disquiet about its implications. Replacing international with local capacity meant hoping that both Albanians and Serbs would agree on power sharing, and trusting local actors to take on such roles in good faith. Yet Kosovo Albanians rapidly replaced internationals in positions from where they could influence the peace process. This subverted the liberal peace agenda by solidifying two parallel societies.[118] The central elements of the state are ethnically divided and sustained by foreign assistance and/or donor governments. This illustrates a paradox: local ownership of the peace process is 'more effective, cheaper and more sustainable'[119] but in a highly politicised environment such as Kosovo the neutrality or benign intentions of civil society actors and NGOs may be misleading.[120]

Because parallel civil societies (in particular the Kosovo Albanian version) evolved as a reaction and counter to the dominance of the Serbian government, they have developed as exclusive ethnic organisations. The implications of this are clear:

The powerful hybrid role of the LDK – simultaneously a resistance move-ment, a civil society and a one-party state bureaucracy, is one source of the difficulty Kosovo has had establishing a pluralistic civil society in the post-settlement period.[121]

This is compounded by the post-communist culture of distrust of central government, breeding a tradition of non-communication and non-cooperation with central government structures.[122] Furthermore, a situation developed similar to the 'autonomy' period in the 1990s, where the strength of the parallel structures at local level means that most local NGOs became an intrinsic component of LDK services to the Kosovo Albanian community.[123] This further jeopardised the independence of the peacebuilding process and the development of a pluralist civil society.

The rule of law also presents an array of difficult technical problems for UNMIK. These also were not adequately tackled, due primarily to these parallel structures. The rule of law has become a hybrid between international and local legal structures, and because of the strength of the parallel Kosovo Albanian legal system, 'Kosovo Serbs look directly to Belgrade'.[124] As a result, it is widely believed that the 'only solution is an ethnic approach, and to draw a line between the ethnic com-munities and legitimise the divisions'.[125] This is compounded by the existence of the TMK (Kosovo Protection Corps or Kosovo Liberation Army, UCK) which although intended as an unarmed 'protection corps' and successor to the KLA has metamorphosed into an illegiti-mate (Kosovar) 'law' enforcement organisation and in some cases is a de facto municipal authority. According to the OSCE, 'From killing to eviction and tax collection, there were apparently few areas into which the power and control of the UCK/Provisional TMK allied to the self-styled administration, did not reach.'[126] Needless to say, UNMIK has been widely criticised for failing to prevent the physical growth, cor-ruption and ethnic violence of this organisation, to the detriment of multi-ethnicity and the rule of law.[127]

Human Rights

The difficulties encountered with respect to a coherent human rights programme are also due to the development of parallel societies: 'the continuing tide of violence, fear, uncertainty and spiralling insecurity; and the continuing exodus and enclavisation of the province's remain-ing non-Albanians, threaten to result in the creation of ethnically homogenous pockets.'[128] The principal problem has been the inability of UNMIK and the PISG to reconcile the two ethnic communities. The ethnic barriers that have been erected in the parallel communities, coupled with the monopoly of central politics by Kosovo Albanians, have made the struggle for human rights particularly difficult.[129] This dimension should not be underestimated. It relates directly to the ethnic cleansing of the Kosovo Albanians by the Milosevic regime, at the same time underwriting the humanitarian intervention and NATO bombing of Serbia in a 'humanitarian war' – and now indicates the potential for reverse ethnic cleansing of Serbs by Kosovo Albanians.

As a result, both communities view the other with suspicion, fear and hostility whilst blaming the other and maintaining their own culture of victimhood. This 'ideology of victimisation' underpins the dangers immanent in the politics of delivering security, peace and human rights.[130] The hollow shells of houses stripped of everything but their concrete skeletons that litter the landscape are a constant reminder of this. Blame is still being apportioned, but it is not a psychological burden that is being eased by reconciliation. Instead, it is firmly entrenched in community-based distrust. This is a failure for human rights, which were supposed to replace this tragic – possibly cultural – structure and Fanonian cycle.

Ethnic polarisation is not necessarily the sole reason and should not be seen in isolation from other factors, of course.[131] Five dynamics are identified by ICG as being responsible for the continuing destabilisation: 'radicalised Kosovo Albanians, the KLA, Serbian paramilitaries, criminals from Albania and political rivals in the intra-Kosovo Albanian conflict'.[132] Human rights are frustrated by these elements, led by ethnic entrepreneurs who exploit the ethnic tensions to support their own agendas. This failing is unsurprising because UNMIK had no coherent plan for human rights education or promotion of initiates to prevent further abuses of basic concepts, such as the presumption of innocence, individual and not collective guilt, non-discrimination and tolerance.[133] This is partly because cultural and historical barriers in Kosovo preclude human rights from being understood as individual rights. Instead they are seen as collective or group rights.[134] This in turn relates to Kosovo Albananian minority status in the past, and is a result of political authority having overridden individual rights because 'self-governance in mono-ethnic units seems safer than enjoying minority rights in a multi-ethnic unit'.[135] The view is now common amongst the local human rights community that the internationals themselves are violating human rights simply because of their presence, by holding reserved powers and being unaccountable.[136]

The interpretation of minority rights represents the key to the Kosovo knot, and became central to Kosovo's final status negotiations. The Kosovo Serbs do not accept that they are a minority but rather consider themselves as a majority within a 'greater Serbia' (even if this idea appears dead) in which the Kosovo Albanians are the minority.[137] The latter, of course, argue that the Serbs are a minority within Kosovo. Mertus argues that a 'human rights culture', which cultivated respect for the Serbs as a part of society, has developed in the Kosovo Albanian community since the 1980s. However, UNMIK leadership failed to recognise and take advantage of this trend.[138] Instead, the internationals were seduced by the leadership and influence of the KLA (UCK/TMK). Internationals failed to prevent extremist elements within UCK/TMK from monopolising and corrupting governance:

> In the early days authority slipped out of the hands of the internationals and into the hands of the armed factions disgruntled at having to share power with the internationals and moderate Albanians, and aghast at the prospect of working with the Serbs.[139]

The KLA is the strongest power grouping, not just as a former 'army' with mass support from Kosovo Albanians, but also as a self-declared political force, combining a populist party and national liberation movement that seeks to govern an independent Kosovo.[140] However, they have no agenda for multi-ethnicity. In fact, it is in their interest to maintain the ethnic division in order to monopolise political power and influence. The polarisation of the communities is exploited by these elements, indirectly supported by the internationals, and has now become a de facto barrier to human rights.[141] The situation in Kosovo needs to be seen outside of the ethnic matrix because the evocation of ethnic categories silences discussion of alternatives,[142] and has not prevented one ethnic group, albeit a majority, from co-opting the peacebuilding process.

Economic Liberalisation and Development

After 1999, the main focus was on reconstruction rather than development. The fact that Kosovo was not a state hindered these processes because, for example, the World Bank could only give grants because of the lack of sovereign status.[143] Donor contributions fell and poverty rose as the international community contemplated 'draw down' even though final status had not been settled, on independence declared. Investment was minimal, unemployment is around 50 per cent according to the Ministry of Labour, and individuals register as unemployed but receive no benefits.[144] Indeed, there are no real institutions to deal with social welfare issues. Certainly, before the recent declaration of independence, Kosovo was in economic limbo. For example, World Bank officials noted that the Ministry of Finance had at one point asked for loans but had been told that that status needed to be resolved before any investment could occur. They acknowledged that Kosovo needed a viable economy regardless of its status.[145] It is clear that development was caught in a paradox: no development without status, no status without development. How far the declaration of independence will change this development situation remains to be seen, but the ambiguity of status certainly had a detrimental effect on the development of the economy. Even more problematic was the fact that Belgrade argued that if Kosovo did become sovereign it would own about $1 billion of Serbia's national debt. UDI has not settled these issues so far.

The 'national' economy has stagnated rather than reaping a peace dividend, and the population suffer the consequences of underdevelopment, unemployment, poverty and lack of opportunity. This is partly because the institution building and civic administration in Kosovo has been political, not economic.[146] The lack of economic opportunities and the absence of jobs, coupled with the overwhelming number of young people, is a dangerous mix for a region already unstable with ethnic tension. The current privatisation of Kosovo's assets, in which former 'state' assets, such as mines, factories and production plants – locations for possible employment – are 'sold off' by the Kosovo Trust has not produced the trickle-down effect neoliberal economics (a crucial part of the liberal peace) predicts. Instead, these go to the highest bidder with a proportion of the realised monies reserved for competing claims over ownership, historical liabilities dating back to the pre-socialist system of private ownership, and compensation for former socially owned enterprises. This reform of a socialist economy has not so far had an impact on economic opportunities. Socially and state-owned enterprises have passed into private hands and led to decreased economic opportunity, at least in the short term. The reality of the internationally imposed neoliberal model has been that there is no place (nor financial support) for the impoverished and needy. It has paid little attention to the consequences of socio-economic degradation for the broader peace process and for the unravelling of ethnic polarisation. According to a particularly critical UNMIK economic advisor, these problems are caused by 'weak institutions, inadequate infrastructure and lack of skills in the labour force'.[147]

The short-term result of attempting an accelerated transformation from a socialist post-communist agricultural state economy into a formal capitalist, market-based version has been to increase poverty, unemployment and a decline in the standard of living. Neoliberalism after all is configured via decentralisation, privatisation and stimulation of market forces to create a trickle-down effect of wealth. It requires competition in the market place, the private sector and employment zones, but above all, it needs an injection of foreign capital. The cause of poor economic performance and poverty are seen as 'an exasperatingly anaemic private sector' with 'very low levels of investment in productive activities'.[148] Yet the view of international officials was that public funds are simply not available because 'with a slim budget and rising commitments, Kosovo cannot afford extensive social assistance and poverty reduction programmes'.[149] Liberal peacebuilding creates economic expectations of wealth in line with political freedoms and rights, but the former have not been satisfied by its processes.

Other problems have arisen from the collapse of the manufacturing sector, the decline of public enterprises, the contraction of construction activities and the limited growth of the service industry due to the shrinking donor community.[150] Outside investment in the economy has been stunted due to ambiguity over sovereignty, and borrowing from international financial institutions or the capital markets is restricted. There are also no venture capital or research development funds so a 'budget straightjacket' has been created.[151]

The existence of parallel institutions undermines the economic process and the attempt to create a single unified economy under the umbrella of one state. The 'national' economy is divided between formal and informal, as well as between the Kosovo Albanian and the Kosovo Serb sector funded by Serbia. This causes artificial discrepancies in the economy: for example, Serbia 'employs' Kosovo Serb teachers, bureaucrats and technocrats, maintaining their pay at an artificially high standard to encourage them to continue to work for a Serbian solution, but also to prevent defection to the Kosovar 'state' system. Generally, much hope has been placed upon the resolution of final status in order to improve the economic situation, though it is hard to see where foreign direct investment would come from or why sovereign borrowing would necessarily make a short- to medium-term difference to socio-economic hardship amongst the population. Again, UDI has not resolved these uncertainties. Following independence hundreds of enclave Serbs resigned from UNMIK and Kosovo institution jobs,[152] which does not bode well for the future economic development of the region. All of the above problems are amplified in the Serb enclaves where nationalist opposition to the government in Pristina as well as the involvement of the Belgrade authorities have muddied an already difficult situation.[153]

Conclusion

The liberal peacebuilding project in Kosovo (as the recent declaration of independence demonstrated) has, for specific reasons and mainly because of the support of powerful Contact Groups members and a general sympathy for the Kosovo Albanians, underlined one of its key dilemmas. Increasingly, because of the failures of such projects elsewhere, calls are being made for more local ownership, custodianship and participation, and a move away from heavy-footprint neocolonial style approaches to peacebuilding and statebuilding. Yet, the Kosovo case shows that local negotiation over the nature of the liberal peace occurs even where externally controlled institutions are supposed to control a broad range of governance functions. Although these functions do not necessarily produce the results intended, local co-option and increasing participation and control of them can substitute for international government.

Yet, local co-option is politically motivated, and may well reify the very roots of the conflict peacebuilding was trying to assuage. Peacebuilding brings a range of material and abstract resources to a post-conflict zone, comprising money, knowledge, assistance, recognition, support and advice, which local actors may try to control in order to further their pre-intervention objectives, or to gain an approximation of them. These devious objectives[154] involve local actors treading a fine line between cooperation with internationals and manipulation of them, and the outcome may not be recognisable as the liberal peace intended by the internationals. Locals actors are capable of co-opting internationals though the liberal peacebuilding process and thus via the aim of building a self-sustaining orthodox liberal peace. As a result internationals become complicit in building a self-sustaining majoritarian and ethnicised peace. This occurred because of both local and international dynamics, but Kosovo Albanian elites became adept at dominating the subtle negotiations that occur between the local and international in the various areas of reform in their favour. Local NGOs also become adept at manipulating 'multi-ethnicity' in order to attract funding.[155] This co-option occurred despite the fact that most international actors are of the opinion that local institutions have a very limited capacity as yet.[156]

Serbian elites saw the opportunity to withdraw from the political process in protest at the construction of an ethnic majority through liberal peacebuilding. This happened partly because of the final status problem. Yet, this co-option appears to be a common factor across many other cases: the dynamics of ethnic majoritarian exclusion and ethnic minority withdrawal from politics, and the ethnic contest over sovereignty have perhaps been most notable in the extended and protracted peace process over the Cyprus conflict.[157] Also similar to the Cyprus case is the intention to use EU accession to stabilise the Kosovo entity in the long term, whereby the EU is seen to be a regional entity into which normalising states can be embedded.[158] It might well be that such dynamics are built into the very architecture of liberal peacebuilding itself, rather than the active fault of one party or other. There are still too many opportunities within the process for exclusive rather than inclusive forms of politics.

In the haste to provide local participation and ownership, the peace process may actually have sowed the seeds for future ethnic strife between Kosovo's ethnic groups. UDI in Kosovo, though widely recognised as of late 2008, means that like in Cyprus, both parties still feel that material sovereignty is a plausible prize (though for both it takes very different guises). In other liberal peacebuilding processes the control of sovereignty has often already been settled, though it may still be contested at the discursive level, sometimes between internationals and locals, or through political groupings at the local level. As a result, the liberal peace in Kosovo is a virtual peace and internationals may even be complicit in their co-option over suspect and local practices which have reproduced ethnic divisions in their efforts to close a chapter.

The liberal peace discourse assumes that its principal components will eventually serve to alleviate the perceived causes of conflict, thus creating a sustainable peace. This claim is based on several assumptions: that the tenets of liberal peace are correctly implemented and that the steps required to do this – no matter how difficult – are actually taken; that the host community is broadly receptive to these tenets; and that the polity that emerges is sovereign but governed by international liberal norms and conditions. As this chapter has illustrated, these are problematic assumptions. Liberal peace processes lead to established and recognised 'western' solutions to the causes of a conflict and thus have become the universal blue print, via the liberal peace discourse, for reconstruction. But the question is whether they can actually be implemented and operated as they are designed to be by the user community. For example, can a post-communist, post-conflict, contested entity such as Kosovo, with little or no experience of parliamentary democracy or a market economy and, despite the best efforts of the international community, develop such a political system without reverting to ethnic exclusion, with all the inconsistencies, nuances and idiosyncrasies that have been long compensated for by the local processes of donor states?[159] Would the new political elites in such an environment actually want this, given that it means that their state would have to be shared with minorities – historical enemies in fact? According to OSCE officers, long before UDI, this was unlikely.[160] A recognised Kosovo state or not, it is clear that the entity is a hijacked entity which has developed mono-ethnic, majoritarian sovereignty, a weak economy and a marginalised minority. These are not indicators of a sustainable peace, liberal or otherwise.

This also connects to the issue of economic liberalisation. Neoliberal models provide little in the way of social security or financial support for a population who mostly live on or below the poverty line with no income and in a subsistence economy. Coupled with this was the inability of UNMIK to take the necessary steps to engage with the cultural aspects and idiosyncratic elements of Kosovo, be they parallel institutions that needed to be employed and developed in the case of human rights or replaced for the benefit of pluralism and democracy.

Instead of applying an understanding of Kosovo – as a historical, political, social and cultural entity to the liberal peace model, the liberal peace was imposed on Kosovo – and inconsistently at that. Peacebuilding thus collapsed into the Kosovo Albanian project of statehood. This did not encourage a self-sustaining peace. At best, this indicates an externally sustained, conservative and very limited form of the liberal peace, which perpetuates an ethno-national matrix.[161] The situation in Kosovo remains a Gordian knot, prejudged by the fact that liberal peacebuilding is predicated upon the existence of the institutions of the state, and resisted by the Serb community.[162] This has formed the basis for the co-option of peacebuilding, pressure for independence, and the unilateral declaration of independence. It is also reflected in the recent adoption of a new constitution for Serbia that includes the province of Kosovo. Such basic issues remain unresolved, despite lengthy international governance aimed at constructing a liberal peace. This is a situation the current EULUX mission will need to rectify if it has any hope of creating self-sustaining peace in the region.

Notes

1. A short version of this chapter was published as 'Co-opting the liberal peace: untying the Gordian knot in Kosovo', *Cooperation and Conflict*, 43: 1, 2008.
2. In accordance with official UN language and spelling, we will use the word Kosovo to describe the territory in question in a neutral sense, while recognising that this label is contested. Kosovo Albanians use 'Kosova' and Serbs 'Kosovo and Metohija'. We will also follow UN practice to describe members of each ethnic group. For a detailed history of the region, see N. Malcolm, *Kosovo: a Short History* (London: Macmillan, 1998); M. Vickers, *Between Serbs and Albanians, a History of Kosovo* (New York: University Press, 1998). For debates on historical narratives, see J. A. Mertus, *Kosovo: How Myths and Truths Started a War* (Berkeley, CA: University of California Press, 1999).
3. The World Bank, *The World Bank Group in the Western Balkans* (Washington, DC: World Bank, 2005), p. 20.
4. The initial strength of KFOR was 50,000. This was later reduced to 30,000. The NATO-led mission of four multi-national task forces is now comprised of thirty-six nations and more than 16,000 peacekeepers. See www.nato.int/kfor/kfor/kfor.
5. Confidential Source, KFOR, *Personal Interview*, Pristina, 7 April 2006.
6. The Yugoslav constitution of 1974 made Kosovo an autonomous province; this lasted until the collapse of Yugoslavia in 1989. See Malcolm, *Kosovo*, p. 327.
7. Of the population of Montenegro, 55.53 per cent voted for independence from Serbia in a referendum. *The Guardian*, 1 June 2006.
8. ICG, 'Kosovo's fragile transition', Europe Report 196, 25 September 2008, p. i.
9. The Contact Group comprises the US, UK, France, Germany, Italy and Russia.
10. On 24 October 2005, the UNSC appointed former Finnish President

Martti Ahtisaari to start a political process to determine the future status of Kosovo.

11. Confidential Source, OSCE Political Affairs Officer, *Personal Interview*, Pristina, 5 April 2006.
12. Indeed, one interviewee (who did not want to be identified) for an international organisation told us that there was great pressure not to report on negative developments to hasten conditional independence. We were even told by an interviewee that it looked like the Serb community were being 'sacrificed' for this.
13. Oliver P. Richmond, *Transformation of Peace* (London: Palgrave, 2005), ch. 5.
14. It is very clear that local employees who work for internationals in Kosovo often identify with independence professionally as well as personally.
15. This term is used to denote the various actors comprising UNMIK, donors and the NGOs they support.
16. See Security Council Resolution 1244, 10 June 1999: UNMIK website, www.unmikonline.org/.
17. Ibid.
18. Roland Paris, *At War's End* (Cambridge: Cambridge University Press, 2004), p. 123.
19. M. Llamazares and L. Reynolds Levy, *NGOs and Peacebuilding in Kosovo* (Bradford: University of Bradford, 2003), p. 19.
20. UNDP, *Human Development Report – Kosovo 2004* (Pristina: UNDP, 2004), p. 54. However, our own fieldwork indicated that it was much more difficult for Kosovo Serb NGOs to gain funding than for Kosovo Albanian NGOs.
21. W. O'Neill, *Kosovo: an Unfinished Peace* (London: Lynne Rienner, 2002), p. 37.
22. 'Constitutional framework for provisional self-government', UNMIK/ REG/2001/9. See www.unmikonline.org/constframework.htm.
23. For more detailed information on how the constitutional framework is constructed and ultimately operates, see www.unmikonline.org/ constframework.htm.
24. www.unmikonline.org/2ndyear/unmikat2p7.
25. OSCE Mission in Kosovo, Elections: see www.osce.org/kosovo/13208.
26. Confidential Source, OSCE, Political Affairs Officer, *Personal Interview*, Pristina, 5 April 2006.
27. See www.unmikonline.org/constframework, p. 10.
28. O'Neill, *Kosovo*, p. 38.
29. www.osce.org/kosovo/13376.
30. Ibid.
31. www.osce.org/kosovo/13215.
32. O'Neill, *Kosovo*, p. 39.

33. See 'The EU Pillar in UNMIK', at www.euinkosovo.org/uk.
34. UNMIK have launched a privatisation process run by the Kosovo Trust Agency which is to privatise and liquidate socially owned enterprises and administer publicly owned enterprises to allow a faster decision-making process. See www.euinkosovo.org/uk/invest/invest_privat.php.
35. UNMIK has signed free trade agreements with Macedonia, and Bosnia and Herzegovina. See Kosovo Economic Outlook 2006: www.euinkosovo.org/uk/docu/docu.php.
36. www.euinkosovo.org/uk.
37. Confidential Source, UNMIK, Economic Advisor, *Personal Interview*, Pristina, 5 April 2006.
38. One source argued that this was a holding mission rather than a peace-building mission, given that there was no reconciliation process, and no real attempt to build civil society.
39. Confidential Source, House of Representatives, *Personal Interview*, Pristina, 5 April 2006.
40. See F. Bieber and Z. Daskalovski (eds), *Understanding the War in Kosovo* (London: Frank Cass, 2003); P. Latawski and M. Smith, *The Kosovo Crisis and the Evolution of Post-Cold War European Security* (Manchester: Palgrave, 2003); M. Waller, K. Drezov and B. Gokay (eds), *Kosovo: the Politics of Delusion* (London: Frank Cass, 2001).
41. See Mertus, *Kosovo*, pp. 231–4.
42. UNDP/USAID/Institute For Development Research, 'Early Warning Report Kosovo', Report 12, October–December 2005, pp. 1–2.
43. UNDP, *Human Development Report – Kosovo 2004*, p. 3.
44. Ibid. p. 50.
45. Seventy-nine per cent in 2000 to 54 per cent in 2002. UNDP, *Human Development Report – Kosovo 2004*, p. 57.
46. Confidential Source, OSCE, Democratisation Officer, *Personal Interview*, Pristina, 4 April 2006.
47. Ibid.
48. Ibrahim Rugova died in office 22 January 2006. He was replaced by Fatmir Sejdiu, also the leader of the LDK.
49. The other Kosovo Albanian party is the Alliance for the Future of Kosovo (AAK) – led by Ramush Haradinaj, the former prime minister who was recently indicted for war crimes. The main Serbian political entity in Kosovo is the Return Coalition – 'Povratak' (KP) – consisting of twenty parties and led by Dragiša Krstovic.
50. ICG, 'Kosovo after Haradinaj', Policy Report, 26 May 2005: www.crisisgroup.org.
51. Confidential Source, OSCE, Democratisation Education Officer, *Personal Interview*, Pristina, 5 April 2006.
52. UNDP, *Human Development Report – Kosovo 2004*, p. 58.

53. The World Bank, *The World Bank Group in the Western Balkans*, p. 23.
54. Confidential Source, World Bank, Operations Officer, *Personal Interview*, Pristina, 3 April 2006.
55. UNDP, *Human Development Report – Kosovo 2004*, p. 65.
56. Ibid. p. 54.
57. Confidential Source, World Bank, Operations Officer, *Personal Interview*, Pristina, 3 April 2006.
58. Confidential Source, OSCE, Democratisation Education Officer, *Personal Interview*, Pristina, 5 April 2006.
59. Confidential Source, LDK, MP, *Personal Interview*, Pristina, 3 April 2006.
60. Ibid.
61. O'Neill, *Kosovo*, p. 75.
62. Ibid. p. 76.
63. Ibid. pp. 79–81.
64. UN, Brahimi Report: www.un.org.
65. See OSCE, Kosovo: Review of the Criminal Justice System, 2000: osce.org.
66. OSCE, Kosovo: First Review of the Civil Justice System, June 2006: www.osce.org/documents/mik/2006/06/19407.
67. We were quoted an unbelievable 90 per cent, although this has been difficult to verify. Agon Vrenezi: NCSC, Programme Officer, *Personal Interview*, Pristina, 4 April 2006.
68. Ibid.
69. See UNMIK Police at www.unmikonline.org/civpol/factsfigs.htm.
70. See Kosovo Police Service at www.unmikonline.org/justice/police.htm.
71. O'Neill, *Kosovo*, p. 113.
72. www.unmikonline.org/2ndyear/unmikat2p4.
73. O'Neill, *Kosovo*, p. 51.
74. www.osce.org/kosovo/13215.
75. There is a distinct and notable difference in the road quality, house building and general condition of the villages between Kosovo Serb and Albanian districts.
76. O'Neill, *Kosovo*, p. 55.
77. It is often wrongly related just to missing Kosovo Albanians. The suggested figure is 3,600, which includes 2,772 Kosovo Albanians and 549 Kosovo Serbs. O'Neill, *Kosovo*, p. 58.
78. ICG, 'Bridging Kosovo's Mitrovica divide', Report 165, 13 September 2005, p. 1.
79. Ken Booth (ed.), *The Kosovo Tragedy: the Human Rights Dimension* (London: Frank Cass, 2001), p. 18.
80. The World Bank, *The World Bank Group in the Western Balkans*, p. 21.

81. UNMIK, Kosovo Economic Outlook 2006, Economic Policy Office, March 2006, p. 6.
82. UNDP, *Human Development Report – Kosovo 2004*, p. 19.
83. UNMIK, Kosovo Economic Outlook 2006, Economic Policy Office, March 2006, p. 6.
84. The World Bank, *The World Bank Group in the Western Balkans*, p. 21.
85. UNDP, *Human Development Report – Kosovo 2004*, p. 14.
86. Confidential Source, OSCE, Democratisation Officer, *Personal Interview*, Pristina, 4 April 2006.
87. Vickers, *Between Serbs and Albanians*, p. xiv.
88. ICG, 'Collapse in Kosovo', Europe Report 155, p. i: www.crisisgroup.org.
89. D. Held, *Democracy and the Global Order* (Oxford: Polity, 1995), p. 5.
90. It has been suggested that a final settlement might involve an 'exchange' of territory with a partition of Northern Kosovo, which is predominantly Serb, to Serbia for succession of the south.
91. Confidential Source, OSCE, Democratisation Officer, *Personal Interview*, Pristina, 4 April 2006; Confidential Source, OSCE, Education Officer, *Personal Interview*, Pristina, 5 April 2006; Confidential Source, OSCE, Political Affairs Officer, *Personal Interview*, Pristina 5 April 2006.
92. Confidential Source, OSCE, Democratisation Officer, *Personal Interview*, Pristina, 4 April 2006.
93. Confidential Source, OSCE, Political Affairs Officer, *Personal Interview*, Pristina, 5 April 2006.
94. Vickers, *Between Serbs and Albanians*, p. 178.
95. Confidential Source, LDK, MP, *Personal Interview*, Pristina, 3 April 2006; Confidential Source, Institute of Political Studies, Executive Director, *Personal Interview*, Pristina, 4 April, 2006.
96. F. Fanon, *The Wretched of the Earth*, 5th edn (London: Penguin, 2001), p. 41.
97. Confidential Source, OSCE, Political Affairs Officer, *Personal Interview*, Pristina, 5 April 2006.
98. Confidential Source, OSCE, Democracy Education Officer, *Personal Interview*, Pristina, 5 April 2006.
99. UNDP, *Human Development Report – Kosovo 2004*, p. 88.
100. Ibid. p. 91.
101. J. Linz and A. Stepan, *Problems of Democratic Transition and Consolidation* (Baltimore, MD: Johns Hopkins University Press, 1996), p. 28, quoted in Latawski and Smith, *The Kosovo Crisis*, p. 77.
102. Latawski and Smith, *The Kosovo Crisis*, p. 84.
103. A. Holohan, *Networks of Democracy* (Stanford, CA: Stanford University Press, 2005), p. 16.

104. Quoted in Holohan, *Networks*, p. 16.

105. J. Snyder, *From Voting to Violence: Democratization and Nationalist Conflict* (London: Norton, 2001).

106. Mr Janovitch: Serb National Party, Leader, *Personal Interview*, Mitrovica, 6 April 2006.

107. www.unmikonline.org/2ndyear/unmikat2p6.

108. Confidential Source, OSCE, Political Affairs Officer, *Personal Interview*, Pristina, 5 April 2006.

109. For example, a number of government and NGOs interviewees in Pristina, in response to questions about statebuilding, independence or governance, often replied with the prefix 'we' instead of the expected 'Kosovo' as would be expected from independent advisors. Confidential Source, World Bank, Operations Officer, *Personal Interview*, Pristina, 3 April 2006; Naim Rashiti: International Crisis Group, Researcher/Manager, *Personal Interview*, Pristina, 4 April 2006.

110. ICG, 'Collapse in Kosovo', Europe Report 155, p. i: www.crisisgroup.org.

111. P. Besnik, 'The UN in Kosova: administering democratisation?', in F. Bieber and Z. Daskalovki, *Understanding the War in Kosovo* (London: Frank Cass, 2003), p. 205.

112. See F. Fukuyama, *State Building: Governance and World Order in the Twenty-First Century*, 2nd edn (London: Profile Books, 2005).

113. Holohan, *Networks*, p. 160.

114. Llamazares and Reynolds Levy, *NGOs and Peacebuilding in Kosovo*, p. 13.

115. UNDP, *Human Development Report – Kosovo 2004*, p. 53.

116. See P. Stubbs, 'Partnership or colonisation? The relationship between International Agencies and Local Non Governmental Organisations in Bosnia-Herzegovina', in B. Deacon *et al.*, *Civil Society, NGOs and Global Governance*, Globalisation and Social Policy Programme occasional paper, 2000, p. 24, quoted in Llamazares and Reynolds Levy, *NGOs and Peacebuilding in Kosovo*, p. 16.

117. Holohan, *Networks*, p. 136.

118. Mertus, *Kosovo*, p. 262.

119. S. Barakat and M. Chard, 'Theories, rhetoric and practice: recovering the capacities of war torn socities', *Third World Quarterly*, 23: 5, pp. 817–35, quoted in Llamazares and Reynolds Levy, *NGOs and Peacebuilding in Kosovo*, p. 16.

120. Ibid. p. 16.

121. Ibid. p. 3.

122. Ibid. p. 5.

123. Ibid. p. 20.

124. Agon Vrenezi: NCSC, Programme Officer, *Personal Interview*, Pristina, 4 April 2006.

125. Ibid.
126. OSCE, *Human Rights in Kosovo: As Seen As Told*, vol 2, 5 November 1999, p. 61, quoted in O'Neill, *Kosovo*, p. 74.
127. See O'Neill, *Kosovo*, p. 118.
128. J. Husanovic, 'Post-conflict Kosovo: an anatomy lesson in the ethics/ politics of human rights', in Booth, *The Kosovo Tragedy*, p. 226.
129. Booth, *The Kosovo Tragedy*, p. 1.
130. Husanovic, 'Post-conflict Kosovo', in Booth, *The Kosovo Tragedy*, p. 276.
131. Ibid. p. 267.
132. ICG Report, 'Violence in Kosovo: who's killing whom?', 2 November 1999: www.intl-crisis-group.org/,p.1, quoted by Husanovic in Booth, *The Kosovo Tragedy*, p. 267.
133. O'Neill, *Kosovo*, p. 129.
134. Ibid. p. 129.
135. Ibid. p. 130.
136. Ibrahim Makolli: Council of the Defence of Human Rights, *Personal Interview*, Pristina, 6 April 2006.
137. Confidential Source, SDP (Serb), Leader, *Personal Interview*, Mitrovica, 6 April 2006.
138. J. Mertus, 'Human rights culture in Kosovo', *Global Governance*, 10: 3, pp. 333–52.
139. Holohan, *Networks*, p. 13.
140. Husanovic, 'Post-conflict Kosovo', in Booth, *The Kosovo Tragedy*, p. 266.
141. Ibid. p. 274.
142. I. Blumi, 'Ethnic borders to a democratic society in Kosovo: the UN's identity card', in Bieber and Daskalovski, *Understanding the War in Kosovo*, p. 219.
143. Confidential Source, World Bank Officials, *Personal Interview*, Pristina, 3 April 2006.
144. Ibid.
145. Ibid.
146. Holohan, *Networks*, p. 135.
147. Confidential Source, UNMIK, Economic Advisor, *Personal Interview*, Pristina, 5 April 2006.
148. Ibid.
149. Ibid.
150. Ibid.
151. Ibid.
152. ICG, 'Kosovo's fragile transition', Europe Report 196, 25 September 2008, p. 25.
153. Confidential Source, Representative of Serbian Democratic Party, *Personal Interview*, Mitrovica, 6 April 2006.

154. For more on this concept, see Oliver P. Richmond, 'Devious objectives and the disputants' views of international mediation: a theoretical framework', *Journal of Peace Research*, 35: 6, 1998; Oliver P. Richmond, 'Spoiling and devious objectives in peace processes', in Oliver Richmond and Edward Newman (eds), *Spoilers in Peace Processes* (UN University Press, 2006).

155. D. Falloni: OSCE, Youth Education Officer, *Personal Interview*, Pristina, 5 April 2006.

156. Confidential Source, OSCE, Political Affairs Officer, *Personal Interview*, Pristina, 5 April 2006.

157. See Oliver Richmond, 'Shared sovereignty and the politics of peace: evaluating the EU's "catalytic" framework in the eastern Mediterranean', *International Affairs*, January 2006.

158. See Confidential Source, OSCE Official, *Personal Interview*, 4 April 2006.

159. For further analysis, see J. Stilhoff Sorensen, 'Questioning reconstruction: reflections on the theoretical foundations for conceptualising reconstruction in Kosovo', in Bieber and Daskalovski, *Understanding the War in Kosovo*, p. 262.

160. Confidential Source, OSCE, Political Affairs Officer, *Personal Interview*, Pristina, 5 April 2006. Confidential Source, OSCE, Democracy Education Officer, *Personal Interview*, Pristina, 5 April 2006.

161. Husanovic, 'Post-conflict Kosovo', in Booth, *The Kosovo Tragedy*, p. 269.

162. 'Patience wanes for Kosovo's Albanians', *Financial Times*, 10 November 2006, p. 4.

5

Building/Rejecting the Liberal Peace: State Consolidation and Liberal Failure in the Middle East

Introduction

It is widely assumed that 'peace' is ambiguous in nature in the Middle East, and indeed it cannot be thought of as any more than a negative peace. This is part of a general exceptionalism that is directed towards some polities around the world in the broader milieu of the conditionalities of global governance. Thus, peace in the Middle East need not be liberal, though there has been movement in this direction. Exceptionalism remains but liberal conditionalities are making their mark in a somewhat less obvious manner than in other conflict regions.[1] Though some in the academic community in Israel are generally critical of securitised strategies and policies, which they believe to be counter-productive, 'peace' has been seen by the conservative and military elites of the region as something which potentially undermines long-held political beliefs and interests. The state framework in the region tends to represent peace as highly militarised and centralised, discriminatory, and privileging certain groups and their internal solidarity. This has led to internal ambivalences within these states as to their own use of violence and coercion of the 'others' it identifies, resulting in broader nationalist, linguistic, ethnic, cultural and religious cleavages. These provide the basis for the organisation of politics and result in securitisation rather than an emancipatory or even orthodox form of the liberal peace. The response to this – the mechanisms of peace through liberal governance and its institutions – have appeared in a limited fashion, with little success. Peace is associated with state security, and the usual institutions associated with a liberal peace (the UN, EU, OSCE, World Bank) have little or no capacity to use their usual conditional or trusteeship-style methods as in other locations. This is partly because such tools and institutions are not trusted or are seen as a political or cultural anathema.[2]

The general assumption has been that Israel is a liberal state, despite its long-standing problems with the Palestinians and the Arab world more generally, which have necessitated a high level of securitisation within the state itself. It has also been clear that the various 'peaces' that Israel has so far arrived at with its neighbours are not liberal, but tend to be rather illiberal, resting on ceasefires and fraught relations with non-democratic governments. The latter are taken to be representative of non-liberal entities, and while it is commonplace for Israeli politicians and policymakers to openly favour 'strategic' and conservative modes of analysis over orthodox and emancipatory ones, these are still taken to require reform while Israel is already generally perceived as a liberal state. Because of long-standing disagreements between a wide range of international actors and the Israeli government dating back to the late 1940s, international institutional involvement in the Israeli–Palestinian conflict has been minimal; there has not been a UN peacekeeping operation, or any real peacebuilding mission. With the advent of post-Cold War liberal interventionism some progress was made on a peace agreement and on the construction of a liberal proto-Palestinian entity, along with minimal institutional change within the Israeli state. However, since the second intifada, coinciding with a new security discourse post-9/11, any peace process has been undermined, rolled back and blocked, and any institutions that may have been created have been progressively dissolved by a return to the pre-peace process, pre-Oslo positions. Indeed, as a result of these contradictory processes, a two- (liberal-) state solution, which is effectively a confirmation of partition and of the outcome of a long-standing historical process of separation, appears to be emerging. This falls into line with a broader global process, connected with the liberal peace project, in which partition into mono-identity nation states appears to be its result, representing a corruption of the supposedly pluralist and cosmopolitan, liberal state project. While we accept that the Palestinian polity is far from achieving the level that is suggested by the liberal project to achieve peace, we argue that Israeli state institutions also need addressing in this context. Partition and the exacerbation of the roots of the conflict appear to be connected to the current approach to peace, liberal or otherwise.

For these and other reasons, the liberal peace framework has not produced the results many expected in the heady, post-Oslo days. The situation does not compare well with the liberal peacebuilding missions in Cambodia, Kosovo, East Timor and Bosnia.[3] This is particularly curious given the longevity of the Palestinian-Israeli conflict and the critical importance attached to its resolution by prominent members of the international community. Despite twelve United Nations Security Council Resolutions (since 1967), three General Assembly Resolutions (since 1948),[4] the failed Oslo peace settlement in 1992, various ongoing peace initiatives[5] and the continuous work of local and international actors and NGOs, the peace process in the Palestinian-Israeli conflict is 'the worst it has ever been'.[6] According to the recent end of mission report by Alvara de Soto – the UN special coordinator for the Middle East peace process – perhaps stating the obvious, the future prognosis is bleak.[7] Partly, this may be due to the absence of any coordinating peacebuilding agency, and because of the clash of claimed territorial sovereignties in an unhelpful and inflexible international legal and normative environment, which automatically favours the liberal self (however militarised) over non-liberal others. If nothing else, this case study provides, over its long course, many insights into the pitfalls of putatively liberal peacemaking.

The liberal aspiration for emancipation of the Palestinians and the form of a territorial liberal democratic state connected to this project has not generally been problematised. So focused are calls for the so-called two-state solution – which assumes a functioning Palestinian state – that the danger of the liberal peace model trap in respect to this is unnoticed. This chapter examines the liberal assumptions and the opportunities that all parties have exploited in their subversion of the Middle East peace process. They have deployed a 'liberal camouflage' for their little-changed pre-negotiation objectives in some cases. In this context, this chapter produces a further critique of liberal peace transitions centred on its tendency to reconstruct formal territorial sovereignty in situations where exactly this is at the heart of the conflict.

Building Liberal States through Peace Agreements: Oslo

The 1947 UN General Assembly Resolution 181 (UN partition plan) laid down the basis for the creation of both a Jewish and an Arab state in Palestine, and a new peace.[8] Though this was not formulated as a liberal peace in these fraught times, as the Cold War came to a close it became clear that this was what was now envisaged. The Oslo Accords of 1993 represented the first concerted opportunity to invest in the liberal peace model for the international community. The majority of subsequent international peace initiatives since then, such as the Wye River agreement (1998), the Camp David Summit (2000), the Road Map (2002), Sharm el Sheik (2005) and most recently Annapolis (2007), can be seen as attempts to further reproduce the liberal peace, and indeed to use it to set an example for a 'new' Middle East.

The Oslo peace process or Declaration of Principles (DoP), famously signed on the White House lawn in September 1993, grew out of the Madrid conference in 1991 and months of secret discussions hosted by the Norwegian government. It represented a watershed in the nature of the peace process, which now moved from a focus on strategic and diplomatic issues, overshadowed by violence, to the liberal peace and statebuilding agendas, by which violence, particularly committed by Palestinian groups, was both to be ended and to be the incentive for a peace process.[9] However, what distinguished it from all other attempts at making peace in the past was the decision to hold face-to-face talks between the Palestine Liberation Organisation (PLO) and Israel rather than depend exclusively on secret back channels as before. This was in keeping with the new era of peace processes, which were self-legitimating even if non-state actors and 'terrorists' were involved, because their objective was to create a liberal state. Indeed, it has been argued that the Palestinian elites were starting to think in terms of a liberal peace from the late 1980s.[10] This meant that they would contribute to the liberal order of states and its inherent guarantee of peace, which also required local and regional elites, actors and communities to abide by democratic norms, enter the global market, respect human rights, and accept international law and mutual recognition. It was also clear that the notion of mutually recognised liberal states was now coming to the fore in the thinking of the Israeli negotiators and their international advisers.[11] Even more importantly, it required that each actor accepted a territorial configuration that determined their status in the international system. This reciprocity – growing legitimacy of key actors in return for a peace process which promised a new liberal state configuration vis-à-vis sovereignty and territory – was a formula that paid dividends across the world in the 1990s. This also began a 'peace industry' in the Middle East, compromising many different types of externally funded, conflict-resolution-oriented NGOs. In this it has been argued that local people, especially Palestinians, were treated as followers rather than partners.[12]

This represented the first time that the Palestinians, represented by Yasser Arafat and the PLO, were able to speak as an independent party – a development that conceivably laid the foundations for the future Palestinian state.[13] For this reason, as much as the actual declaration of principles, Oslo represented a major turning point in the Palestinian-Israeli peace process in keeping with this wider trend. Prior to official negotiations, groundbreaking progress had been made through mutual recognition. For this prerequisite to talks, Arafat renounced terrorism and violence, accepted UNSC Resolutions 242 and 338 as a basis for negotiation and, most significantly, recognised the existence of the state of Israel. In turn, the Israeli Prime Minister, Yitzhak Rabin, officially recognised the PLO as the representative of the Palestinian people and expressed willingness to negotiate within the framework of the peace process.[14] Noticeably, however, Rabin did not refer to the UN resolutions or the right of the Palestinians to an independent state, even though the aim of the Oslo talks was to establish a limited National Authority for Palestinian self-rule in the form of statebuilding. Although it involved particularly complicated negotiations and resulted in a complex initial agreement,[15] the intention was to create Palestinian autonomy, or at least a limited form of it, and accept the consequences of this. This was acknowledged by all the parties. As Article 1 of the negotiations suggests,

> The aim of the negotiations . . . is to establish a Palestinian interim self-governing authority for the Palestinian people . . . in the West Bank and Gaza . . . for a transitional period . . . leading to a permanent settlement based on Security Council Resolutions 242 and 338.[16]

This was to be achieved in three stages: Oslo I (1993), comprising initial diplomacy tools to establish principles and strategies as well as a timetable for implementation; Oslo II or the Interim Agreement (1995),[17] which was to lay the foundations for the Palestinian National Authority and the establishment of self-rule through functioning institutional and territorial power; and Oslo III, which was intended as the final stage of conflict termination and was to deal with the 'real issues' such as the permanent status of the Occupied Territories, Jerusalem and refugees. Needless to say, Oslo III, due to begin in May 1996, did not happen. Despite the historic and groundbreaking negotiations and the establishment of the Palestinian National Authority and a form of limited self-rule in areas of the West Bank and Gaza, the promises of the Oslo Accords and the declaration of principles, to the delight of some and the lament of others, failed to come to fruition.

There has been a great deal of commentary on the failure of the Oslo peace process. Much of it deals with the historical events and naturally places the breakdown of the process in the familiar political and historical context of the ongoing cycle of conflict – where it can be easily understood. For example, it is commonly explained that the ongoing violence, in the form of terror attacks and targeted killings and incursions, continued on both sides, as did settlement building, and when the political situation shifted[18] a second intifada erupted in 2001. This armed insurrection led to the dissolution of the Palestinian National Authority and the actual destruction of Arafat's PLA compound, which effectively heralded the end of the Oslo Peace Accords.[19] Others suggest a number of policy reasons, of the problem-solving type, associated with the implementation of the Oslo agreement to explain why it failed.[20]

Undoubtedly the violence and problematic technical reasons influenced the suggested failure of Oslo, but more detailed and perhaps critical analysis has examined the asymmetry of the Accords and suggested that it was not an agreement between equal partners but between 'an occupying power and an occupied people'.[21] As the 'mutual' agreements demonstrated, Arafat's concessions were much more extensive than Rabin's. Nevertheless, both leaders were making unprecedented compromises and were under tremendous pressure from the opposition among their own people, particularly as the violence on both sides escalated (indeed, Rabin's perceived treachery cost him his life).[22] The importance of the Oslo process as a representation of the liberal peace model seems to be that both the Palestinian and Israeli leadership recognised for the first time – in public at least – the necessity to work together to find a mutual solution. Such a solution was supposed to be based on a compromise with each other within a specific form of politics, not necessarily predetermined by the tragic model of territorial sovereignty, but more focused on a reconstruction of what a politics of peace at that time meant. This was contrary to exclusive Israeli and Palestinian claims of territorial sovereignty over the same land, and represented a major, but brief, shift away from old-fashioned notions of state and sovereignty. Unfortunately, what then followed marked an attempt to return to these older norms of statehood, which the subsequent clamp down on terrorism and the later 'war on terror' endorsed in local and global contexts. Yet, Oslo represented a policy shift from political independence to the recognition of mutual political dependence. The main issue became no longer whether power should be shared but rather how and on what terms.[23]

Notwithstanding, the relationship of the actors remained asymmetric in traditional terms, and this is often regarded as the reason for the failure of the process. The Oslo agreement heralded the construction of a Palestinian 'state' that was so fractured and divided (into areas of varying Israeli control) that Palestinian 'autonomy' was effectively a fallacy and day-to-day operation would have been virtually impossible without direct Israeli involvement or the support of international actors and donors. The asymmetric construction of the Oslo agreement itself was designed to reflect the strength and existing structure of the Israeli state. Lustick suggests that Israeli opponents of the Oslo process were able to treat it not as a political framework for compromise but as a rigid legal codex. It became 'an array of legalistic and definitive limits for the opposing side versus an array of loopholes and opportunities for the aggressive, adversarial exploitation of opportunities for one's own side'.[24]

Clearly, there was in practice a failure to engage fully with the root causes of the conflict. The Oslo talks ignored the final status issues, and although it has been suggested that this was deliberate in order to get the process on track, it proved a false political reality; those issues could not be so easily ignored and thus 'were on everyone's mind all the time and dominated the agenda'.[25] Fatally for the peace agreement, this followed Kissinger's dictum of 'constructive ambiguity', which each side used in order to 'sell' the agreements to their own constituencies. In doing so, each side was also allowed to interpret what they perceived to be unwritten agreements regarding the final or permanent status that would emerge at the end of the process.[26]

The shift of what initially began as a behind-the-scenes process, namely Track II, was based upon mutual recognition and on an agreement that a compromise was plausible if debate could occur within a more flexible set of parameters, towards a more traditional high-level diplomatic process. This soon raised familiar obstacles to such formal peace processes. In addition, and partly because of this shift, the Oslo Accords also failed to deal with the deeper socio-economic issues, particularly among the Palestinians at the grass-roots level, which had been developing in the fifty years of the conflict. This amounted to a rejection of one of the root causes of the conflict. Previous peace processes had been generally unsuccessful for just this reason, given that the regional Arab states had been negotiating largely for their own agenda, rather than for the concerns of the Palestinian people. However, since the first intifada[27] and the withdrawal of Jordan from its former role of representing the Palestinians,[28] the concerns of the Palestinians became the main issue and Palestinian politicians were directly negotiating for them, or so it seemed. This was seen by some Palestinian commentators as an 'internal peace movement' aimed at two states, which opened the way for liberal conditionalities to be introduced. Clearly, the core issues of sovereignty, territory, refugees and the status of Jerusalem were still important but what the intifada brought to the surface were the contemporary, structural reasons for the conflict, such as the socio-economic condition in which the Palestinians had lived for decades. In this way, the intifada represented a Palestinian grass-roots rebellion against the Israeli occupation, which was regarded as the cause of their socio-economic problems. Nevertheless, the Oslo Accords were no exception to the trend of political solutions that neglected such issues, even if this process was one negotiated by Palestinian national politicians. Indeed, Oslo has been referred to as 'a solution to strategic problems and dilemmas' and it is uncertain 'whether the leaders understood and represented the fundamental interests and rights of their people'.[29] Certainly Palestinian feelings about the Oslo Accords are not particularly positive: it was suggested that Oslo could never be taken seriously because it was primarily a political settlement when what was needed was a socio-economic one.[30] Hence, the ultimate Palestinian grass-roots response to Oslo was the second (al-Aqsa) intifada. What this suggests about the failure of Palestinian politicians to alleviate the suffering of their own people is all too clear.

Despite these shortcomings, the Oslo Accords can be regarded as an attempt to introduce the liberal peace framework to the Middle East, laying the foundations for the creation of a Palestinian state. Born on the wave of post-Cold War optimism and the (re) creation of a new world order that was being applied to other world conflicts,[31] Oslo followed in the mould of *An Agenda for Peace*,[32] encompassing a new vision for dealing with the conflict, which by 1992 was also underway in Namibia, Nicaragua, Angola, Cambodia and El Salvador. The influx of international donors, actors and particularly NGOs into the Middle East on the signing of the Oslo Accords brought the conditionalities and expectations of the liberal peace into the region. The West Bank and Gaza received major investment packages through the UN, EU, World Bank and other major donors – familiar players now in the established world of post-conflict peace- and statebuilding. Indeed, the total funding was on a huge scale. A 1993 World Bank report, *Developing the Occupied Territories: an Investment for Peace*, recommended that the donor community provide technical assistance to public sector economic investments in the West Bank and Gaza. This included transport, power, education and health and was estimated at US $1,350 million for the medium term and US $1,600 million for the long term.[33]

This was consistent with the liberal peace aim of state formation though economic investment. Indeed, a closer examination of the DoP confirms this. Even though most of the articles are concerned with the nature of the interim self-government arrangements, there is a close link to a language related to liberal peacebuilding missions. Article III states, 'In order that the Palestinian people in the West Bank and Gaza Strip may govern themselves according to democratic principles, direct, free and general political elections will be held . . . under international observation.'[34] It is also emphasised in this article that this development is 'a preparatory step towards realization of the legitimate rights of the Palestinian people and their just requirements'.[35] This promotes democratisation and human rights, and in terms of the rule of law – another pillar of liberal peace theory – Article VIII requires the creation of a strong police force by empowering the interim council with legislative powers.[36]

Article VI calls for 'promoting economic development' and Palestinian control of 'education and culture, health, social welfare, direct taxation and tourism, while Article VII calls for the promotion of economic growth through the establishment of, among others, a Palestinian sea port, development bank as well as water and electricity authorities.'[37] Furthermore, Article XI suggests 'Israeli-Palestinian cooperation in economic fields' by 'recognizing the mutual benefit of cooperation for development'.[38] Interestingly the Annexes to the Accords also place emphasis on the necessity for Israeli-Palestinian cooperation, particularly in the regions of economic development and regional growth programmes, including social rehabilitation, business development and infrastructure.[39] This certainly reads like the UN mandates in Cambodia, Kosovo or East Timor, with the only major difference being the absence of an international authority to implement it.

The Oslo Accords clearly reflect the liberal peace model for post-conflict statebuilding. Although they were presented as a political solution promising peace between Israel and the Palestinian leadership (they would certainly guarantee continued PLO and Fateh domination in the short term through the creation of a Palestinian National Authority), the Accords actually heralded a new era of political, economic and social accountability for the Palestinian and

Israeli leadership – because, and perhaps unbeknown to these princi-ple actors at the time, the liberal peace model introduced criteria by which the statebuilding project could be judged. Although the politi-cal conditions of the Accords failed in the medium term, Oslo set new parameters as the internationals introduced a liberal statebuilding mechanism into the Middle East peace process.

Comparing the Liberal Peace Model in Palestine and Israel

The liberal peace model claims to offer both a political framework and a practical multi-level and multi-dimensional tool for creating self-sustaining peace. It is actively being deployed at the political level by all actors as a way out of the conflict via the so-called 'two [liberal] state' solution – which might also be seen as partition[40] or the fracturing of political communities (which has been observed in several other contexts, too). Through this, the general acceptance of a Palestinian state is almost inevitable. However, the liberal peace model has a propensity for not creating what it promises, nor for sat-isfying its own stringent institutional criteria (regarding democracy, human rights and rule of law).

A first concern is the actual peace process itself. As with many processes, it has been monopolised by the political elites, who of course have much to gain and lose from a settlement. Their agendas are often in disregard of the people for whom any future settlement is supposed to benefit. For the Palestinians who suffer from dire socio-economic conditions this is more serious. Certainly, solutions to the Palestinian-Israeli conflict are overly focused at the political level, indeed on the most prominent actors – perhaps the only actors – in the official peace process, which are the 'established' political elites. Approaches to peace, based on individuals and communities, and political, human or socio-economic rights and solidarity, although tackled in some degree by NGOs at the grass-roots level and rhe-torically at the state level, are not necessarily engaged with. They are instead assumed to be solvable at the state level through the 'final status' process. Progress in these vital areas – via development loans and investment – is thus dependent on a final status solution, which implies liberal state creation. This is perhaps a familiar critique of the inconsistency and contradictory nature inherent in the liberal peace framework, where references to the individual/community are often subsumed within the statebuilding process and the creation of a state with which to defend these rights. The obvious problem, however, is how to protect these rights when there is no state entity; where the state does not value the rights of 'others' or of minorities in a manner that satisfies such groups; and where the likelihood of this occurrence is low, given the local and regional political implications – indeed a strong possibility in Palestine.

In both Israel and Palestine, but particularly Israel, there are a number of peace NGOs and 'independent' think tanks whose remit is to support the peace process. Although their agendas (and staff) employ the language of liberal peace, they adopt an overtly political top-down approach to peace and advocate political solutions based on familiar state-centric notions, such as national and personal security.[41] Once again this process could be acceptable if state creation were a real possibility or end point which would not contravene the rights of some groups. However, when it leads to divided polities which offer rights inequitably, as is the case in Bosnia and Kosovo, the position of the Palestinian people, trapped in political no-man's-land with no real protection of rights, is unlikely to lead to a viable state supported by a liberal social contract.

Other independent peacebuilding NGOs expressed to the authors their lack of confidence in the ability of Track II approaches to create incentives for peace, thus effectively undermining the grass-roots process altogether.[42] Similarly, at the governmental level there is a relatively unsophisticated view of what a peace process entails – focused again on the Track I conflict management approach, and the avoidance of, rather than negotiation of, concessions. This is curious, given the extent of literature on the development of peace processes in places as diverse as the Middle East, Cambodia, Sri Lanka, Cyprus, Bosnia, East Timor and Kosovo.[43] Or perhaps, and certainly from the Israeli perspective, it is understandable, given the propensity of the government to preserve their political position and closely guarded state sovereignty – in direct contrast to the culture of concessions inculcated by peace processes. The fervently negative responses to our questions about a UN mission in Israel-Palestine certainly confirmed this suspicion to these researchers.[44] This raises the issue that without a formal UN peacebuilding mission, responsible also for security, how can agency be created for NGO actors and local civil society when the political process is monopolised by the power-seeking elites? Even the respected human rights organisation BT'Selem adopts a particularly Israeli understanding of human rights in the Palestinian regions.[45]

The liberal peace model launched at Oslo is leading to virtually liberal state creation process. In the Palestinian-Israeli context, it is creating a regional imbalance – a powerful Weberian and more or less unitary state in terms of identity, and a weak, divided and unsupported and under-resourced quasi-state that simulates a liberal state in name and dependencies only. Israel as a 'liberal democratic' state continues to be placated by the internationals, and the Palestinians continue to be a forgotten 'other' shrouded within their own quasi-state. Their international status is limited, they are politically divided, and their territory is reduced and contained (by Israel) for security reasons.

Against this background, the next section will examine some of the individual components of the liberal peace model (democracy, human rights and the rule of law) and argue that the liberal criteria of the framework have been subverted, and in many cases ignored, in order to move the process forward to the creation of a stable security situation for Israel. The internationals' aim, as a consequence, is the creation of a Palestinian state. But given the reality of the situation on the ground, vis-à-vis settlements in the West Bank and the course of the security wall, this does not represent two independent states coexisting side by side. Instead, in this context the liberal peace model favours reinforcing the securitised status quo and is camouflaged by the liberal peace framework in its conservative guise.

Smoke and Mirrors? Democracy and Governance in Israel

'Israel is a liberal democracy' is a statement that is frequently used to describe the political system in the country, particularly in response to our questions on the liberal peace.[46] Certainly, the state functions in a similar manner to many liberal democracies: it has a democratically elected government and Prime Minister, a parliament (Knesset) with all-party representation and has a separation of powers between this institution and the President and Supreme Court. However, perhaps the two unique difficulties (although clearly related) that Israel has to contend with are how to separate religion from the state and the issue of how to deal with Palestinian claims (both inside Israel proper and within the Occupied Territories).

Israel has no written constitution although a number of fundamental laws exist. This is due primarily to the difficulty of separating Judaism from the state. Israel, in this respect, refers to itself as 'Jewish and democratic', and although this is certainly the basis of the Israeli state by virtue of its very nature, which considers faith as a prerequisite, religion is exclusive. This undermines the status of non-Jewish ethnic groups, particularly Israeli Arabs who make up approximately one fifth of Israel's population. This question, often referred to as the 'Jewish question', has been the source of debate over how the Jews, as an ancient religious people, should fit into a political order such as the one provided by liberal democracy. Critics suggest that national self-determination for Jews in a state of their own can no longer be part of a morally acceptable answer.[47]

Tied into this debate is obviously the question of the Palestinians: this creates another problem for democracy and has a serious existential dimension for Israel. Commonly termed the 'demographic question', this refers to the absorption of the Occupied Territories along with approximately 3.5 million Palestinian people. For Israel, with an approximate population of 7 million that already includes approximately 1.4 million Arabs, this is a serious issue.[48] Whilst the occupation of the West Bank and Gaza is politically untenable – as Israel is increasingly compared with apartheid-South Africa – more concerning for the Jewish nation is that long-term occupation could eventually undermine the desired, but already problematic homogeneity of the Israeli state. In order to maintain its Jewish identity, Israel might need to sacrifice either democracy or its exclusivity as the Jewish homeland. In an unprecedented statement, the Israeli Prime Minister vocalised this growing concern as he suggested that unless a two-state solution was achieved, '[Israel would] face a South African-style struggle for equal voting rights, and as soon as that happens, the state of Israel is finished.'[49]

It is certainly a difficult task to interpret and identify the stimulus for Israeli political activity. The Jewish state, often appearing so homogenous and unified, is in fact a particularly composite, diverse and fractured political community and indeed it might only be the conflict with the Palestinians and the wider perceived threat from the Arab world that maintains some cohesion.[50] The divergent groups within Israeli politics and society have very different views on the nature of peace that might be achieved. Similarly, it is difficult to assess the impact of liberal peacebuilding on a state where the burden of liberal democracy weighs heavily on an occupying army oppressing a Palestinian population in contravention of international law. Are we witnessing an engagement with the ideology of the liberal peace model and the relinquishment of Zionism? It would certainly seem that Israel is abandoning its Zionist goal of a greater Israel (which includes the Palestinian areas as the 'promised land') and is concentrating on securing the territory it already has, perhaps engaging with the so-called two-state solution. This is being achieved not just rhetorically by the construction of a 'security fence'[51] and is perhaps also conversant with the disengagement plan and the unilateral withdrawal from Gaza, which Sharon oversaw in September 2005.

The author of *The Iron Wall*, the revisionist historian Avi Shlaim, argues that the Israeli Zionist policy toward the Palestinians has been based on the understanding that the Arabs would never voluntarily give up land they saw as their own. He suggests the Zionists have always intended to employ settlement by the use of force to construct a metaphorical iron wall, which the Arabs would be powerless to break down.[52] With the construction of the security fence, this is now a reality. Predictably, there is a great deal of debate about the purpose of the fence. The official Israeli explanation is the need for security and the prevention of terrorism. However, the course of the wall does not follow the 1967 green line and annexes a great deal of Palestinian land (and actual Palestinians), not to mention the Old City of Jerusalem. The wall debate raises a familiar theme in Israeli policy toward the Palestinians in regard to security and land, while the actual wall conveniently provides both for Israel. It effectively emasculates the Palestinian territory to such an extent that its inhabitants are probably now unable to create a functioning state. This outcome of partition denotes the limits of the liberal peace model, where the framework is unable to reconcile different ethnic communities and instead divides the territory into emaciated and internally divided separate states or states in waiting. This came about because the liberal peace does not promote trust and cooperation between communities as its starting point – or indeed within them. Instead, it focuses on zero-sum institutions, which disputants must enter even if doing so disadvantages them. This might work if liberal peacebuilding created a social contract by recognising and responding to the needs and identities of individuals and communities within those institutions. Yet it fails to provide them with basic needs, hence preventing the emergence of sustainable peace in an environment of pre-existing social, political and economic inequality.

Claims of liberal democracy are overshadowed and certainly corroded by the Jewish and Palestinian questions – which includes, from the Palestinian perspective of course, the continued military occupation of the Palestinian lands (pre or post 1967). Emphasis on democratic reform is continually focused on the Palestinian leadership, particularly by Israel and the United States, often as a pre-condition for negotiation in any peace process. However, questions relating to democracy and governance in the liberal peacebuilding process should also be asked of the Israeli state. It might be claimed that Israel is free-riding on the discourse of liberal peace, using it as a subtle vehicle for a 'greater Israel' (Eretz-Yisrael) and to ensure the survival of the Jewish state. A walled division would clearly satisfy the democratic, demographic and Palestinian problems for the state of Israel.

Palestinian Versions of Democracy

Democratic governance in the Palestinian Territories is predicated upon two main factors: the role of Israel as the occupying power in the region; and the political and cultural system of the Palestinian Arabs – both of which result in a form of 'selective democracy'.[53] Employing its disproportionate strength, Israel is able to dominate and control the socio-economic conditions in the West Bank and Gaza. This was particularly apparent following the success of Hamas in the Palestinian Legislative Council (PLC – Parliament) elections in January 2006. Since then the Israelis have led an international boycott of the Hamas government, withheld tens of millions of dollars in vital tax revenues,[54] and closed the border to trade and commerce. Unsurprisingly, this greatly exacerbated the socio-economic situation in Gaza and arguably triggered the civil war between Hamas and Fateh that led to Hamas taking complete control of Gaza.

The Israeli military and government is also able to use its military strength to kill those it regards as unacceptable Palestinian political leaders, politicians and individuals,[55] and also to, quite literally, demol-ish the Palestinian government, which it did in September 2002 by destroying almost the entire infrastructure of the fledgling Palestinian National Authority. This asymmetry is not unnoticed by the interna-tional community, 'Each time the Palestinians come close to achieving any level of institutional empowerment and democratic governance, it is expected that the Israeli occupation forces will redouble their efforts to destabilize Palestinian society.'[56] Nevertheless, despite such recognition there is a distinct lack of support from the international community. For example, following the parliamentary elections that resulted in Hamas winning seventy-six of the 132 seats in the chamber (the ruling Fateh party won only forty-three), the response of the inter-nationals was quite the reverse of what it should have been to enable a democratic process, particularly when an election with 77 per cent electoral participation unseated the established ruling elites. Instead of upholding the result, the election results were seen as a disaster for the region and were condemned by the international community, particularly the United States and Europe. The paradoxical nature of the situation was clearly illustrated by the British Prime Minister, Tony Blair, who stated, 'I think it is important for Hamas to understand that there comes a point and the point is now . . . where they have to decide between a path of democracy or a path of violence.'[57] Thus, internationals place emphasis on the democratic process in liberal statebuilding yet fail to support it when the outcome is not to their liking. The liberal peace model only supports 'liberal' partners; the phenomenon of allowing the election of the 'wrong' leadership has been termed 'illiberal democracy'.[58]

Of course, Palestinian democratic governance to date has been far from free of criticism, with much of it being aimed at the Palestinian political, cultural and religious system. The incumbent political system in Palestine is a barrier to the development of democracy, which in turn influences the social and economic situation. UNDP suggests the need for 'democratization of all aspects of political life within a pluralistic system that includes rotation of power and leadership . . . separation of powers, conducting periodic elections that prevent monopoly over power, revamping of political institutions and structures'.[59]

Although Palestine is not yet a state entity, the existing Palestinian Fateh leadership claim (although without a democratic mandate) the political leadership of the Palestinian people. The provisional constitution suggests engagement with the liberal peace model. Article 8 (March 2003) states,

> The Palestinian political system shall be a parliamentarian representative democracy based on political pluralism. The rights and liberties of all citizens shall be respected, including the right to form political parties and engage in political activity without discrimination on the basis of political opinions, sex, or religion.[60]

How far this constitution is influenced by international conditionality[61] to placate both the radicalised Palestinian public and the internationals, and to consolidate power for Fateh is difficult to judge. A UNDP report in 2004 suggested, somewhat contrary to the requirements of the 2003 constitution, that the traditional structure of the Palestinian political system 'is based on an alliance of political elites, security apparatuses and traditional social structures and on a network of relations of loyalty and personal and interest-oriented connections with people in power at all levels'.[62] These criticisms are culturally insensitive, the insinuation being of endemic and widespread corruption. They demonstrate the classic liberal peace approach to statebuilding, namely a failure to engage with the local cultural and political systems and instead looking to replace them, from above, with western patterns of liberal democracy and civil society. Needless to say, the democratic elections in Gaza that were supposed to enact western democracy returned a Hamas government. This was not only a shock to the sensibilities of the international liberal peacebuilders but it demonstrated that democracy was replicating the already existing form of the political system and reiterating a zero-sum power struggle. This should not have been a surprise: it has been a common occurrence when democracy is applied to a traditional patronage and clientelism-based autocratic system of governance, such as in Cambodia or East Timor, and as also seen in Bosnia after Dayton.[63] A revealing interview with a Fateh former National Legislative member suggested that democracy was a difficult concept to apply to the Palestine National Council (PNC) and that a form of 'interior democracy' existed.[64] The attempt to introduce democratic reform has been hindered by the complete absence of a UN mission or Office of the High Representative that could institute constitutional change. In this case, of course, reform might be better than the problems of external conditionality as has occurred in other cases. But, paradoxically, reform without external conditionality appears very unlikely. Even when the UN has had direct involvement in the local political system, such as in Cambodia, Bosnia or East Timor, a similar situation of democracy, replication of the existing power structure occurs.[65] As UNDP point out, 'The incentive to create institutions designed to empower society remain weak and efforts to modernize Palestinian life are symbolic and/or superficial.'[66] In this context, a central peacebuilding actor would have difficulties in persuading both the Israeli government and Palestinian authorities, not to mention the main interest groups they represent, of its authority or of the sanctity of the liberal peace model.

There is little doubt that these recommendations are particularly applicable to the Palestinian political system and represent criticisms voiced not just by the international community but by many Palestinians themselves who see their national leadership as corrupt, undemocratic and unrepresentative. Indeed, the second (al-Aqsa) intifada can be regarded as a reaction against Israel and the failings of the

peace process as well as against the perceived corruption and ineffec-
tiveness of Arafat and the Fateh leadership – at both national and local
levels – and their failure to deal with the socio-economic conditions in
the territories. The success of Hamas, as a grass-roots socio-political
movement is also indicative of the weariness of the Palestinian public
with the corrupt and ineffective old-guard Fateh regime.

Perhaps the recent division between the West Bank and Gaza
is actually a product of the liberal peace model. The promise of a
'state' built with Israeli acquiescence and international assistance is
obviously attractive to Abbas and Fateh who control the West Bank
and claim to represent the Palestinians. However, this would be a
state without Gaza that serves to further weaken the Palestinians as
a political entity as well as reducing the chances of a workable state.
Fateh are attractive to the internationals as 'liberal Palestinians'
because they employ the language of the liberal peace model and also
to the Israelis, who can further divide and weaken the Palestinians by
supporting them. Fateh, in turn, are probably subverting the liberal
peace framework to reinforce their own position of control of an
emerging Palestinian state. The reluctance to engage in dialogue with
Hamas is perhaps indicative of this. Hamas in Gaza, conversely, are
viewed as the 'unacceptable other' in the liberal model. They are an
example of a politically legitimate group and electorally mandated
representatives of people, who, due to their political orientation
are not recognised by the liberal model, or indeed internationals,
and are therefore sidelined and ignored. Ironically, as a non-liberal
other, Hamas is a grass-roots Palestinian organisation with deep
socio-economic roots and widespread support due to their attempts
to engage with social and welfare issues, an area neglected by the
elite level Fateh and indeed the liberal peace model. Once again, the
liberal peace model in Palestine, as in Bosnia, Kosovo and elsewhere,
is unable and indeed perhaps unwilling to deal with these issues and
so instead it reinforces them.

Civil Society, Human Rights and the Rule of Law

Palestinian human rights and civil society are severely curtailed by
the conflict with the state of Israel. Indeed, local activists have made
the general claim that the peace process has continually collapsed
because its human rights element has not been addressed properly.
Some see such a framework as biased towards the Palestinians.[67]
Palestinians see the security forces of the state as one of the main

obstacles to human rights by contrast. These also impede the development of the rule of law, besides the free market and private property ownership it promotes. Palestinian representatives claim that most aspects of the liberal peace (including democratization) are blocked by Israeli attitudes to both security and the Palestinians, who might prefer a UN peacekeeping force rather than an isolated mediation process.

Palestinian civil society's practices of substitution for the lack of a state provider are very developed, and civil society advocacy and human rights groups are quite active within the Israeli state. On the other hand, basic aspects of a liberal polity, such as separation of powers and an independent judiciary, are very suspect on the Palestinian side, and within the Israeli polity extensive exemptions are made for certain communities (i.e. settlers) and for issues relating to Palestinian rights.[68]

Indeed much civil society activity in the areas of advocacy and the provision of basic resources and facilities, particularly for Palestinian communities, also represents a form of resistance to the militarised and securitised approach of the Israeli state. A 2006 UN report was particularly scathing of Israeli violations of human rights and international humanitarian law, pointing to a litany of abuses. These included military incursions, destruction of civilian infrastructure, levelling of agriculture land and high civilian deaths. The report also focused on the economic sanctions in Gaza, which have led to 70 per cent unemployment and over 80 per cent of the population living below the official poverty line.[69] Accordingly, the siege of Gaza is considered a form of collective punishment in violation of the Fourth Geneva Convention, while the indiscriminate use of military tactics against civilians and civilian targets has resulted in serious war crimes.[70] The report also highlights the continued construction of settlements in the West Bank and East Jerusalem, the situation of Palestinian prisoners in Israeli jails, targeted assassinations and the daily discrimination and injustice against Palestinian civilians.

The liberal peace framework is subservient to state interests, international politics and the continued appeasement of Israel by the international community, and in particular the United States. This has undermined the credibility of the liberal peace framework for peace in the region, as well as a universal model for peace, rather exposing it as a form of western ideological control. This inconsistency between the theory and practice of liberal peace and the revelation of its ideological orientation has serious implications, as the Special Rapporteur on the situation of human rights in the Palestinian territories points out:

> The Occupied Palestinian Territory is the only instance of a developing country that is denied the right of self-determination and oppressed by a Western-affiliated State. The apparent failure of Western States to take steps to bring such a situation to an end places the future of the international protection of human rights in jeopardy as developing nations begin to question the commitment of Western States to human rights.[71]

Due to the unique ethnic nature of the Israeli state, it also has internal human rights issues relating to the representation of ethnic groups. Although there is representation of ethnic minorities, particularly Arab-Israelis in the Knesset, human rights questions arise in reference to the exclusive nature of Zionism and Jewish nationalism, and indeed the function of the Israeli state as a national homeland for Jewish people. Certainly, the symbols of state such as the Israeli flag, emblem, anthem and coinage seem to have little space for any other minorities to be included – ethnic, religious or otherwise. Indeed, it is ironic that the state requires religion to be so clearly stated on their national identity cards. If other nationals wish to become an Israeli citizen (and receive full citizenship rights) they are required to relinquish their former nationalities. For this reason, many Arab-Israelis are forced to reject citizenship and choose to remain Palestinian by nationality. This in turn affords them few rights in Israel and gives them the status of a refugee. As a result, many are treated as second-class citizens.[72]

The liberal peace model does not challenge this outcome, because it is ultimately a state discourse and naturally supports recognised and established international status, the dominant human rights model and the western version of these. Alternative forms are not entertained by the current liberal peace model, which is, despite the rhetoric of universal rights, actually exclusive. The Palestinian frameworks for human rights and rule of law in the West Bank and Gaza do not fit the liberal peace model either. A UNDP report suggests these rest on 'a host of illegal practices, such as bribes, corruption and various means of bypassing or disregarding the rule of law. In spite of a nominal level of pluralism in this system, features of authoritarianism are still present.'[73]

The historical and cultural legacy of Jewish human rights is particularly sensitive, and was perhaps the reason for the creation of the state of Israel in 1948. Nevertheless, the liberal peace model, as a western state discourse, is inconsistent in relation to minorities or non-western cultures but conversely, when employed in support of a western dominant version, serves to reinforce the status quo by marginalising alternative voices, minorities and 'others'.

Free Market Reform and Development

Economic liberalisation and development as key tenets of the liberal peace have certainly been on the agenda of the international peacebuilders in the Middle East. But free market reform and development are not necessarily a concern for the Israeli economy, which is taken to be developed and neoliberal in structure and form. This is far from the case in Palestine. In the context of the economy in which the Palestinians work, the situation is very different, particularly as their interaction with the formal Israeli economy is now very limited or at least subject to Israeli conditionalities. Thus, the focus has been on developing Palestinian capacity through the usual mechanisms, and according the prescriptions built into World Bank, IMF, UNDP and EU engagements in this area, into a neoliberal economy, which attracts foreign direct investment (FDI) and trickles down to the general population after the regulatory frameworks and economic elites have emerged. Neither, of course, has occurred at a significant level, though different stages of the peace process have brought in large amounts of foreign assistance (much of which appears to have been misused or misdirected particularly by the Arafat regime). Although economic development was regarded as vital to the success of the peace process, it was not until the Oslo Accords in 1993 that concerted efforts could be made in developing the Palestinian economy. Even by this time though, the economic situation was serious. A 1993 World Bank report entitled 'Developing the Occupied Territories – an investment in peace', stated,

> The economy of the Occupied Territories is currently in turmoil. Income levels have stagnated over the past decade; unemployment and underemployment are rising rapidly; public infrastructure and services are grossly overstretched; and the fragile natural resource base is threatened with irreversible damage.[74]

The report goes on to discuss prospects for sustainable development in the future and outlines the priority agenda of policies and programmes needed to promote such development.[75] A major part of this was the creation of the Trust Fund for Gaza and the West Bank (TFGWB) in 1993, which was designed to allow the Palestinian Territories – as a non-sovereign state – access to financing from the IMF and World Bank. Since the establishment of the TFGWB, the Bank has committed over US $500 million to thirty-four projects and disbursed US $433 million.[76] The approach of the World Bank and other international institutions to the peacebuilding mission in Palestine was to try and avoid the difficult political issues at the root of the conflict by establishing a technical mission and focusing on policies, institutions and investments. International development has focussed on developing Palestinian capacity through the usual mechanisms into a neoliberal economy. Since the failure of Oslo and the second intifada, the continuing cycle of violence has not allowed the economy to develop at a significant level, despite the large amounts of foreign assistance. Indeed, the current socio-economic situation is hardly an example of the merits of liberal peace. According to the UNDP (2008) real GDP growth is minus 1.0, the poverty rate is 68 per cent – with 35 per cent in extreme poverty – unemployment is 30.3 per cent and the HDI is 106.[77]

Despite much humanitarian and emergency assistance to plug the gap between the emergence of a free market and everyday life, economic difficulties on the ground continue to be one of the most significant problems faced by individuals and communities. Of course, these difficulties are also intricately related to security problems in the region. The neoliberal component of the liberal peace model allows for security to take precedence over everyday life, however, reducing the responsibility of international actors, agencies and donors to actively work towards dealing with poverty, the lack of jobs and opportunities, and the deficiencies in public services, broadly defined. These issues are rather relegated to the neoliberal terrain of self-help, ironically to arise from dispossessed and heavily regulated communities, and the fragile quasi-state that represents them. Thus, the breaking of the cycle of poverty and violence has not been successfully achieved, just as the cycle of violence, occupation and further violent resistance has not been broken at the political level. This has had a knock-on effect for the Palestinian Authority, for the emergence of a social contract and for the stability of the regional environment.

The reasons for the disastrous economic situation are directly related to the ongoing conflict and the failure of the Israeli and Palestinian governments, as well as the internationals, including the Europeans, Americans and Arabs, to secure a lasting peace in the region. However, on a local level, the key factor for understanding the economic situation in Palestine – much like the political one – is the inescapable fact that no progress can be made in developing the Palestinian economy without the support of the Israeli government. Unlike other liberal peacebuilding missions where the UN was able to assume some form of governance and directly guide economic development, in this instance, the internationals have been unable to sufficiently influence the security concerns of the Israeli government nor control the financial management of the Palestinian Authority. As is characteristic of the asymmetric nature of this conflict, economic development has been sacrificed in favour of reinforcing the security status quo. This has been particularly apparent after the construction of the security barrier and the blockade of Gaza. Indeed, Israeli government restrictions on the movement of goods and labour to and from the Palestinian territories have stunted any hope of developing the Palestinian economy – despite the best intentions of the donor community. As a UNDP report stated,

> The deterioration of the situation in the Gaza Strip and the building of the Separation Wall in the West Bank have both especially affected poor villagers and farmers in rural areas. The poverty rate increased from 56% to 69% in villages between November 2004 and July 2005, while extreme poverty reached 32% as compared to 23% in November 2004.[78]

This affects both Palestinian economic development and threatens donor funding. As Baskin points out, 'the losses to the Palestinian economy equalled and even surpassed the total amount of donor funds that were pumped into the process'.[79] Interaction with the formal Israeli economy, particularly since the formation of a Hamas government in Gaza, is now very limited or at least subject to Israeli conditionalities. Despite promises of huge amounts of funding – international and Arab communities recently pledged $7.4 billion to revive the moribund economy[80] – it seems unlikely that they will break of the cycle of poverty, which is connected to the need for a successful peace process.

This is not to say that there is not potential for a Palestinian economy. One observer argued that they have actually been successful, given their constraints, in maintaining a shadow economy built on small and medium-sized enterprises, and operating within and around Israeli control, to negate the worst aspects of day-to-day life, though this was not flexible enough to provide a peace dividend in the face of local corruption.[81] On the other hand, it was also argued that the 'process of peace' had failed even though, as a concept, it retained wide appeal in terms of democracy and trade, mainly because the peace process had made 'beggars of Palestinians', particularly through the adoption by Fateh of neoliberal strategies. In short, 'the fruits of peace were never delivered to the plates of the average Palestinian citizen.'[82] Current international efforts to shore-up the Fateh government in the West Bank and ostracise the Hamas one in Gaza is a further indication to Palestinians that peace is a process of division rather than cooperation, and one of impoverishment rather than development.[83] This means that the peace backed by the west is seen as predatory rather than community, social or welfare oriented, and any state that emerges as a result of this may be more designed for regional stability than to deal with the economic problems of Palestinian communities.

Conclusion

On close examination the chaos of the Middle East peace process is related to the unintended consequences of the liberal peace framework. Most western diplomats have assumed that it applies easily to the Israeli state but not to the Palestinian entity (similar to their assumptions in the case of Cyprus over the failed UN Annan Plan of 2004, where it was assumed that the Greek Cypriot government had accepted the liberal assumptions behind the plan).[84] A more radical argument might be that the liberal peace is not 'failing' in Israel/ Palestine, but is actually doing exactly what its conservative graduation is supposed to do – to protect the legal, diplomatic, military and territorial status of a pre-existing sovereign against non-sovereign, secessionist and irredentist minorities. Again, this is exactly the dynamic that has developed in the case of Cyprus and in Sri Lanka. In Northern Ireland, it was the decoupling of this implied inflexible version of sovereignty from peace that allowed progress in the 1990s, and the same looked to have been plausible post-Oslo Accords in the Middle East.

It is the state-centric aspect of the liberal peace model – an auto-bias towards building the state and existing state entities – that has caused the most difficulty. This aspect, tied in with territorial and intellectual sovereignty, means that liberal peacebuilding replicates states as its core conflict management mechanism, which then replicates epistemic patterns of inclusion and exclusion. This is most recognisable in the state system, where a precarious negative peace is held together in the best tradition of liberal-realism and conflict management by boundaries, divisions and walls, as well as a pre-emptive security and threat discourses. The liberal peace model actually subverts an emancipatory graduation of the liberal peace process by favouring existing states and sovereign entities over its supposed emancipatory focus on the production of a social contract. This is brought about by the obvious incompatibility of a western-centric approach to statebuilding that has limited relevance to the wide range of existing cultural, political and socio-economic structures of a region. Coupled with the distinct lack of local ownership – apart from supporting the already established local elites who were part of the problem in the first place – the process is destined to fail. It legitimates the displacement of the peace process and its replacement with a negative and conservative notion and process of peace, which in most cases rests on security, securitisation and exclusive forms of governance. The result is a very conservative form of the liberal peace at best, representing a virtual peace in the form of an emaci-ated, virtual state as the endpoint of the peace process, rather than a transitionary point.[85]

This indicates that under such circumstances the liberal peace model can only ever be a form of the victor's peace, where the primary objective is security as well as the maintenance of the inter-national status quo and international system. In other words, our suspicion is that where the statebuilding model begins in such cir-cumstances is where it also comes to rest. It consolidates the status quo, with all of its attendant injustices. Preventing stagnation in peacebuilding, if insecurity and the issues that the conflict is rooted in in the first place are to be addressed, requires a broader approach. Indeed, there is much evidence that dealing with social, economic, identity and cultural issues, in parallel with security, territory, and governance issues, is likely to placate more disputants more quickly. Against this background, it is thoroughly anachronistic that most (especially in the post 9–11 environment) peace processes start from security issues and subsequently fail to progress. Indeed, it is also concerning that such reductionist processes continue to be deployed when there is so much well-known evidence as to their limitations, their complicity in maintaining ugly status quos, and what might be done about this. Thus, such peace processes are rarely about genuine compromise and addressing root causes, but confirming the superi-ority of the actor that has most of the conflict's political resources – normally territorial sovereignty. Indeed, the norm of dealing with political and military issues and actors first introduces a bias against peace processes developing beyond ceasefires; the peace process then becomes the justification for offensive acts, such as the exclusion of certain actors and issues, wall-building, and introducing painful, and probably contextually unsuited, conditionalities.

How compliant international actors have been in this process remains to be fully assessed, but flexible creative alternatives to notions of sovereignty, territory, legitimacy and so forth, that could help complicated protracted conflict find lasting or positive peace are not entertained in this framework. Instead, the liberal peace model is focused on statebuilding, state creation, international recognition, division, borders, territory, population, rights and markets, and other familiar components in the mantra of liberal-realist international order and security. The deviancy of the liberal peace model, especially in its more conservative forms, is that it promises so much to the actors in the process, particularly at the individual level, in the form of democracy, human rights and rule of law, and liberal economics – particularly the disposed, marginalized and oppressed – who may have deployed violence to achieve this in the first place. In place of these promises the liberal peace actually delivers exclusive forms of these, designed for the dominant majority or politically acceptable groups who can shore up the state and regional system. This is to the detriment of non-liberal others: the politically weaker minorities and socio-economically deprived individuals (sometimes encompassing a whole population or nation) whom the liberal peace process was supposed to protect and lift out of violence. Instead, they remain, marginalised and socio-economically vulnerable. This is particularly apparent when the liberal peace model connects neo-liberalism to 'peace' in a statebuilding process. This economic model helps stabilise the incumbent political and socio-economic structures as it supports the existing economic elites by clearly benefiting those already in the economic system, not those outside it.

Looking at the poor record of the limited liberal peacebuilding that has been deployed in the Middle East more generally, this raises the issue of whether it can coexist and indeed cooperate with a hybrid system, for example, a non-liberal version of peace? Indeed, this may well be a necessary ambition; otherwise, to non-western, non-liberal actors the liberal peace will merely appear to be an ideology of state security camouflaged by eurocentric claims of emancipation and universal rights. From this perspective, the liberal peace process in the Middle East can be regarded as a Trojan horse, camouflaging an ideologically powerful state discourse. This is actually very fragile

174

when the actors, in this case the Palestinians, buy into the liberal peace process and look forward to its claimed emancipation and all the benefits that come with international state recognition. The outcome is often a non-state limbo. The territory suffers *de jure* or indeed de facto internal division along ethnic or cultural lines along with the emergence of autonomous ethnic regions that exist within an emaciated, ineffective and indeed, internationally unrecognisable state. This 'non-state' hangs in an international shadow with an uncertain future, and is neither able to function as a state economically nor able to afford protection to its people. It is more often than not dominated by the established elites, often with extremist and nationalist agendas, who actively subvert the process of democracy, undeterred (or even implicitly encouraged) by internationals. They provide a political class that, when supported, will stabilise and provide a manageable security situation in the short to medium term at best.

Such dynamics are apparent in Palestine. Despite the continued promises of a Palestinian state, the distinct lack of engagement at the political level with the 'final status' issues that define the Palestinian-Israeli conflict – the future borders of the Palestinian state (including Israeli settlements), the right of return of Palestinian refugees, and the status of Jerusalem – is an indication of either the subversiveness of the liberal peace model or, more innocently, the subversion of the liberal peace model by the disputants, or one dominant disputant.

Yet the belief of the internationals in the liberal peace model is also apparent particularly in relation to requests, and indeed demands, for democracy, human rights and rule of law, based on the assumption that once introduced it should naturally develop and become self-sustaining, thus providing stability in the region. Calls for democracy and a 'new Middle East' have formed a major part of the recent US neo-conservative liberal 'civilising mission' to reshape the entire region. Yet, this is very problematic in a region made up of states that traditionally privilege national security thus re-ordering and securitising society, and so see peace in terms of land and security which act as buffers against violence and terrorism, rather than engaging with the needs of everyday life.[86] Thus the 'neo'-liberal peace model reproduces a counterproductive security order predicated on combating, but also aiming at maintaining, a state of war as a way out of having to engage with sorts of issues that a focus on everyday justice and equity would engender. The notion of two liberal states is similarly anomalous, given local power relations.

The liberal peace model supports Israel as a liberal state whilst attempting to shape the foundations for a liberal state in Palestine. Generally speaking, all of our interviewees for this chapter supported the institutions and goals that make up the liberal peace, but also saw it as subservient to security, the existing Israeli state, and the sacrifices this entailed, in positive and negative forms. This circumscribes the applicability of the liberal peace model and the role of the alphabet soup of institutions and organisations that are usually deployed in other post-conflict situations. The unintended but perhaps natural outcome for the liberal peace model has been to create division, leading to exclusivity as the basis for (re)inclusion into the international state system. As in other cases, the partition of polities, communities and territory has become the basis for 'peace' in its most conservative, if scarcely liberal, form. The framework is unable to deal with the complicated features of state creation, which in this case would mean dealing with the core issues of territory, refugees and the status of Jerusalem as well as the socio-economic problems of the Palestinian people. This might also point to the need for alternatives to dominant discourses of sovereignty and legitimacy. The most likely outcome now is that the Palestinians will remain divided between the West Bank and Gaza in a fragile polity that is controlled by Israel but is 'on track' to statehood. This territory may remain in international limbo as the international community, and indeed the local and regional actors, are unable (or unwilling) to grant recognition, particularly given the conditionality of the liberal peace model. The result has been the continuation of the cycles of violence that the Middle East is currently subject to, rather than joint or shared forms of sovereignty and a sustainable everyday form of peace.

Notes

1. Confidential Source, Van Leer Institute, *Personal Interview*, Jerusalem, 28 June 2007.
2. Confidential Military Source, *Personal Interview*, Jerusalem, 1 July 2007. This source saw the possibilities of an UNMIK-style operation in Gaza, but not in the West Bank. Jesse Helms, 'Saving the UN', *Foreign Affairs*, 75: 5, 1996.
3. Although these are post-conflict situations, they can also be seen in actuality as forms of imperfect 'virtual liberal peace'. See Oliver Richmond and Jason Franks, 'Liberal hubris: virtual peace in Cambodia', *Security Dialogue*, 38: 1, 2007; 'Co-opting the liberal peace: untying the Gordian knot in Kosovo,' *Cooperation and Conflict*, 43: 1, 2008;

'Liberal peace in East Timor: the emperors' new clothes?', *International Peacekeeping*, 15: 2, 2008.

4. There have been a number of Security Council and General Assembly Resolutions; the most important for peace have been UNSC Resolution 242 and 338. See http://www.un.org/documents/scres.htm.

5. In the almost 14 years since the Oslo Accords, there have been eleven additional peace initiatives, such as Camp David, Taba and the Road Map. There have also been bilateral and multilateral negotiations, unilateral actions, and initiatives by Israeli and Palestinian private citizens.

6. Confidential Source, PASSIA, *Personal Interview*, Jerusalem, 28 June 2007.

7. Alvaro de Soto, End of Mission Report, May 2007.

8. See http://daccessdds.un.org/doc/RESOLUTION/GEN/NR0/038/88/IMG/NR003888.pdf?OpenElement.

9. Confidential Source, Peres Centre, *Personal Interview*, Jerusalem, 27 June 2007. Our interviewee mentioned that what was crucial about post-Oslo discussions for Israelis was that 'the system would speak peace'.

10. Confidential Source, PASSIA, *Personal Interview*, Jerusalem, 28 June 2007.

11. Confidential Source, Peres Centre, *Personal Interview*, Jerusalem, 27 June 2007

12. Confidential Source, PASSIA, *Personal Interview*, Jerusalem, 28 June 2007.

13. B. Morris, *Righteous Victims: a History of the Zionist-Arab Conflict 1881–1999* (London: John Murray, 2000), p. 613.

14. Ibid. p. 612.

15. For a detailed explanation of the agreement, see ibid. p. 627.

16. Nils Butenschon, 'The Oslo Agreement: From the White House to Jabal Abu Ghneim', in G. Giacaman and D. Jørund Lønning, *After Oslo – New Realities, Old Problems* (London: Pluto Press, 1999), p. 19.

17. This also included the Wye Summit.

18. In May 1996 the minority Labour government of Shimon Peres was defeated by the right-wing Likud party (Netanyahu became Prime Minister).

19. See A. Shlaim, *The Iron Wall: Israel and the Arab World* (London: Penguin, 2000), pp. 512–604; Morris, *Righteous Victims*, pp. 612–69.

20. Gershon Baskin, 'Why Oslo failed', *The Jerusalem Post*, 13 and 20 August 2007.

21. Butenschon, 'The Oslo Agreement', p. 22.

22. In November 1995, Jewish extremists assassinated Prime Minister Yitzhak Rabin.

23. Butenschon, 'The Oslo Agreement', p. 23.

24. Ian Lustick, 'The Oslo Agreement as an obstacle to peace', *Journal of Palestinian Studies*, XXVII: 1, Autumn 1997, pp. 61–6.

25. Butenschon, 'The Oslo Agreement', p. 23.
26. Gershon Baskin, 'Why Oslo failed', *The Jerusalem Post*, 13 August 2007.
27. Confidential Sources, PASSIA, *Personal Interview*, Jerusalem, 28 June 2007.
28. The Jordanians concluded their own bi-lateral peace treaty with Israel in 1994.
29. Butenschon, 'The Oslo Agreement', p. 17.
30. Mahadi Abdul Hadi: Director, PASSIA, *Personal Interview*, Jerusalem, 28 June 2007.
31. Roland Paris, *At War's End: Building Peace After Civil Conflict* (Cambridge: Cambridge University Press, 2004).
32. B. Boutros-Ghali, *An Agenda for Peace: Preventative Diplomacy, Peacemaking and Peacekeeping* (New York: United Nations, 1992).
33. World Bank, *Developing the Occupied Territories: an Investment for Peace. Volume I: Overview* (Washington, DC: The World Bank, September 1993): www-wds.worldbank.org.
34. See http://www.jmcc.org/research/series/dop.html.
35. Ibid.
36. Ibid.
37. Ibid.
38. Ibid.
39. Ibid.
40. Confidential Source, PASSIA, *Personal Interview*, Jerusalem, 28 June 2007.
41. Ron Pundak: Director, Peres Centre for Peace, *Personal Interview*, Tel Aviv, 27 June 2007.
42. Shimshom Zelniker: Director, Van Leer Institute for Peace, *Personal Interview*, Jerusalem, 27 June 2007.
43. Abu Vilan: MK – M'eretz, *Personal Interview*, Tel Aviv, 1 July 2007; Kadura Fares: Fateh, *Personal Interview*, Ramallah, 30 June 2007.
44. Alon Dumaris: IDF, *Personal Interview*, Tel Aviv, 1 July 2007.
45. 'The Palestinians have human rights the Israelis have security'. Jessica Montell: Director, BT'Selem, *Personal Interview*, Jerusalem, 26 June 2007.
46. Abu Vilan: MK – M'eretz, *Personal Interview*, Tel Aviv, 1 July 2007.
47. Gadi Taub, 'Liberalism, democracy, and the Jewish State', *Chronicle of Higher Education*, 10 August 2007.
48. Although not as serious as first thought following a recount of the 1997 consensus in which the number of Palestinians and Israeli Arabs was thought to match the Israeli population. Now it seems there is a 1.5–2 million gap.
49. *The Guardian*, 30 November 2007.

50. Jason Franks, *Rethinking the Roots of Terrorism* (London: Palgrave, 2006), p. 7.
51. The security fence is in reality a network of fences with vehicle-barrier trenches surrounded by an on average 60 metre-wide exclusion area and up to 8 metre-high concrete walls, that carves it way through the territory.
52. Avi Shlaim, *The Iron Wall: Israel and the Arab World* (London: Penguin, 2000).
53. Gershon Baskin: Director, IPCRI, *Personal Interview*, Jerusalem, 29 June 2007.
54. Israel began releasing these funds in July 2007 – although to the Palestinian President and Fateh in the West Bank and not to Hamas in Gaza.
55. These are euphemistically termed 'targeted assassinations'.
56. United Nations, *Human Development Report – Palestine* (UNDP, 2004), p. 67.
57. 'Hamas sweeps to election victory', *The Guardian*, 26 January 2007.
58. Fareed Zakaria, *The Future of Freedom* (New York: Norton, 2003), p.17.
59. United Nations, *Human Development Report – Palestine*, p. 69.
60. Constitution of the State of Palestine, Third Draft, 25 March 2003.
61. See Richmond and Franks, 'Co-opting the liberal peace: untying the Gordian knot in Kosovo'.
62. United Nations, *Human Development Report – Palestine*, p. 69.
63. See Oliver Richmond and Jason Franks, 'Liberal hubris: virtual peace in Cambodia', *Security Dialogue*, 38: 1, 2007; 'Liberal peace in East Timor: the emperors' new clothes?', *International Peacekeeping*, 15: 2, 2008.
64. Kadura Fares: Fateh leader, *Personal Interview*, Ramallah, West Bank, 30 June 2007.
65. See Richmond and Franks, 'Liberal hubris: virtual peace in Cambodia,'; 'Liberal peace in East Timor: the emperors' new clothes?'
66. United Nations, *Human Development Report – Palestine*, p. 69.
67. Gershon Baskin: Director, IPCRI, *Personal Interview*, Jerusalem, 29 June 2007.
68. Ibid.
69. United Nations Human Rights Council, 'Report of the Special Rapporteur on the situation of human rights in the Palestinian territories occupied since 1967', UNDoc A/HRC/4/17 29 January 2007, p. 2.
70. Ibid. p. 3.
71. Ibid. p. 4.
72. See Franks, *Rethinking the Roots of Terrorism*.
73. United Nations, *Human Development Report – Palestine*, p. 70.
74. World Bank, *Developing the Occupied Territories – an Investment in Peace* (Washington, DC: World Bank, 1993), p. 1.
75. Ibid.

76. The World Bank, Country Brief, West Bank and Gaza: www.world-bank.org.
77. See www.undp.ps/en/index.
78. Ibid.
79. Gershon Baskin, *The Jerusalem Post*, 27 August 2007.
80. 'Donors pledge billions in aid for Palestine', *The Economist*, 18 December 2007.
81. Gershon Baskin: Director, IPCRI, *Personal Interview*, Jerusalem, 29 June 2007.
82. Gershon Baskin, *The Jerusalem Post*, 27 August 2007.
83. PNA Representative, Fateh Leader, *Personal Interviews*, Ramallah, West Bank, 30 June 2007.
84. This turned out not to be the case and a referendum saw a broad rejection by the Greek Cypriots and acceptance by the Turkish Cypriots. See Oliver P. Richmond, 'Shared sovereignty and the politics of peace: evaluating the EU's "catalytic" framework in the eastern Mediterranean', *International Affairs*, 82: 1, 2006.
85. For further arguments on 'virtual liberal peace', see previous chapters.
86. Confidential Source, Coalition of Women for Peace, *Personal Interview*, Jerusalem, 27 June 2007. Indeed, it was argued that the Israeli state cannot afford or sustain such a peace.

Conclusion: Evaluating the Achievements of the Liberal Peace and Revitalising a Virtual Peace

This book has focused on five case studies that have been examined in order to empirically ground the liberal peace framework, and to begin to open up a better and broader understanding of the problems that have plagued it since the liberal peace project of the post-Cold War environment began. What we have found is extremely worrying, especially for those who support the argument that conflicts can be resolved or transformed by focusing on the international and institutional levels as a priority, and that international actors can do much to assist in this process if only coordination, efficiency and sequencing were better. This is not to deny the plausibility of this agenda, but to point to the ease with which this approach is subverted into ideological and implausible, not to say unethical, choices and processes by international actors as well as by local elites who have invested much in their conflicts – or their peace processes. This is often despite the best individual efforts of many within what has effectively become an international civil service of peacebuilders and statebuilders. Statebuilders are far more partial to these problems than those involved in the more everyday aspects of peacebuilding within society.

What we have found is that the progress of statebuilding is extremely slow, such that it cannot really be called 'peacebuilding'. This is partially because it is not localised, cannot engage with the non-liberal subject or their needs, and fails to build a liberal social contract or develop customary and hybridised understandings of a viable, context-driven, rather than internationally or donor-driven, form of peace in a local and everyday context. The elision of the two terms peacebuilding and statebuilding has legitimated statebuilding practices of a top-down, externally driven nature, whereupon their problems have actively discredited the broader agendas of peacebuilding at the expense of the local, its everyday context, the customary, and of hybridity. For this reason, active steps need to be taken by academics and policymakers to address these issues, otherwise there is a risk that the liberal state itself will cease to have universal translatability even at the institutional level in theory, let alone practice. We have found major gaps in an empathetic connection between statebuilding and the everyday aspects of peace, which include areas such as transitional social welfare, the enablement of a social contract and civil society, in development and marketisation, and a reluctance to engage with the local – along with the usual concerns about democracy, efficiency, sequencing and corruption.

We are all too aware of the failings of the global statebuilding and peacebuilding industry and the hidden ideological camouflage of its technical expertise. This is not to say that all is lost, but clearly that the local, the everyday, the customary, human needs, human security and the social contract need to be positioned far higher up the practical agenda than they currently are. Far more attention needs to be paid to peacebuilding and longer-term engagements with specific conflict and post-conflict contexts, with a more hybridised meeting of the 'liberal' and the 'local' than currently appears to have occurred.

In what follows we return to the key lessons of each of our cases in order to provide some points for the potential reconstruction of the peacebuilding agenda. One of the big questions that emerges out of this study, is whether statebuilding and peacebuilding should be conceptually and practically separated, as they were before the end of the Cold War. The statebuilding agenda is focused on political, economic and security architecture, and determines its outcomes as a neoliberal, sovereign and territorial state. This is in contrast to peacebuilding, which, we argue, focuses on the needs and rights of individuals, on sustainable communities and on the requirements for a self-sustaining polity of equitable representation without placing sovereignty, territory and the institutions of the state before that of the mundane needs of everyday life. It was these latter aspirations that motivated many in the UN system and in the international community to become interested in peace processes, peacekeeping, peace support operations, development, the rule of law, human rights and peacebuilding. This has led to a compromise agenda between statebuilding and peacebuilding, now known as liberal peacebuilding. It tends to veer towards statebuilding approaches, but uses peacebuilding a framework for its legitimation, resulting in the uncomfortable compromises of liberal peacebuilding.

The tendency to treat these components as separate from their local context and always contained within a formal Westphalian state has undermined the legitimacy on the ground of the statebuilding/ liberal peacebuilding project. Against this background, our research has thrown up strong evidence for a necessary rethinking of the relationship between peacebuilding and the contemporary project of statebuilding, and for a debate on the relationship between liberalism and the contextualisation and representative capacities of both the local and the everyday. This requires international personnel, actors, officials, diplomats, peacekeepers and aid workers to reflect on the baggage they bring to 'peace' activities, and to instead work as enablers for localised dynamics of peace rather than enablers for an international architecture of peace that has effectively treated the people on the ground as guinea pigs in international engineering projects. This may involve very difficult choices and conversations in a transitionary moment between war and peace, and also a reflection on the liberal project itself, as well as the nature of the liberal state; it also necessitates localised reflection and reform to avoid repeating the dynamics that led to the conflict in the first place, as well as undermining hard won rights or needs. Between these two dynamics, we find that there is space for a hybridised form of peacebuilding and statebuilding that can develop international approaches and consensus for peace, while also developing and assisting the localised dynamics for peace. This hybridised evolution must occur in a close relationship focusing on political agency for individuals rather than institutions. Otherwise, we will continue to see the dynamics of an international praxis of peace from Cambodia to East Timor, and now Afghanistan and Iraq, leading to the creation of the empty shells of states, which have little impact during the transitions from violence on the everyday lives of the vast bulk of their populations. Often, as our research has underlined, half or more of the population of a post-conflict state have not gained a share of the peace dividend if poverty and unemployment indicators are anything to go by.

Many might argue that the limited progress in security affairs is more than enough in terms of achievements for peacebuilding. Others might add that limited interventions are more practical than the ambitious goals of peacebuilding actors. Many think that even 'empty' state institutions are preferable to the local anarchy they perceive would supplant them, on the grounds that they offer future potential for an orthodox or even emancipatory liberal peace. Even if this does resemble international trusteeship, neocolonialism or the suppression of self-determination or self-government, they may think that the security advantages of the model are significant. We argue that this misrepresents the global and local intertwining of the emancipatory agendas of peacebuilding and the more securitised agendas of statebuilding. Without peacebuilding of a sophisticated nature, which is able to comprehend its transnational, local, regional and global dynamics, security and state projects will forever be reactionary, struggling to respond to and pre-empt the next escalation often by depoliticising political subjects. Even worse, they may lead to local dissent, dissatisfaction and resistance. In security and state terms, the world is bounded, static and divided into separate entities. In peacebuilding terms, the world is organic, social and very closely connected, so that problems in one area – particularly in the context of variations of the human needs and human security debates – constantly spill over. Peacebuilding of a localised and context-specific nature produces an everyday dynamic that spills over positively into future social, economic, political and cultural wellbeing. Security strategies and the current policies of building empty states simply replicate themselves, their exclusion of key casual factors and large segments of global and local populations, stratified in a wide range of ways, often according to religion or other forms of identity, class and geographic location. Yet, security is necessary for peacebuilding to occur. Beyond this paradox it is in the international-local stratification that the inconsistencies and inequalities of the liberal peace model become most evident.

Though this inconsistency is not a direct source of conflict in the sense that has been experienced in all of our cases, it plays some role in undermining the localised legitimacy of the liberal peace project, amongst both elites and local communities. Thus, what tends to happen is that elements or roots of the conflict continue to exist, though they are now directed through the statebuilding process, and are fed by its own blindspots and the resources that are brought to each post-violence environment. This, of course, can also be read as a success: the politics of violence are converted to democratic politics, albeit limited. But our research shows that this has failed to have a significant impact on people's everyday lives, or to develop meaningful participation in liberal institutions or the market for many. A big question therefore arises: how far can the empty liberal state manage conflict, in the absence of conflict transformation or resolution, in the long term?

We found little confidence in any of our cases, amongst internationals or locals, that a reversion to violence was unthinkable. We found little confidence amongst civil society that people's lives had or would improve, or that their politicians had their human needs or rights foremost in their mind. We found little confidence amongst the political elites that internationals understood the local context, that security and institutional needs had been met sustainably, and that the risk of conflict had been completely averted. Amongst international actors, we also, tellingly, found little confidence in their own approaches, methods, organisations and achievements, or their own relations with local counterparts. Indeed, what this indicates is a high degree of dissonance between local communities, political elites and international peacebuilders in the context of a very fragile status quo in which internationals had become a vital part. They often concur on the difficulties of their projects, but are unable or unwilling to develop their approaches and consider unpalatable and detailed exploration of alternatives, hybrids or significant modifications to their models. Much of the assessment and evaluation that takes place is conducted by internationals, not locals or even independent organisations, from within the liberal peacebuilding system, meaning that these processes become circular. They are supposedly failing or faltering because of procedural matters or the 'dysfunctionality of the local', but not because of their concepts, theories or material matters. The local is absent from this process of evaluation except in very negative ways. Because the starting point is that the liberal state is the only solution to contemporary conflict, the evaluation of the liberal state as a solution to a particular conflict in a particular context does not occur in an open or transparent manner. As a consequence, the peace dividends that persuade local populations to support liberal peacebuilding are very limited and circulate mainly amongst internationals and their local counterparts.

Culture and Needs: Ambiguity in Cambodia

Peacebuilding in Cambodia represents one of the longest running of the attempts, directly and indirectly, to construct a broader peace housing all of the trappings of the liberal state. Since 1993, the early post-Cold War triumph for the UN and for the emerging liberal peace framework has turned into a quagmire in which the success in local and regional security has not translated into the creation of a liberal state. Instead, what has emerged has defied the intentions of its planners, and represents a quasi-liberal, fairly authoritarian state in which the needs of its communities remain marginalised. Though the regional dynamics of the conflict have been mitigated (at least to a large degree) and the Khmer Rouge have dissolved, the peace that remains is very much a negative or conservative peace, and the newly built state has some very problematic dynamics. The former are major achievements, but the state itself is probably not sustainable in the long term. Though it has the shape of a liberal state, it also houses a predatory elite with the population suffering from acute poverty and a lack of democracy, human rights, resources and law. A liberal social contract has not been achieved and the citizens of the state remain subjects of the peace process. One of the key issues that emerges from our analysis is the ontological and methodological problem of whether the liberal peace is at all transferable into such a non-liberal context via consensual methods. It may be that this is a long-term prospect or unlikely, or that there are specific problems with certain elements of the liberal peace, but not with others.

Clearly, UNTAC's mandate was both revolutionary and unprecedented. Its mission aims represented a new-found hope that the UN and the international community could use its new-found freedom to develop a mechanism whereby peace could be instilled in unstable regions. This rapidly took the shape of replicating the liberal state as a condition for material assistance, leading to ever more intrusive methods (though less so in the case of Cambodia). Even so, the UN's overall command of the Cambodian socio-political and economic infrastructure via its intervention in human rights, electoral, military, civil administration, police, repatriation and rehabilitation issues indicated international confidence in what was rapidly to become known as statebuilding, but was then seen as third-generation peace-keeping, which incorporated aspects of peacebuilding and aimed at 'conflict resolution' by dealing with issues relating to human needs. It is no surprise that in this atmosphere of post-Westphalian praxis human security was to replace more traditional notions of security. Yet what occurred was that the peacebuilding process merged into statebuilding, which in turn became a vehicle for elite competition, not to mention corruption, at the expense of civil society and local populations, all clearly within the gaze of international actors. It might be more appropriate to see Cambodia as a neo-feudal state presided over by internationals who are more concerned with preventing elite-level destabilisation than dealing with everyday needs and problems of the population itself. Though this is a caricature, it is also to a large extent the case. The conservative and hybrid semi-feudal 'liberal peace' that has emerged compares poorly with the original aim of the UN, and for the most part excludes local voices, communities and society. An extreme interpretation, but one that requires some consideration, is that it has validated and reproduced a quasi-feudal system that requires a degree of western complicity.

The international community's faith in the ability of the components of the liberal peace to take root and produce a stable and sustainable polity has not yet come to fruition. Indeed, during our fieldwork we found widespread disillusionment and frustration amongst the peacebuilding community, both on and off the record. Much of this was directed towards local civil society and local politicians, but some was also aimed at the international model itself, and at issues of coordination, overlap and the lack of material resources. A conservative version of the liberal peace has at best been achieved in most cases, but even this is virtual because the state, which has been the target of so much international attention, has very limited capacities to act as a mechanism for a legitimate social contract. As David Chandler has implied in another context, the state merely exists for its own sake, and has yet to be internalised to reflect its citizens and their rights or a civil society. It defers rather than facilitates local politics, or at best gives certain elites absolute control over politics and the state.[1] Given its elite co-option, it might even be said to be an obstacle to achieving a liberal state grounded in a social contract and democratic norms.

Of course, in terms of the more limited goal of provision of security and very basic stability and order, even this might be said to be a success. But given that liberal peacebuilding has adopted a much broader agenda since the end of the Cold War, it has to be evaluated against a more sophisticated set of goals. As a validation of the universality of the liberal state model, Cambodia illustrates its core difficulties in transference, the limits of its capacity, the opportunities for predatory elites it presents, the lack of capacity of internationals, and the hubris of the neoliberal model of the state in such development and non-western contexts.

It also illustrates the hybridity that emerges as a result of this encounter between the exported blueprint or package of liberal peace with development and non-western contexts, which have recently emerged from catastrophic regional and civil conflict. This hybridity presents some very interesting opportunities, especially if the peacebuilding/statebuilding model can find ways of responding to it. At the moment hybridity represents a compromise with the ideals of the liberal state and local, self-interested, sometimes predatory, sometimes authoritarian elites, and an 'asset-stripping' of the state and often even of international donors. Lip service to liberal ideal and western strategic interests are its quid pro quo. But a far more interesting picture opens up when the traditional elite's political views are replaced by a localised perspective focused on civil society and everyday life. With the exception of major gains in security, this is where the liberal state project has proven the weakest. This contrast is nowhere more evident than in the hinterlands of Cambodia as compared to its enclaved capital, the main site of its new state 'politics'. The institutional setting of a liberal democracy is visible as also are the trappings of a developing market economy. Further away from the capital, its limited reach, cultural difference and predominantly subsistence economy is far more visible.

So, the simplistic claim of a linear progress of the liberal peace project from a conservative to an emancipatory graduation is not evident. Instead, what can be observed is a multiple speed, geographical model where certain locations mirror the liberal state while others reflect a pre-liberal, feudal or subsistence polity. This 'uneven development' might spread outwards from its centre, or instead it might merely represent a façade in a virtual peace situation, where an orthodox liberal peace exists for elites and for the capital, while a conservative liberal peace or a completely different form of polity exists for more peripheral others. In the cultural setting of provincial and rural Cambodia, it is hard to see where the years of liberal peacebuilding have made an impression in terms of institutions, development and everyday life. This suggests an alternative form of polity – or indeed peace – is in existence, representing a peace marginally connected to the liberal peace model, but also separate, and one that tolerates inequalities, a lack of opportunities and a lack of human security. Local customary, societal and cultural dynamics associated with local configurations of power, knowledge, resources and institutions are unaccounted for by this rather naive teleology. Even so, liberal peacebuilding automatically assumes it carries the technical and normative legitimacy to bring peace – although this is a western, liberal, state-centric narrative of peace with all of its related ethical meta-narratives.

These have not been completely meaningless in the Cambodian context, but they are far from institutionalised or internalised. Cambodia has had reasonably successful elections, and it has established a working government, but neither reflect the intentions of international peacebuilders, who have been forced into uncomfortable relationships with rather undemocratic processes and actors, and an authoritarian, not to mention corrupt, elite. Advances have emerged, but not in the manner expected by internationals. Civil society is developing, though mainly in spaces and styles determined by internationals and the NGO community they sponsor and can view. A human rights consciousness is emerging. Thus, a hybrid form of peace exists which incorporates the components of the liberal peace at a level perhaps not appreciated by international actors and very strongly modified by its local context, social and power configurations, and cultural norms. This is modified most strongly by an authoritarian streak that runs through politics, and the weakness of economic development, which means that a vast cross-section of society remains politically and economically marginal to the state project.

Given that Cambodia represents one of the longest-standing post-Cold War peacebuilding 'experiments', the liberal peace model and its progressive graduations should have proceeded from the conservative end of the liberal spectrum to an orthodox or more emancipatory liberal peace. This is not to say that much has not been achieved, but there are no grounds to believe that the Cambodian polity has progressed from a conservative version of the liberal peace to an orthodox version. Politics is still undemocratically contested, poverty is rife, human rights regimes are weak, development is limited, and the free market, despite drawing in limited foreign investment, still works against the localised economy and the vast bulk of its members, rather than for them. Deep wounds from the conflict have persisted, and there are still border tensions, particularly with Thailand. This does not represent a self-sustaining and orthodox version of the liberal peace, and it certainly does not represent an emancipatory project. Instead, it represents very uncomfortable compromises: the state houses a still a very fragile polity upon which the peacebuilding community should reflect, especially if the legitimacy of the peace project that Cambodia has been part of is to remain.

Fundamental problems exist in reconciling the Cambodian polity to the orthodox liberal peace model, which is what one would expect to have been achieved after almost two decades of the liberal peace project there. The vast majority of its population have not seen such associated benefits, though of course they have received the basic peace dividend of a stable security situation, even if this has not translated into much progress in the broader realm of human security. What is notable is that there are still deep-rooted issues, factors and dynamics that have not yet been addressed, many related to local societal and socio-economic issues rather than merely technical, bureaucratic, political or institutional factors. Local contextualisations of the liberal peace almost seem to be absent, since there is a two-speed peace, pseudo-liberal at the elite and institutional level, and very basic or virtual for most parts of society. Perhaps the latter may be more accurately termed a liberal–local hybrid. Ultimately, the focus has been on building the state rather than a social contract. The institutions of the state have been a priority after security, and thus the universal contractual nature of the liberal peace ideal – as a system derived from citizenship – has been lost. It might even be said that the latter is not in the interests of statebuilders, because it demands an ethical dimension to peacebuilding which empowers individual agency rather than a technocratic contest over statebuilding. The result has been the focus on political power as a zero-sum game, and a weak democratic process. This implies that either more time is required for the liberal peace project, or that it is terminally unsuited to non-liberal, non-western and non-developed environments. It may well be that focus on the territorially sovereign state could be moderated by an enhanced legitimacy through closer attention to building a social contract. Or, that the aims of peacebuilding might be better addressed through a far more contexutalised approach that does not rest solely on liberalism, but on bottom-up approaches that engage with highly localised versions of needs and rights.

What has emerged is a virtual liberal peace, as outlined in Richmond's earlier interrogation of the liberal peace.[2] Chandler has termed this 'peace without politics', and others have pointed to quasi or shadow states.[3] This has the advantage of allowing international intervention, conditionality and dependency creation, as well as a demonstration of the supposed superiority of the liberal state model. The trouble is that this lacks a meaningful connection with the local, the cultural and needs of everyday life. If these later aims could be achieved – as the emancipatory and civil strands of the liberal peace aim to create – then the peace would be much more stable and sustainable.

Instead, because of material and coordination issues, and because of wide-ranging local resistance or marginal levels of cooperation, the international community appears to have adopted a conservative version of the liberal peace in the Cambodian context, focusing on security, state and institutions, and wary of more orthodox or emancipatory ambitions. This limited approach has almost automatically had the effect of undermining the liberal project, laying it open to easy accusations of hypocrisy, western interests and ideology, and biopolitical governmentalism aimed against the non-western/liberal other. The effect has been to create an authoritarian virtual state, and one which has little impact on civil society, or concern with indigenous patterns of politics other than to demonise them, or with needs as well as rights. This might be recognisably liberal from the perspective of the international community, but it does little in the way of achieving a liberal social contract or of inviting the loyalty and support of its social, political and economic groups. Such a top-down process rests on the imposition of external norms and defers executive and administrative functions. Empty liberal institutions coexist with semi-feudalism, free market reform with corruption, acute poverty and subsistence, while accountability, human rights and the rule of law struggle to emerge. This has led to a 'virtual liberal peace hybrid', rather than a liberal–local hybrid, which is a phenomenon comprised of a superficial overlay of the liberal peace. This prioritises experts, functionaries, and executors and elites over local indigenous norms, needs, culture and tradition in both negative and positive forms. A very conservative version of the liberal peace exists as a result indicative of its elite-level hijacking, of acute poverty and corruption, as well as limited human rights and rule of law. There are prospects of progress towards a more orthodox graduation of the liberal peace, but this depends on these problems being addressed, which looks to be a very difficult task.

This assessment of the 'liberal experiment' in Cambodia indicates the need for a much more reflective international role in peacebuilding, as opposed to merely liberal peacebuilding or statebuilding, and in particular a more symbiotic, transparent, accountable and unscripted relationship of the full range of peacebuilding actors with local actors (and not just elite local actors). These openings need to allow for a consideration of how the current practices associated with the liberal peace are a virtual front for statebuilding, which unfortunately but actively defers the many benefits that would legitimise peace for its citizens.

East Timor: Capacity, Poverty, Welfare and the State

The events in East Timor represent a very poignant validation and critique of the liberal peacebuilding project. It was clear that self-determination, self-government and statehood were widely accepted in East Timor by those who wanted to see the end of Indonesian rule. When the peacebuilding and statebuilding project finally began, after the turmoil and violence of 1999, there seemed to be a wide, local and strong basis for success after the violent withdrawal of Indonesian troops and of pro-Indonesian militias. This smooth progression towards statehood appeared to be confirmed for the new state of Timor Leste in May 2002. As became clear, building the infrastructure of a state was not enough to contain violence related to very basic and well-known problems with respect to political competition, the control of institutions such as the army or police, unemployment and poverty. The experience of East Timor marks the end of widespread acceptance that neoliberal states were suitable responses to conflict, as recent government and World Bank policies on welfare and capital reforms illustrate,[4] though the blueprint transferral of the institutions of the liberal state and its aspirations for civil society remain intact.

The UN statebuilding mission was deemed a success in 'attaining self-sufficiency for East Timor' very prematurely.[5] Its failure was partly due to institutional deficits, but also because of its neoliberal economic and social implications, as well as cultural dissonance between Timorese identity groups and the new state. Indeed, it might well be that East Timor illustrates Wood's point that neoliberalism undermines many crucial areas of democracy and puts them beyond its reach.[6] As a result, the peacebuilding mission was scaled down in 2005 and was hoped to be fully completed by 2006. Instead, such deficiencies contributed to the violence of 2006, which brought the UN back to East Timor, causing a hasty reassessment by it, UNDP, the World Bank and other donors of their roles, the sustainability of liberal peacebuilding, priorities and timing.

Even so, the violent events of the spring of 2006 are generally portrayed as the result of disgruntled members of the Timorese armed forces (F-FDTL) claiming discrimination in the upper echelons of the organisation rather than relating them to the deeper divisions within the ruling party, Fretilin,[7] and within East Timor society, or to socio-economic difficulties. Belatedly, internationals have started to recognise that the roots of such political crises lie in chronic and deep-rooted problems that the liberal statebuilding project has so far failed to respond to, and in areas that it is ill-equipped to engage with. Such issues only really came to the attention of internationals when they caused open violence and a collapse in both the army and police force, which in turn led to the breakdown of law and order. Warning signs had been noticed, even by those contributing to the statebuilding operations, though they were not acted upon, probably because they had implications beyond the liberal, technocratic and biopolitical models (or fads) of the day. What emerged was a 'new' conflict and a further division within society between easterners and westerners.[8] The violence presented new opportunities for political manipulation, but for the most part was a damning statement on the lack of a social contract, the cultural dislocation of the new state, and chronic socio-economic problems.

It was belatedly recognised by the UN after the violence of early 2006 that the 'underlying causes' of the crisis were 'political and institutional'.[9] Yet this is a confusion of cause and response. Political and institutional reform had failed to address the actual underlying causes such as poverty, deprivation and long-term unemployment, as well as identity issues or the actual connection of the state to the epistemology, the local, or to the worldview of the Timorese communities. Such statements illustrate the near obsession with institutionalisation and the faith placed in institutional capacity to operate whatever the socio-economic, cultural or political circumstances are. This reflects the notion that they are universal and unalterable once in place, regardless of the local environment. East Timor once again demonstrates the need for viable institutions, but these cannot survive or sustain order without being vehicles, not merely for governance, but for the redress of basic needs and rights issues, and a contract amongst the citizens and the state – for their political agency, no less. Not addressing such root causes and basic needs and their connection with liberal institutional design, even after the failure of liberal peacebuilding in Timor, begins to look like western hypocrisy in such post-conflict and development settings, or at least a blind spot and ideological obsession. Events since 2006 also illustrate how easily lost gains in basic security are (this is common defence of those who support the liberal peace paradigm, claiming the 'alternative' would be much worse).

Liberal peacebuilding in East Timor has succeeded in creating only a virtual peace, which has had minimal impacts on everyday life, and though it has reduced violence it has not eradicated it. This might well be related to a number of other issues that emerged with the statebuilding project (and in our other cases, such as Kosovo) including local exclusion from the statebuilding project and the lack of local social and cultural legitimacy for the project overall – especially with the growing monopoly of power by Fretilin. The neglect of the socio-economic situation and social justice because of the imbalance of the free market and institutional priorities of the peacebuilding process left a mass of discontent in addition. Of course, these factors have undermined the social contract that the liberal state is supposed to be based upon, in a context where protest, resistance and violence have often been resorted to. As a result, a very conservative version of the liberal peace exists, mainly propped up by external intervention to prevent the dynamics of acute poverty, unemployment and political, cultural and ethnic contestation destroying the state. There is little prospect of progress under the current approach to peacebuilding towards a more orthodox category of the liberal peace. Indeed, any stability that exists currently can be attributed more to the more traditional patterns of social power and support systems that exist at the local level than to the state itself.

A major dynamic of this weakness has arisen through the damaging unintended consequences of neoliberal economic orthodoxy and its wholesale grafting onto the liberal peacebuilding agenda. Neoliberalism effectively takes many issue areas out of the democratic purview, and encourages the liberal institutionalist urge to replace local culture and identity with institutional design. This epistemology also negates the political significance of difference, needs and poverty, attempting to displace them with democracy, law, human rights and the market. Culture, needs and custom, and their relation to the liberal edifice of the state are far more significant in post-violence, development settings than has often been argued. They have been displaced by the commodification of needs in everyday life, and a focus on rights over needs. It is somewhat contradictory to claim that inalienable rights for citizens are open to interpretation according to local context but then to develop a liberal state that is based mainly on universality and internationally imported mechanisms. The claim for a similar set of inalienable needs rooted in the local context, but provided for by the same state and international mechanisms, is however, treated as implausible. Instead, needs are left to non-existent or dangerously distorted markets in post-conflict environments, thus undermining the very social contract and rights that citizens may have fought hard for.

In addition, this prevents the emergence of a social contract between the institutions created by liberal peacebuilding and the broader population (not to mention the international community). This means that while the state has some legitimacy as a national idea, even if power is contested as much as the 'idea' itself, some of the state's most basic representative, recognition and redistributive functions have failed. Here is where much of its legitimacy has been lost. So in the realms of regulation and freedoms, the state apparatus exists (if only on paper), but in the realms of representation, recognition and redistribution there is little capacity. Though this is now changing in Timor Leste, according the policies of the new government and a revised international approach, the failing is as much that of the internationals who themselves need to recognise the importance and immediacy of these areas of politics if a social contract is to be created and peace is not to be virtual. Perhaps the time has come to reassess the nature of the state in such transitional contexts and to look anew at human security in its broader senses, at human needs and dignity in an everyday rather than state context. Otherwise the state merely becomes (as has been bemoaned across sub-Saharan Africa) a vehicle for elite interests and predation. As we said in our chapter on Timor Leste, a clearer attempt to ask local people, not merely elites, what they want and how to achieve this in a more contextually 'authentic' manner would be a good starting point.

Bosnia: Local Politics, Sovereignty and Trusteeship

Bosnia and Herzegovina still remains ethnically polarised, with swirling separatist political agendas. The government is perceived by internationals to be weak and constantly deadlocked. Local politicians defer difficult decisions to internationals because they are unwilling to make any concessions on their positions. The Serb entity (RS) has continued its separate agendas, while Croat parties threaten to do the same. As a result, Bosnia-Herzegovina is an orphan of the international community's liberal ambitions, of the UN, OSCE and NATO, and now the EU. Such a wealth of actors and resources over more than a decade appear frustrated by the slow pace of reform in Bosnia, and by the local rejection of pluralism. Even the existence of a sovereign state is contested in some quarters – not least by RS, but also by those who claim that the lack of local ratification means that what does exist does not reflect localised legitimacy.

It is hard not to agree with this allusion to the centrifugal forces that seem to be at work. A weak, dependent and contested state exists, which is fragmented and diffuse. It may reflect a future possibility of a western-style, liberal democratic state, but this is certainly far from its current reality. The key tasks identified at the time of Dayton still remain: Bosnia is divided and polarised, its legitimacy is contested, as are its common institutions and borders.[10] There is not as yet a functioning liberal state, despite limited progress. Some argue that this has been held back by the attitudes and actions of the international community, while others place the blame on the shoulders of local political actors.[11] A familiar pattern has emerged across the Balkans, not least in Bosnia, which is to await the impact of the EU harmonisation and accession process, particularly in dealing with the twin issues of a lack of development and pluralism. It is clear that the relationship between international governance, the national/local political leadership and the Bosnian peoples is polarised, and there has been a growing tendency on the part of local actors to opt out of the liberal peacebuilding process. As a result, the causes of some aspects of the conflict are unresolved, and there is a fragile socio-economic and security environment.

There is a much bigger question here, running through all of our cases. It is apparent that many of the institutions or opportunities inherent in liberal peacebuilding are not taken up by elites or populations or at best are manipulated. The question is why, and what might be done to resolve this problem, which is damaging to the project of peacebuilding overall. In Bosnia, the usual mix of power-seeking rather than sharing, nationalism, predatory elites, poverty and cultural obstacles prevails over the liberal project. This is the paradox of local versus international ownership of the statebuilding process, whereby both levels wait for the other to take decisive actions required for progress, while both also effectively claim that sovereignty is needed by them to effect any real change. Thus the qualitative nature of the peace itself appears ambivalent about ordinary people's agency, and also about its own standards. More than ten years after Dayton there appears to be an underlying resistance to the liberal peace project, in terms of how it is run by external actors, what it suggests for Bosnia's boundaries, how it endeavours to ethnically categorise while instilling pluralism, and its lack of delivery of jobs and basic needs.

There has been constitutional failure and local elites may have actually benefitted from the political stagnation that has arisen from the Accords. Yet, their desire to engage with the EU also suggests that Bosnia has the potential to achieve an orthodox liberal state if elites can be weaned off their nationalist sentiments and the tendency towards separation can be dealt with. Even here, however, liberal peacebuilding continues to rest on elite politics (which are often predatory in different ways) rather than building a local social contract. This is the paradox of the trusteeship and devolving type approach that internationals have adopted in Bosnia. The failure to empower individual citizens in social, economic and cultural terms, has meant that liberal politics rests far away from them, and has made it extremely difficult for the Bosnian state to progress in the manner that international peacebuilders desire. Clearly, though, there is the potential for this to happen, but there is also similar potential for the Bosnian state to fall apart. Again, Bosnia has to be categorised as subject to a conservative version of the liberal peace, with the potential, albeit fragile, to progress towards the more orthodox category.

Kosovo: Liberal Peace, Statehood and Local Co-option

Though our previous cases have emphasised the contradictory and top-down nature of the liberal peace, and shown this to be often to the detriment of local needs, identity, customs and welfare, this does not mean that local political elites do not have agency. They have in fact the capacity to either block or co-opt the liberal peacebuilding process. In the case of Kosovo, because the preceding military inter-vention favoured the Kosovo Albanian victims over Serb forces, the subsequent peacebuilding operation provided more political oppor-tunities for them than for the Serbs. The Kosovo Albanians became adept at adopting the praxis of the liberal peace, and exploited the support, credibility and sympathy of the international community to construct their own state conforming to liberal 'standards', even though it was clear from very early on that the Serb population might not cooperate with its institutions. Since the peacebuilding operation was skewed towards the Kosovo Albanian community, their declara-tion of statehood, with strong support from the US, UK and other states, became the goal of their involvement in peacebuilding, leading to further secession becoming the potential goal of the Serbs' political strategy. Yet, this contravenes the basic pluralist and power-sharing expectations inherent in the liberal state, while the usual problems relating to international control of much of the political process, ethnic politics and high unemployment remained, though the latter were less significant than what had become a race for sovereignty and recognition. Peacebuilding in Kosovo essentially became a race for power and statehood, and marginalisation for other internal identity groups and their agendas.

The situation in Kosovo is far from an orthodox liberal peace as intended by international actors, especially with their 'standards before status' approach.[12] Kosovo Albanian officials and actors took the state-in-waiting they were handed, and used it to develop their own claims for sovereignty, regardless of regional implications and international dissensus. In these specialised circumstances, resting on the overt support of the US and many European states, statehood and sovereignty were placed before a qualitative peace, meaning that little more than a virtual peace came into being, and a new round of violence, displacement, population movements and border skirmishes might easily break out. Root causes have not been addressed, and the liberal state package has divided and categorised the populace in ways that reproduced political and ethnic tensions rather than placating them.

This indicates a paradox in the current attempt of the peacebuilding and statebuilding community to resolve such deficiencies via more local ownership, custodianship and local participation. If this occurs in a manner which favours specific elites, ethnic groups, social groups or general populations, then it simply becomes another, albeit more sophisticated, mechanism via which the conflict continues, and original prenegotiation objects may well continue to be significant in this process. The material, intellectual, philosophical and methodological resources of the liberal peacebuilding/statebuilding nexus are the armaments of this process. Indeed, it may well be that the virtual peace and empty states so far produced in contexts such as Kosovo, Cambodia or Bosnia (to varying degrees) are beneficial in this continuing contest that blurs the boundaries between liberal peace, liberal war and political violence, structural or otherwise. The very concepts of liberalism, pluralism, multi-ethnicity, democracy, human rights, development and marketisation, and the rule of law, have taken on overtones relating to their subtle manipulation and bias towards one group or another, often adjudicated by unaccountable (and often ill-informed, whether in terms of the balance of information or methodological bias they relate to) international personnel, policymakers and officials. The liberal peace in Kosovo has hence become implicated in the ethnic, sovereign and territorial dynamics of inclusion and exclusion, cooperation and rejection, and there is little space for democratic politics in between these positions. Perhaps the mitigating effects of the EU may unravel these conflictual dynamics, but this would depend upon coordinated policies from the EU being implemented across the region. So far the signs for this do not bode well and as peacebuilding has collapsed into the Kosovo Albanian project of statehood, so too may EU accession.

As a result, peacebuilding in Kosovo has become statebuilding, and is mainly located at the conservative end of the liberal peace spectrum. The potential to progress to the orthodox graduation would be plausible if the Serb community could be brought into local politics (along with their international supporters) and the current self-declared state entity and its supporters became amenable to the pluralism this implies. Until this happens, it is very unlikely that Kosovo will represent a success for liberal peacebuilding. Liberal politics in the region rests upon the defence of mutually exclusive identities and concurrent institutions within which 'liberalism' is acted out in connection with international, rather than local, actors.

The Middle East: Two Liberal States?

This case study is very different to our other cases in that there has been no formal peacebuilding operation, though of course there have been long-standing attempts towards a formal peace process, and towards statebuilding for the Palestinian entity, as well as the involvement of a range of actors who are also instrumental in the liberal peacebuilding consensus (i.e. the US, UK, various donors and agencies, and the EU). We included this case in this book because we were interested in how far the liberal state model was being deployed in contexts where the key liberal peacebuilding actor – the UN – did not have access for political reasons, and whether the same normative framework that has been instrumental in the praxis of liberal statebuilding might apply in a more tenuous type of peace process: seemingly a more traditional high level diplomatic, security and territorially oriented approach. We have found this to be the case, though the tools through which liberal processes are inculcated in the Middle East are far more limited because of the lack of a coordinated peacebuilding project – apart from the post-Oslo period where the Palestinian Authority (PA) was enticed along this road for a while at least.

Though the Middle East has been exceptional in the broader liberal peacebuilding/statebuilding project, liberal expectations and conditionalities have been present. This is apparent in the fact that 'peace' has been constructed as a zero-sum concept by the political and military elites of the region. Thus, as opposed to the orthodox or emancipatory versions of the liberal peace, it has been perceived as highly militarised, centralised, discriminatory and privileging certain groups and their internal solidarity – even a form of 'apartheid' and commensurate with a conservative version of the liberal peace. This conservative version has resulted in broader nationalist, linguistic, ethnic, cultural and religious cleavages, which provide the basis for the organisation of politics. These politics, it has been claimed, are actually liberal, at least when they are looked at within the borders of the identity group – whether Jewish or Arab. This claim does not stand much scrutiny, especially given that the key aim of the liberal peace is regional peace and stability as its primary goals with domestic order and peace following in a secondary position. This approach explains the regional and local securitisation of the Middle East.

Yet, in this acutely conflictual and heavily securitised territorial framework, the most recent strategy has been to follow the logic of liberal statebuilding in its territorial and normative form. This means that the normative framework of orthodox liberalism, including pluralism, representation, human rights and prosperity, is present but has been made secondary to security and territorial boundaries. This more conservative and traditional form of the liberal state is an unlikely place to look for a solution to one of modernity's longest standing conflicts.

There is a certain asymmetry in this more conservative approach. As there is no coordinated international peacebuilding mission, it rests on diplomacy, mediation and negotiation, which themselves rest on the balance of power and asymmetry in resources and recognition between the main actors. The general assumption that Israel is a liberal state while the PA is subject to all of the usual non-liberal proclivities that mark such entities, also skews any attempt at building peace, reproducing the general securitisation of the peacebuilding and statebuilding projects in the Middle East. This is probably why the various 'peaces' that Israel has so far been party to with its Arab neighbours have not facilitated liberal institutions, but instead have rested on high-level diplomatic processes, ceasefires, demarcation of boundaries and recognition. These are the sorts of dynamics reminiscent of an earlier epoch of peace agreements, focusing on the bare minimum of a negative peace rather than the more positive forms of peace that the liberal peacebuilding framework claims to offer. The regional or international claims attributed to the liberal peace are only faintly present in this region. However, it is generally thought that as Israel is at least a minimally liberal state, though limited by its security restrictions, this dynamic will have a knock on effect in pacifying the region. Without international organisations being present in a more direct manner, however, this has very limited potential and the post 9/11 period has been particularly difficult, especially in the light of the possibilities in the 1990s post Oslo, which appeared to point far beyond the conservative version of the liberal peace. Thus, the creation of a two-liberal-state solution looks more like partition, being non-pluralist and accentuating nationalism and other forms of 'national identity', rather than a viable and consensual settlement of the conflict. This confirms the dynamics identified in Bosnia and Kosovo relating to the divisive side effects of the liberal state model and its inability to promote pluralism over identity, ethnicity and religion.

Thus, the liberal peace framework has not been able to find a foothold in the Middle East, nor has the peace process produced the results that were expected after Oslo. This is why it does not compare well with the liberal peacebuilding missions elsewhere even despite their weaknesses. It is perplexing as to why internationals have not developed greater access to the Middle East given their claims as to the universal validity of the liberal peace model. The ability of the Israeli government to shape the peace process explains why the focus has been not on the liberal peace as such, especially in its orthodox or emancipatory terms, but rather on its conservative and securitised form, and on regional stability rather than domestic reform. It has also selectively focused on the liberalisation of Palestinian institutions and norms as the pathway by which the liberal peace transition might reconstruct a region based on formal territorially sovereign states. Thus, the focus of peacebuilding is on institutions and state boundaries, in a context where both are so heavily contested in multiple ways that chances of peace on these terms are slim. In the meantime, the needs *and* rights of peoples are postponed or simply ignored, even though rights in our other cases have often been a key concern (while needs have been secondary). It might well be argued that the bias of liberal statebuilding exacerbates the roots of the conflict and heightens its local costs in this context, moving statebuilding far away from the objectives of peacebuilding, and even of liberal peacebuilding (if it is taken that liberal peacebuilding aims to achieve an orthodox or even emancipatory goal). Indeed, the statebuilding project and its liberal institutions may even provide a reason or excuse as to why peace still so distant.

This is the basis for the more radical argument we outlined in our chapter on the Middle East: that such dynamics are the indirect or even direct result of the liberal peacebuilding and statebuilding project, and not commensurate with peacebuilding as a needs-based, grass-roots oriented process. The conservative graduation of the liberal peace is a compromise on outright war and the orthodox graduation but does not actually have to induce a progression along the linear liberal peace spectrum towards a more emancipatory position. In this sense, and contrary to the cases we examined in the Balkans, the conservative graduation of the liberal peace has protected the legal, diplomatic, military and territorial status of a pre-existing claim of sovereignty. The basis of the liberal peace is inherently state-centric, replicating its territorial and identity based patterns of inclusion and exclusion, rather than reconciliation and social justice often assumed to be inherent in orthodox and emancipatory liberal thinking about peace. Here, the 'victor's peace' seems to be a more apt description.

This illustrates the key problem of liberal modernity as conceptualised in mainstream theoretical and policy-related international relations, statebuilding and peacebuilding literatures: can it coexist and indeed cooperate with a hybrid system representing other identities or cultures? In the case of the Middle East, would this mean an engagement with non-liberal versions of peace, even an 'Islamic peace model'? Otherwise, the liberal peace appears in a comparative context to be representative of external interests rather than those of its local citizens – the post-conflict individuals. Thus, what has somewhat predictably emerged is that liberal strategies of peacebuilding, where they have occurred, have favoured what has already been identified as a liberal state (Israel) and called for significant reform from non-state non-liberal, actors (the Palestinian entity) in order to become a recognised state in its own right. But this version of the peace process has been blocked by the fact that the way the state is conceptualised, even in its liberal form, means agreement on boundaries, territory, and of course its capital, as well as its political framework (not to mention the general reluctance to countenance new state formation). Thus, it is inextricably tied up in the contest of identities in the region and in conflicts between the way politics and justice are understood by disputants. While there may well be a mutual agreement on democracy, human rights, the rule of law and the state as the vehicle required for such norms and institutions, the liberal peace has simultaneously sustained old and unresolved issues (indeed, these may be termed the root causes of the conflict itself).

If the peace process in the Middle East is a tenuous example of liberal peacebuilding and of viable statebuilding, it places the process at its most conservative end, barring the actual use of force or pre-emptive war (as in Iraq or Afghanistan). Indeed, it is most clearly an example of a victor's peace upon which division and sovereignty becomes the basis for liberal, rather than local, states. Here, the paradox of the liberal peace – as a security oriented, territorially defined state, where democracy, the rule of law, human rights and development are crucial but secondary – becomes most clear. Reconciliation, justice and needs (as well as rights) represent the most obvious gaps in this version of the liberal peace project.

Comparison of the Five Cases

All of our five cases represent long-standing laboratories for different aspects and styles of liberal peacebuilding. The priority has been regional stability and local security, inducing elite-level compromises, and building the institutions of the liberal state housed in internationally recognised sovereign states. These dynamics are common to all of the cases. Yet none of these goals has been comprehensively achieved. In none of these cases – chosen as a fairly representative sample of the whole chronology of post-Cold War liberal peacebuilding – can there be said to be much more than a negative peace, focused on the conservative end of the liberal spectrum. This is not to negate all of the important efforts that have so far been made. Indeed, it is clear that more effort and engagement is needed, in the context of a more sensitised and contextual understanding of each case. This points to the fact that a comprehensive pattern across such a sample gives rise to some telling questions, not least about the models that have been deployed and the mechanisms that have been employed. In each case, international or dominant local elite actors have moved towards more coordination, efficiency, conditionality and more coercion in order to smooth the path to the creation of the liberal state. This, we argue is a problematic turn. What is required is actually a much more context-specific peacebuilding operation leading to a more locally 'authentic' polity which houses the institutions necessary for democracy, self-determination, the rule of law, human rights and prosperity, rather than a blueprint state and the resulting top-down statebuilding project.

In each of our cases, a state has been built, perhaps with the exception of the Palestinian case, and basic but fragile security has been achieved (again with the Palestinian exception). This has been frequently upset by incidents, major or minor, and has generally represented a very narrow form of security rather than institutionalised human security. In each, democratic institutions have been formed, but in none have they worked in the manner internationals intended: they have generally converted violent conflict into political conflict. In each a rule of law has slowly been established, but one that is often biased towards a set of elite actors, or is not completely enforceable or consensual because of the incapacity of the judicial system, the failure to engage with customary practices, or limitations in the provision of security. Respectively, institutions for human rights have been developed, though in each, with only limited effect, often because of a conflict between the imported form of liberal individualism and the common local tendency towards a community orientation and patronage. In all cases, marketisation has been introduced and development strategies put in place that have failed to reduce unemployment, subsistence or even poverty. In all of these cases, these strategies have failed to make a major difference to the everyday life of the general population affected by conflict. In each of these cases, attempts have been made to support and develop a civil society, but this has generally had very limited effects in an environment of structural (and sometimes overt) violence, and in the face of elite predation or co-option of the political process. Civil society remains an internationally supported artifice of liberal norms rather than a locally rooted expression of a social contract or of political, social and economic agency. All of these cases combine political instability and conflict with low levels of development, with poverty, with non-liberal cultures, with anti-democratic practices, and with the tendency of international engagement to be limited to formal peace process and institutions in a sovereign context.

In each case, there have been major incidents of violence, of corruption, or obvious resistance to liberal institutions or their co-option that risked – without external intervention at least – the viability of the liberal state itself. As a result, poverty has continued, development has failed to significantly improve citizens' prospects, and the gap between elites and citizens has significantly increased rather than reduced. Gains have been relative to a very low original base and generally are seen as marginal by those who have experienced them. The overall balance sheet offers some prospects for progress but shows very limited progress so far, as well as the continuing fragility of the peace that has been induced. This sheds doubts on the universal legitimacy and effectiveness of the liberal peace project as well as on the capacities of the liberal state when introduced in violent and non-liberal contexts, where sovereignty, territory, society, politics and the economy are locally regarded in very different ways.

Thus, liberal peace transitions effectively appear to be more about a 'transition' to statehood and regional stability than about the norms and institutions of the liberal peace and their implications for the post-conflict individual; they are indeed far from producing an emancipatory form of peace. What is common to these transitions are the following:

1. Sudden political violence, low levels of security, the proliferation of militias and small arms;
2. limited security provided by national armies and police forces – some compensation by international forces;
3. justification of liberal peacebuilding processes and progress based upon its offer of a future security, self-determination, democracy, rule of law, human rights and prosperity;
4. the blurring of peacebuilding into liberal peacebuilding and again into statebuilding;
5. a focus on the state, recognition and territorial sovereignty;
6. an international civil service taking up key political and economic roles;
7. an international move towards forms of trusteeship as problems mount;
8. poor international coordination;
9. an international rejection of the significance of causal factors (root causes) outside of the liberal and neoliberal conceptual framework;
10. a focus on the liberal peace and a one-size-fits-all form of conflict resolution;
11. little connection between the state, internationals and local communities' customary practices and tradition; no social contract;
12. very limited progress as defined according to the criteria inherent in the liberal peace;
13. international 'draw downs' based on faulty evaluations of 'success';
14. frequent relapses into violence, often termed 'state failure' or 'state fragility';
15. democratic weakness, political stalemate;
16. corruption, elite predation;
17. poor human rights records;
18. a disabled or virtually absent civil society;
19. the dictat of international donor funding cycles and of international interest;
20. a weak rule of law;

21. poor or absent welfare systems;
22. a limited effect of development strategies;
23. an international tendency to blame local elites or citizens;
24. an international tendency to overplay local difference and identities;
25. a simultaneous international tendency to ignore local voices;
26. local criticisms of the distant position of internationals and international prejudice against local actors;
27. ever-extending 'transitions';
28. the emergence out of all of these problems of a quasi-liberal polity connected to but deviating from the internationals' liberal state model, displaying local cultural and also local pre-conflict qualities; in other words a hybrid local-liberal peace.

Many of the above problems illustrate the limited reach of liberal peacebuilding. They should not be read as an invitation for peacebuilding to become more biopolitical and governmentalising, as some have argued (especially via a recourse to force, illiberalism, conditionality, and anti-democratic and anti-self-determination processes). Social engineering in already very fraught social environments by outside actors with very limited local knowledge and with off-the-shelf peacebuilding systems (of a problem-solving nature) that are designed to maintain a limited connection with the local, and in fact to distance the local, are not destined to make very much progress in our view.

The above analysis allows for a more relevant and plausible evaluation of the situations in the cases we have examined than that often carried out by internationals. Such an evaluation is more attuned to context and so to sustainability. For example, looking at the poor record of liberal peacebuilding in the Middle East generally raises the issue of whether this approach can really achieve a hybrid system, which in this case would mean a combination with a non-liberal version or Islamic model of peace. This requires the liberal peace to adopt maximum flexibility and a notion of emancipation that crosses liberal boundaries and concerns itself more with state or polities that reproduce contextual rights and needs (though we acknowledge this distinction is itself blurred), not merely liberal rights. This is also the case in the post-socialist contexts of our two Balkan cases, where social memories of a political system oriented towards reproducing a form of social justice reflect poorly on the contemporary liberal and neoliberal contexts. In the post-colonial contexts of East Timor and

Cambodia, and though the aspirations for self-determination were so great in both, even internal pluralism and liberal-local hybridity look doubtful (as is also to a lesser degree the case in the Balkans) given the tensions between political elites and between local identity groups – as well as the unattuned approaches of internationals who are intent on liberal statebuilding. In these contexts, the elite compromises that have arisen make the liberal peace appear to be an ideology of state security and western hegemony merely camouflaged by claims of emancipation and universal rights. This is not the case, at least consciously, but a local perception of such a dynamic provides powerful ammunition in local party and democratic political processes. These later then become the medium through which the liberal state maybe locally rejected or modified to reinclude pre-existing political praxis. In such circumstances, the outcome has been the tendency towards a division and fragmentation of the liberal state, so that separate identity groups and their elites can enjoy the privileges of a separate rather than mutual peace. Along with the virtual state that liberal peace-building creates, there also emerge 'non states' which represent the interests of certain groups, often ideologically opposed to liberalism, but accepting and even simulating the notions of statehood and sovereignty. These hang in international limbo, neither providing a functioning state economically nor making the latter capable of affording protection to its people. These entities are dominated by established elites and often follow extremist and nationalist agendas, actively able to subvert the process of democratisation. They are even undeterred by the internationals who seek a political class that can guarantee a minimum of security and a maximum of some form of liberal state institutions. The unintended but perhaps natural outcome for the liberal peace model has been to create divisions and exclusivity as the basis for (re)inclusion into the international state system. As in other cases, the partition of polities, communities and territory has become the basis for 'peace' in its most conservative, if liberal, form. The framework is also biased towards existing states, as we have seen. Its primary objective is security and the maintenance of the international status quo and international system. Tables C.1 and C.2 and Figure C.1 sketch positive and negative aspects of this framework according to liberal claims and actual outcomes during the short, medium and long term.

Table C.1 Who benefits from the liberal peace and when? (short term – from start of peacebuilding for first year; medium term – second year to fifth year; long term – sixth year onwards)

	Claimed	Actual
Actors/Level of analysis		
Security sector	Liberalising actors in the short, medium and long term	Very easily undermined by political violence from fringe and splinter groups
Arrival/presence of internationals	General population in the short to long term	Requires long-term engagement
Political and economic elites	Immediately, as long as they liberalise	Immediately, but liberalisation is not crucial
Civil society	In the short to medium term	Medium to long term
Local society/customary	Relative benefits, immediately	Medium- and long-term benefits marginal and depending on liberalisation rather than local context
Dynamics of the liberal peace/statebuilding		
Democratisation	All liberal actors in medium to long term	Illiberal actors can use democracy for nationalist or sectarian objectives in short to long term
Rule of law	Those with access in the short to long term	Difficulties in establishing RoL, and lack of capacity and access means that customary processes often continue into the long term
Development	Everyone from short term	Mainly elites in any time frame
Free markets	Elites in the short/ medium term; everyone in the long term	Everyone in the long term? Marginal in short to medium term

Conclusion: First Steps towards Revitalising a Virtual Peace

Against the background of our case studies, we conclude that what is needed is the development of a praxis of post-liberal peacebuilding (potentially utilising the eirenist approaches to IR and to peacebuilding that Richmond has detailed elsewhere).[13] These would be designed to capitalise on the core of the original conflict resolution

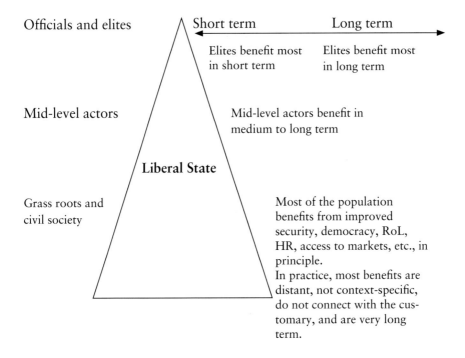

Officials and elites   Short term   Long term

Elites benefit most in short term   Elites benefit most in long term

Mid-level actors   Mid-level actors benefit in medium to long term

Liberal State

Grass roots and civil society

Most of the population benefits from improved security, democracy, RoL, HR, access to markets, etc., in principle.
In practice, most benefits are distant, not context-specific, do not connect with the customary, and are very long term.

Figure C.1 Beneficiaries in liberal states (RoL, rule of law; HR, human rights)

and peacebuilding agendas, addressing needs and root causes, connecting the new liberal state or polity with older, locally recognisable and contextual, customary, political, social and economic traditions, and engaging with grass roots and the most marginalised members of post-conflict polities. This would require a mediation between the local and the international over peacebuilding praxis and social, political and economic practices that both deem plausible and acceptable, rather than a wholesale top-down imposition of an only putatively universal liberal model – the virtual liberal peace. This would enable the development of a post-liberal form of peacebuilding that would counterbalance the core of liberal peacebuilding with the local as well as its needs and cultural patterns. But this would not be to romanticise the local and its capacity for conflict resolution or its dysfunctionality, but rather to enable it to engage in 'unscripted conversations' about what peacebuilding might entail.[14] Rather than representing either an international or even a local bias towards the interests of local elites, this would instead be predicated upon an intimate understanding of everyday life and individual political

Table C.2 Benefits and limitations of liberal peacebuilding

Short term	Long term
Beneficiaries/benefits	
Political elites linked to new state/ internationals	Political elites linked to new state/ internationals
Population affected by security issues	Population affected by security issues
State and government actors, civil service	State and government actors, civil service
Feudal and tribal/clan organisations, warlords, political/ethnic entrepreneurs	Slowly increasing proportion of the population as reform, institutionalisation and development trickles down – but only for a limited proportion of the population
Nationalists, extremists, militias brought into peace process immediately	Warlords, political entrepreneurs, militias, nationalists, extremists, etc. enter the peace process over time
NGO/civil society sector	Civil society and reformed/liberalised traditional culture processes and practices may become recognised
Grey and black markets, legal economy in urban areas may boom	Legal economy may develop and increase in size
Limitations	
Warlords, political entrepreneurs, militias, nationalists, extremists not brought into peacebuilding	Incorrigible actors who deploy violence for extreme ideological ends are excluded but may continue to block progress
The state and institutions are 'empty', unable to provide public service, welfare, or redistribute resources	This remains in the long term unless the state gains resources (i.e. has oil, minerals, etc.)
Populations remote from capital where most internationals are based often remain marginal	Urbanisation occurs in a search for employment, but rural populations remain marginal
Population's welfare not directly engaged with by internationals	Marketisation and development fail to bring general benefits
Traditional culture processes and practices marginalised	Traditional culture processes and practices may become part of limited peacebuilding hybrid
Feudal and tribal/clan organisations are marginalised	Feudal and tribal/clan organisations re-enter peacebuilding
The poor are marginalised by neoliberal ideology, and tendency towards centralised state run by political elites	The poor benefit from democracy (may vote for redistributive measures), human rights, and improved RoL but these remain limited
Nationalists, extremists, etc. may harness liberal institutions	Grey and black markets remain significant, as does subsistence and unemployment

agency and needs in each context, and what a peaceful everyday life might be facilitated by. This might involve liberal peacebuilders facing up to some unpalatable truths about how bias towards geopolitical interests and limited understandings of peace undermine peacebuilding and replicate violence, and would entail some radical shifts of emphasis, not least from a blind faith in the power of political rights and the market for the provision for everyday needs and a better understanding of customary practices.[15] This post-liberal peace, representing a liberal-local hybrid and an interface between the two, would also be constantly called upon to reflect on its own interests and assumptions, and rather than to distance itself ethically and materially from the local, to do quite the reverse.

What has actually emerged in all of our cases is a local hybrid form of the international version of the liberal peace. This may surprise those who regard the local as dysfunctional, the international as ill-coordinated, and the outcome as normally a failed state. Instead, what are emerging are polities in the making, with connections between both the liberal and the local (though both appear to largely resist rather than welcome each other).[16] Both are struggling to find ways of retaining their integrity while also developing relations with each other. So far this hybrid is created through mutual resistance and aversion, rather than the open process of negotiation we envisage a local–liberal hybrid could enable. Rather than promoting the locality of this hybrid, internationals have generally resisted it, and attempted to refine the capacity of the liberal peace to engineer peace in its own image rather than accepting and working on this hybrid form of peace. The latter takes the form of international support for local institutions, for local elites, turning a blind eye to their predations, accepting the focus on state institutions, on rights over needs. It generally hybridises power patterns by not engaging with local culture or needs in the short term at least. Thus, this hybrid looks more like an internationally supported authoritarian state supplanted over a poor and chaotic local polity, rather than a developed liberal state. The bias towards territorial statehood rather than to the formation of local polities adds yet more tension to this process. Yet, local actors, social movements and an embryonic civil society have also been able to exert some agency, ranging from resistance to the liberal peace project, to active calls for its nationalisation, and also to its co-option. But the liberal project forces local voices to adopt such strategies by scripting their reactions and interactions. It is no wonder that all of our cases are frozen at the conservative end of the liberal peace spectrum with limited prospects for progress to the orthodox outcome most internationals have worked assiduously to develop. This means they remain dependent upon international support, and display acute conflictual tendencies internally, raising questions about the success of liberal peacebuilding: what is it really? Does it mean a liberal state or a liberal-local hybrid polity? What is the role of the interface between the two (i.e. international peacebuilding)? How is a virtual peace avoided? How might liberal peacebuilding move beyond this and produce something more than a virtual peace?

Critical policies for a post-liberal peace might thus engage with the following:

1. a detailed understanding (rather than co-option or 'tolerance') of local culture, traditions and ontology; and acceptance of peace-building as an empathetic, emancipatory process, focused on individual political agency, everyday care, human security and a social contract between society and the government, which acts as a provider of care rather than merely security;
2. in addition, a peacebuilding contract between internationals and local actors that reflects this social contract;
3. thinking about peace beyond the liberal state mechanism (rather than using peace to propagate liberal states);
4. 'local-local' ownership of a local, regional and global process of peacemaking, or of an agreement;
5. local decision-making processes to determine the basic political, economic and social processes and norms to be institutionalised;
6. international support for these processes, guidance on technical aspects of governance and institution building without introducing hegemony, inequality, conditionality or dependency;
7. an economic framework, focusing on welfare and empowerment of the most marginalised, should be determined locally. Internationals may assist in free market reform and marketisation/privatisation not on the basis of external expert knowledge but on local consensus, but they should also introduce a socioeconomic safety net immediately to bind citizens and labour to a peaceful polity (rather than to war-making, a grey/black economy, or transnational criminal activities). Otherwise, neoliberalism clearly undermines any social contract and leads to a counterproductive class system;
8. any peacebuilding process must cumulatively engage with everyday life, custom, care and empathy, as well as institutions;

9. points 1–8 should result in a process whereby a hybrid, possibly indigenous peace is installed that includes a version of human rights, rule of law, and a representative political process that reflects the local groupings and their agency and ability to create consensus, as well as broader international expectations for peace (but not alien 'national' interests).

To some extent, this reflects the liberal peace but in a localised, contextual and hybridised form. It might also be said to represent the local. It emphasises the need to construct and translate local consensus before intervention, and so the emergence of a hybrid and post-liberal peace. What this also means is that peacebuilding actors themselves must be subject to a set of requirements to prevent them from treating every case as the same, from depoliticising rather than repoliticising, and to actualise or at least simulate a social contract between internationals and local populations. This needs to rest on contextuality, locality and custom, to provide the emerging polity with authenticity with the groups who matter to it most – its citizens. The above agenda requires the following from peacebuilding actors:

1. A recognition and translation of political agency, of care, empathy, welfare and a consideration of everyday life as the basis of a social contract required between societies, emerging post-conflict polities and internationals.
2. Peacebuilding actors should not work from blueprints but should develop strategies based upon multilevel consultation in each case. They should develop relations with local partners that reach as far as possible in a local society, enabling grass-roots representation. They should endeavour to see themselves as mediatory agents (the interface between the liberal and the local) whereby their role is to mediate the global norm or institution with the local norm before it is constructed. Hence, academics and peacebuilding policy makers should avoid overstating the applicability of blueprint-type models, but instead engage more with local knowledge in an empathetic manner.
3. Peacebuilding actors should also operate at a minimum on the basis of the norms and systems they are trying to instil, such as democracy, equality, social justice, etc. Theorists and policymakers cannot ever be beyond ethics, and must acknowledge the reflexive qualities and responsibilities of peacebuilding, and the tensions these produce.

4. Theorists and peacebuilding actors need to move from an institutional peace-as-governance agenda to an alternative, or at least additional, everyday agenda. Putting communities first entails a rethinking of the priorities of peace. In terms of peacebuilding, this would place contextual agency and human needs, particularly economic and security needs, before free market reform, and in parallel to democracy, second-generation human rights and a rule of law that protects the citizen and not mainly wealth and property. This would probably require the creation of social welfare-oriented peacebuilding institutions and the recognition of customary governance and support institutions.

Peacebuilding should not be used as a covert mechanism to export neoliberalism or even liberalism as a 'neutral' ontology of peace, nor should it assume that the territorially sovereign state is its only vehicle. Instead, a reversion to peacebuilding as opposed to (neo) liberal statebuilding should seek open and free communication between post-conflict individuals and peacebuilders about the nature of peace in each context. Peacebuilding requires a much greater engagement with transitional welfare as an essential peacebuilding mechanism for social support and justice (of course recognising the difficulties inherent in 'welfare institutions'). Peacebuilding also requires the mediation of a recognition and adoption of liberal institutions and connecting them with local and customary contexts without displacing the latter. This contextualisation of peacebuilding in transitional periods may allow for it to become more a process of the representation of post-conflict individuals and communities as opposed to the current glorification of the neoliberal state, and hence be far more democratic, able to support both human rights and needs, and a commensurate rule of law, as well as being culturally sensitive and appropriate. This local-liberal hybrid form of peacebuilding represents an agenda for a post-liberal form of peace.

Notes

1. See David Chandler, *Empire in Denial* (London: Pluto, 2006), p. 36.
2. See Oliver P. Richmond, *Transformation of Peace* (London: Palgrave, 2005).
3. E.g. Chandler, *Empire in Denial*, p. 36.
4. See Confidential Sources, UNDP, World Bank and Government, *Personal Interviews*, Dili, Timor Leste, 2–12 November 2008.

5. See for example, UNMISET: www.un.org/Depts/dpko/missions/unmiset.

6. Ellen Meiksins Wood, *Empire of Capital* (London: Verso, 2003).

7. International Crisis Group, 'Resolving Timor-Leste's crisis', Asia Report 120, October 2006, p. 1.

8. Confidential Source, Australian Government Official, *Personal Interview*, Dili, 25 September 2006.

9. United Nations, 'Report of the Secretary-General on Timor-Leste pursuant to Security Council Resolution 1690', August 2006, p. 9. Undocs, S/2006/628.

10. Sumantra Bose, *Bosnia After Dayton: Nationalist Partition and International Intervention* (London: Hurst, 2002), p. 3.

11. David Chandler, 'From Dayton to Europe', *International Peacekeeping*, 12: 3, Autumn 2005, pp. 336–49.

12. Richmond, *Transformation of Peace*, ch. 5.

13. See Oliver P. Richmond, 'Eirenism and a post-liberal peace', *Review of International Studies*, 35: 3, 2009.

14. Mark Duffield, *Development, Security and Unending War* (London: Polity, 2007), p. 234.

15. For a very interesting project on this in the context of the Pacific, see Volker Boege, M. Anne Brown, Kevin P. Clements and Anna Nolan, 'States emerging from hybrid political orders – Pacific experiences', The Australian Centre for Peace and Conflict Studies (ACPACS) Occasional Papers Series, 2008.

16. For more on this idea of replacing the notion of 'failed states' with 'emerging polities', see Anne Brown (ed.), *Security and Development in the Pacific Islands* (Boulder, CO: Lynne Rienner, 2007), p. 13.

Select Bibliography

ADB, *Country Strategy and Program, Cambodia 2005–9*, Philippines: Asian Development Bank.

Anderson, M. B., *Do No Harm: How Aid can Support Peace – or War*, Boulder: Lynne Rienner Publishers, 1999.

Annan, K., 'Democracy as an International Issue', *Global Governance*, vol. 8, no. 2, April–June 2002, pp. 134–42.

Ashdown, P., 'International Humanitarian Law, Justice and Reconciliation in a Changing World', The Eighth Hauser Lecture on International Humanitarian Law, New York, 3 March 2004.

Barakat, S. and Chard, M., 'Theories, Rhetoric and Practice: Recovering the Capacities of War Torn Societies', *Third World Quarterly*, 23(5): 817–35, 2002.

Bellamy, A. and Williams, P., 'Peace Operations and Global Order', *International Peacekeeping*, vol. 10, no. 4, 2004.

Belloni, R., 'Civil Society and Peacebuilding in Bosnia and Herzegovina', *Journal of Peace Research*, vol. 38, no. 2, p. 169.

BHAS, Labour Force Survey (preliminary data), press release no. 1, 27 July 2006, Sarajevo.

Bieber, F. and Daskalovski, Z., *Understanding the War in Kosovo*, London: Frank Cass, 2003.

Boege, V., Brown, M. A., Clements, K. P. and Nolan, A., 'States Emerging from Hybrid Political Orders – Pacific Experiences', *The Australian Centre for Peace and Conflict Studies (ACPACS) Occasional Papers Series*, 2008.

Booth, K. (ed.), *The Kosovo Tragedy: The Human Rights Dimension*, London: Frank Cass, 2001.

Bose, S., *Bosnia After Dayton: Nationalist Partition and International Intervention*, London: Hurst, 2002.

Bose, S., 'The Bosnian State a Decade after Dayton', *International Peacekeeping*, vol. 12, no. 3, autumn 2005, pp. 336–49.

Boutros-Ghali, B., *Agenda for Peace, Preventative Diplomacy, Peacemaking and Peace-keeping*, New York: Department of Public Information, United Nations, 1992.

Brown, A. (ed.), *Security and Development in the Pacific Islands*, Boulder: Lynne Rienner, 2007.

Burchell, G., Gordon, C. and Miller, P. (eds), *The Foucault Effect: Studies in Governmentality*, Chicago: University of Chicago Press, 1997.

Butenschon, N., 'The Oslo Agreement in Norwegian Foreign Policy', Centre for Middle Eastern and Islamic Studies occasional paper no. 56, Middle East and Islamic Studies, University of Durham, 1997.

Caplan, R., 'Who Guards the Guardians? International Accountability in Bosnia', *International Peacekeeping*, vol. 12, no. 3, autumn 2005, pp. 463–76.

Caplan, R., 'International Authority and State Building: The Case of Bosnia and Herzegovina', *Global Governance*, vol. 10, no. 1, 2004.

Chandler, D., *History of Cambodia*, London: Westview, 3rd edn, 1998.

Chandler, D., *From Kosovo to Kabul: Human Rights and International Intervention*, London: Pluto, 2002.

Chandler, D., *Bosnia: Faking Democracy after Dayton*, London: Pluto, 2nd edn, 2000.

Chandler, D., 'From Dayton to Europe', *International Peacekeeping*, vol. 12, no. 3, autumn 2005.

Chandler, D., *Empire in Denial*, London: Pluto, 2006.

Charters, D., *Peacekeeping and the Challenge of Civil Conflict Resolution*, New Brunswick: University of New Brunswick, 1994.

Chopra, J., 'Building State-failure in East Timor', *Development and Change*, 33, no. 5, autumn 2002.

Chopra, J. and Tanja Hohe, 'Participatory Intervention', *Global Governance*, vol. 10, 2004.

Cox, M., 'State Building and Post-conflict Reconstruction: Lessons from Bosnia', *The Rehabilitation of War-torn Societies*, Geneva: Centre for Applied Studies in International Negotiations, 2001, p. 6.

Curtain, R., 'Crisis in Timor Leste: Looking beyond the Surface Reality for Causes and Solutions', SSGM Working Paper, Canberra: The Australian National University, July 2006.

Curtis, G., *Cambodia Reborn? The Transition to Democracy and Development*, Washington, DC: Brookings Institution Press, 1998.

Debrix, F., *Re-envisioning Peacekeeping: The United Nations and the Mobilization of Ideology*, Minneapolis: University of Minnesota Press, 1999.

De Soto, A., *End of Mission Report*, May 2007.

Dobbins, J. et al., *America's Role in Nation-Building: From Germany to Iraq*, California: RAND, 2003.

Doyle, M., 'Kant, Liberal Legacies, and Foreign Affairs', *Philosophy and Public Affairs*, 12(3): 205–35, 1983.

Doyle, M. W., *United Nations Peacekeeping in Cambodia: UNTAC's Civil Mandate*, London: Lynne Rienner, 1995.

Doyle, M. W., Johnstone, I. and Orr, R. C., *Keeping the Peace:*

Multidimensional Operations in Cambodia and El Salvador, Cambridge: Cambridge University Press, 1997.

Duffield, M., *Global Governance and the New Wars*, London: Zed Books, 2001.

Duffield, M., *Development, Security and Unending War*, Cambridge: Polity, 2007.

Dunn, J., *East Timor: A Rough Passage to Independence*, New South Wales: Longueville, 2003.

Durch, W. J. (ed.), *UN Peacekeeping, American Politics and the Uncivil Wars of the 1990s*, London: Macmillan, 1996.

Economic Institute of Cambodia (EIC), *Cambodia Economic Watch*, issue 3, October 2005.

Fagan, A., 'Civil Society in Bosnia Ten Years after Dayton', *International Peacekeeping*, vol. 12, no. 3, autumn 2005, pp. 406–19.

Fanon, F., *The Wretched of the Earth*, London: Penguin, 5th edn, 2001.

Franks, J., *Rethinking the Roots of Terrorism*, London: Palgrave, 2006.

Fukuyama, F., *State Building: Governance and World Order in the Twenty-first Century*, London: Profile Books, 2004; 2nd edn, 2005.

Giacaman, G., and Jørund Lønning, D., *After Oslo – New Realities, Old Problems*, London: Pluto, 1999.

Goldstone, A., 'UNTAET with Hindsight: The Peculiarities of Politics in an Incomplete State', *Global Governance*, 10.1, January–March 2004.

Gotze, C., 'Civil Society Organisations in Failing States: The Red Cross in Bosnia and Albania', *International Peacekeeping*, vol. 11, no. 4, winter 2004, p. 664.

Hach, S. and Acharya, S., *Cambodia's Annual Economic Review*, Phnom Penh: Cambodia Development Resource Institute, Issue 2, August 2002.

Hainsworth, P. and McCloskey, S. (eds), *The Question of East Timor: The Struggle for Independence from Indonesia*, London: I. B. Tauris, 2000.

Heder, S., 'Hun Sen's "Consolidation Death or Beginning of Reform?"', *Southeast Asian Affairs*, 2005.

Heininger, J., *Peacekeeping in Transition*, London: Fund Press, 1994.

Held, D., *Democracy and the Global Order*, Oxford: Polity Press, 1995.

Hinton, A. L., *Why did they Kill? Cambodia in the Shadow of Genocide*, Berkeley: University of California, 2005.

Hobson, J. A., *Imperialism: A Study*, London: Nisbet, 1902.

Holohan, A., *Networks of Democracy*, Stanford: Stanford Press, 2005.

Hughes, C and Conway T, *Cambodia*, London: Overseas Development Institute, 2005.

Hull, G., 'The Languages of East Timor, 1772–1997: A Literature Review', *Studies in Languages and Cultures of East Timor*, Macarthur: University of Western Sydney, 1999.

International Crisis Group, *Violence in Kosovo: Who's Killing Whom?*, Report 78, November 1999.

International Crisis Group, *Collapse in Kosovo*, Report 155, April 2004.

International Crisis Group, *Kosovo after Haradinaj*, Report 163, May 2005.

International Crisis Group, *Bridging Kosovo's Mitrovica Divide*, Report 165, September 2005.

International Crisis Group, *Kosovo: The Challenge of Transition*, Report 170, February 2006.

International Crisis Group, *Resolving Timor-Leste's Crisis*, Asia Report 120, October 2006.

International Crisis Group, *Ensuring Bosnia's Future: A new International Engagement strategy*, Europe Report 180, 25 February 2007.

Jakobsson Hatay, A., *Peacebuilding and Reconciliation in Bosnia and Herzegovina, Kosovo and Macedonia 1995–2004*, Uppsala: Department of Peace and Conflict Research, 2005.

Jesse, J. K., 'Humanitarian Relief in the Midst of Conflict: The UN High Commissioner for Refugees,' *Pew Case Studies in International Affairs*, no. 471, Washington, DC: Georgetown University, 1996, p. 1.

Kaufmann D., Kraay A. and Mastruzzi, M., *Governance Matters III: Governance Indicators for 1996–2002*, www.worldbank.org/wbi/governance/pubs/govmatters3.

Latawski, P. and Smith, M., *The Kosovo Crisis and the Evolution of Post-Cold War European Security*, Basingstoke: Palgrave, 2003.

Lijphart, A., *Democracies: Patterns of Majoritarian and Consensus Government in Twenty-one Countries*, New Haven: Yale University Press, 1984.

Linz, J. and Stepan, A., *Problems of Democratic Transition and Consolidation*, Baltimore: Johns Hopkins University Press, 1996.

Lizee, P. P., *Peace, Power and Resistance in Cambodia: Global Governance and the Failure of International Conflict Resolution*, Basingstoke: Macmillan, 2000.

Llamazares, M. and Reynolds Levy, L., *NGOs and Peacebuilding in Kosovo*, Bradford: University of Bradford, Dept of Peace Studies, 2003.

Lustick, I., 'The Oslo Agreement as an Obstacle to Peace', *Journal of Palestinian Studies*, XXVII, no. 1 (autumn 1997), pp. 61–6.

Mayall, J (ed.), *The New Interventionism 1991–94*, Cambridge: Cambridge University Press, 1996.

Malcolm, N., *Kosovo, A Short History*, Basingstoke: Macmillan, 1998.

Malcolm, N., *Bosnia, A Short History*, Basingstoke: Macmillan, 2002.

Mandelbaum, M., *The Ideas that Conquered the World: Peace, Democracy, and Free Markets in the Twenty-first Century*, New York: Public Affairs, 2002.

Martin, I., *Self-determination in East Timor: The United Nations, the Ballot and International Intervention*, Boulder: Lynne Rienner, 2001.

Mertus, J., *Kosovo: How Myths and Truths Started a War*, California: University of California, 1999.

Mertus, J., 'Improving International Peacebuilding Efforts: The Example of Human Rights Culture in Kosovo', *Global Governance*, 10 (3), pp. 333–52, 2004.

Miall, H., Ramsbotham, O. and Woodhouse, T., *Contemporary Conflict Resolution*, Cambridge: Polity Press, 1999.

Morris, B., *Righteous Victims: A History of the Zionist–Arab Conflict 1881–1999*, London: John Murray, 2000.

Nissen, C. J., *Living under the Rule of Corruption: An Analysis of Everyday Forms of Corrupt Practices in Cambodia*, Phnom Penh: Centre for Social Development, 2005.

O'Neill, W., *Kosovo: An Unfinished Peace*, London: Lynne Rienner, 2001.

OSCE, *Kosovo: First Review of the Civil Justice System*, OSCE, June 2006.

Palmer, M. and Breuilly, E., (trans.) Chuang Tzu, *The Book of Chuang Tzu*, London: Penguin, 1996.

Paris, R., *At War's End*, Cambridge: Cambridge University Press, 2004.

Paris, R., 'International Peacebuilding and the 'Mission Civilisatrice', *Review of International Studies*, vol. 28, no. 4, 2002.

Peou, S., 'Collaborative Human Security? The UN and other Actors in Cambodia', *International Peacekeeping*, vol. 12, no. 1, spring 2005.

Pugh, M., 'Peacekeeping and Critical Theory', *Conference Presentation at BISA*, LSE, London, 16–18 December 2002.

Pugh, M., 'Transformation in the Political Economy of Bosnia since Dayton', *International Peacekeeping*, vol. 12, no. 3, autumn 2005, pp. 448–62.

Richmond, O. P., 'Devious Objectives and the Disputants' Views of International Mediation: A Theoretical Framework', *Journal of Peace Research*, vol. 35, no. 6, 1998.

Richmond, O. P., *The Transformation of Peace*, Basingstoke: Palgrave, 2005.

Richmond, O. P., 'Spoiling and Devious Objectives in Peace Processes', in Richmond, O. P. and Newman, E. (eds), *Spoilers in Peace Processes*, New York: United Nations University Press, 2006.

Richmond, O P, 'Shared Sovereignty and the Politics of Peace: Evaluating the EU's 'Catalytic' Framework in the Eastern Mediterranean', *International Affairs*, January 2006.

Richmond, O. and Franks, J., 'Liberal Hubris: Virtual Peace in Cambodia', *Security Dialogue*, vol. 38, no. 1, 2007.

Richmond, O. and Franks, J., 'Co-opting the Liberal Peace: Untying the Gordian Knot in Kosovo', *Cooperation and Conflict*, vol. 43, no. 1, 2008.

Richmond, O. and Franks, J., 'The Emperors' New Clothes? Liberal Peace in East Timor', *International Peacekeeping*, vol. 15, no. 2, 2008.

Roberts, D. W., *Political Transition in Cambodia 1991–99*, Richmond: Curzon, 2001.

Sambanis, N., *Making War and Building Peace: United Nations Peace Operations*, Princeton: Princeton University Press, 2006.

Shlaim, A., *The Iron Wall: Israel and the Arab World*, London: Penguin, 2000.

Smith, M., *Peacekeeping in East Timor: The Path to Independence*, Boulder: Lynne Rienner, 2003.

Snyder, J., *From Voting to Violence: Democratization and Nationalist Conflict*, London: Norton, 2001.

Sriram, C. L., *Peace as Governance: Power-sharing, Armed Groups and Contemporary Peace Negotiations*, Basingstoke: Macmillan, 2008.

Steele, J., 'Nation Building in East Timor', *World Policy Journal*, summer 2002.

Suhrke, A., 'Peacekeepers as Nation-builders: Dilemmas of the UN in East Timor', *International Peacekeeping*, vol. 8, no. 4, winter 2001.

Talentino, A. K., 'The Two Faces of Nation-building: Developing Function and Identity', *Cambridge Review of International Affairs*, vol. 17, no. 3, October 2004.

Thakur, R. and Schnabel, A. (eds), *United Nations Peacekeeping Operations: Ad Hoc Missions, Permanent Engagement*, New York: United Nations University Press: 2001.

Traynor, I., 'Ashdown Running Bosnia like a Raj', *The Guardian*, 5 July 2003.

United Nations, *Report of the Panel on United Nations Peacekeeping Operations*, New York: United Nations, 2000.

United Nations, *Human Development Report 2003*, New York: United Nations Development Programme, 2003.

United Nations, *Human Development Report – Palestine*, New York: United Nations Development Programme, 2004, p. 67.

United Nations, *Kosovo – Human Development Report 2004*, Pristina: United Nations Development Programme, 2004.

United Nations, *Early Warning Report: Kosovo, Report 12, October–December 2005*, New York: United Nations Development Programme, 2005.

United Nations, *Investing in Cambodia's Future*, New York: United Nations Development Programme, 2005.

United Nations, Human Development Report – East Timor, New York: United Nations Development Programme, 2006.

United Nations, *Report of the Secretary-General on Timor-Leste pursuant to Security Council resolution 1690*, New York: United Nations, August 2006.

United Nations, *National Human Development Report: Social Inclusion in Bosnia Herzegovina*, New York: United Nations Development Programme, 2007.

UNMIK, *Kosovo Economic Outlook 2006*, Economic Policy Office, March 2006.

USAID, *Anti-corruption*, Phnom Penh: United States Agency for International Development, 2005.

Van der Walle, N., Ball, N. and Ramachandran, V., *Beyond Structural Adjustment: The Institutional Context of African Development*, Basingstoke: Palgrave, 2003.

Vickers, M., *Between Serb and Albanian: A History of Kosovo*, New York: Columbia University Press, 1998.

Waller, M., Drezov, K. and Gokay, B. (eds), *Kosovo: The Politics of Delusion*, London: Frank Cass, 2001.

Wood, E. M., *Empire of Capital*, London: Verso, 2003.

World Bank, *Developing the Occupied Territories an Investment for Peace, Volume 1: Overview*, Washington, DC: World Bank, September 1993.

World Bank, *The World Bank Group in the Western Balkans*, Washington, DC: World Bank, 2005.

Zakaria, F., *The Future of Freedom*, New York: Norton, 2003.

Personal Interviews

Abu Vilan, M. K. – M'eretz, Tel Aviv, 1 July 2007.

Ambassador Davidson, OSCE, Sarajevo, 1 February 2007.

Bannon, I., Manager of the Conflict Prevention and Reconstruction Unit Conflict Unit, World Bank, Washington, DC, 23 February 2007.

Baskin, G. – Director IPCRI, Jerusalem, 29 June 2007.

Cartwright, T., Special Representative, Council of Europe, Sarajevo, 1 February 2007.

Confidential Military Source, Jerusalem, 1 July 2007.

Confidential Source, ACIPS, Sarajevo, 29 January 2007.

Confidential Source, Director – Asian Development Bank, Dili, 25 September 2006.

Confidential Source, Australian Government Official, Dili, 25 September 2006.

Confidential Source, Avocats sans Frontières, Dili, 25 September 2006.

Confidential Source, Centre for Human Rights, Sarajevo, 30 January 2007.

Confidential Source, Coalition of Women for Peace, Jerusalem, 27 June 2007.

Confidential Source, Council of Europe, Sarajevo, 1 February 2007.

Confidential Source, Executive Director – World Bank, Dili, 27 September 2006.

Confidential Source, HDZ representative, Mostar, 2 February 2007.

Confidential Source, House of Representatives, Pristina, 5 April 2006.
Confidential Source, Institute of Political Studies – Executive Director, Pristina, 4 April 2006.
Confidential Source, Independent Economic Advisor, Sarajevo, 30 January 2007.
Confidential Source, International Governmental Advisor, Dili, 27 September 2006.
Confidential Source, LDS Party, Sarajevo, 30 January 2007.
Confidential Source, LDK – MP, Pristina, 3 April 2006 .
Confidential Source, National Dialogue Centre, Mostar, 02 February 2007.
Confidential Source, OSCE – Democratisation Officer, Pristina, 4 April 2006.
Confidential Source, OSCE – Education Officer, Pristina, 5 April 2006.
Confidential Source, OSCE – Political Affairs Officer, Pristina 5 April 2006.
Confidential Source, OSCE, Sarajevo, 1 February 2007.
Confidential Source, PASSIA, Jerusalem, 28 June 2007.
Confidential Source, Peres Centre, Jerusalem, 27 June 2007.
Confidential Source, PDP representative, Sarajevo, 1 February 2007.
Confidential Source, SDP (Serb) – Leader, Mitrovica, 6 April 2006.
Confidential Source, SIDA, Sarajevo, 1 February 2007.
Confidential Source, UNMIK - Economic Advisor, Pristina, 5 April 2006.
Confidential Source, Van Leer Institute, Jerusalem, 28 June 2007.
Confidential Source, World Bank – Operations Officer, Pristina, 3 April 2006 .
Confidential Source, World Bank, Dili, 21 September 2006.
Confidential Source, World Bank, Sarajevo, 27 January 2007.
Deputy SRSG – Bosnia, Sarajevo, 29 January 2007.
Diplomatic Source, OHR, Sarajevo, 29 January 2007.
Dizdarevic, S., President Helsinki Committee for Human Rights, Sarajevo, 31 January 2007 .
Dumaris, A. L. – IDF, Tel Aviv, 1 July 2007.
Falloni, D., OSCE – Youth Education Officer, Pristina, 5 April 2006.
Fares, K. – Leader, Fateh, Ramallah, 30 June 2007.
Fonach, J., HAK – Director, Dili, 28 September 2006.
Hach, S., Economic Institute of Cambodia, Phnom Penh, 11 November 2005.
Hadi, M. A. – Director PASSIA, Jerusalem, 28 June 2007.
Janovitch, M., Serb National Party – Leader, Mitrovica, 6 April 2006.
Laoc, T., NDI – Country Director, Dili, 28 September 2006.
Leslie, E., ACT, Phnom Penh, 11 November 2005.
Montell, J. – Director, BT'Selem, Jerusalem, 26 June 2007.
Pundak, R., Director – Peres Centre for Peace, Tel Aviv, 27 June 2007.

Rashiti, N., International Crisis Group – Researcher/Manager, Pristina, 4 April 2006.

Rougevin-Baville, S., Protection Delegate – ICRC, Dili, 27 September 2006.

Samnang, H., Phnom Penh, 10 November 2005.

Official Source, USAID, Phnom Penh, 8 November 2005.

Senior Advisor, Asian Development Bank, 8 November 2005.

Vannath, C., Director of Centre for Social Development (CSD, Phnom Penh, 7 November 2005.

Vrenezi, A., NCSC – Programme Officer, Pristina, 4 April 2006.

World Bank Officials, Phnom Penh, 7–8 November 2005.

Zelniker, S., Director – Van Leer Institute for Peace, Jerusalem, 27 June 2007.

Index

ABRI, 89–90
Agenda for Peace, 6, 19, 156
aid
  Cambodia, 23, 24, 27, 30, 42
  Kosovo, 132
Alliance of Democrats (AD), 27
Annan, K., 83
APODETI, 95
Ashdown, P., 59, 62, 67
Asian Development Bank (ADB)
  Cambodia, 24, 28, 29, 30, 36
  East Timor, 105

Belloni, R., 72
Blair, T., 164
Blumi, I., 147
Bonn Powers *see* OHR
Bose, S., 55, 56, 63, 64
Boutros-Ghali, B., 6, 19
Brahimi Report, 123

Cambodia People's Party (CPP),
  21
Caplan, R., 67
Centre for Social Development
  (CSD), 27, 28
Chandler, D., 21, 55, 56, 58, 63,
  65, 67, 187, 190
Chopra, J., 85, 91, 92
citizenship
  Bosnia, 63
  Cambodia, 190
  Kosovo, 130
  Middle East, 168
Civilian Police *see* CIVPOL

civil society, 6, 12, 184, 204, 210,
  211
  Bosnia, 71–4
  Cambodia, 22–4, 27, 28, 37–40,
    46, 187, 188, 191
  East Timor, 99–102
  Kosovo, 119, 120, 123–4, 132–3
  Middle East, 159, 166–9
civil war
  Bosnia, 55
  Cambodia, 21, 23
  East Timor, 83, 90, 104
  Middle East, 163
CIVPOL (Civilian Police), 114,
  124, 125
CNRT *see* National Council of
  Timorese Resistance
colonialism
  Bosnia, 68
  neo-colonialism, 183
conditionality, 6–7, 8, 9, 16, 203
  Bosnia, 77
  Cambodia, 28, 36, 44, 45–6, 190
  East Timor, 101
  Kosovo, 116
  Middle East, 149, 156, 165, 169,
    174, 176, 201
conflict management
  Bosnia, 54
  Middle East, 159, 172–3
conflict resolution, 208, 209
  Cambodia, 186
conflict settlement
  Cambodia, 20
Conway, T., 36, 42